THEY PLAYED THE GAME

THEY
PLAYED
THE
GAME

Memories from 47 Major Leaguers

NORMAN L. MACHT

University of Nebraska Press • Lincoln

Library of Congress Cataloging-in-Publication Data
Names: Macht, Norman L. (Norman Lee), 1929– author.
Title: They played the game: memories from 47 major
leaguers / Norman L. Macht.
Description: Lincoln: University of Nebraska Press, [2019] |
Includes bibliographical references and index.
Identifiers: LCCN 2018028079
ISBN 9781496205506 (cloth: alk. paper)
ISBN 9781496214171 (epub)
ISBN 9781496214188 (mobi)
ISBN 9781496214195 (pdf)
Subjects: LCSH: Baseball—United States—History—20th
century. | Baseball players—United States—Biography.
Classification: LCC GV863.A1 .M25 2019 | DDC
796.357/640973—dc23 LC record available at
https://lccn.loc.gov/2018028079

Set in Lyon Text by E. Cuddy.

To all the ballplayers and their teams
who gave us the pleasure and pain of
rooting for them

CONTENTS

PREFACE

AS WE AGE, OUR memories become more selective, self-serving, imaginative. As New York Giants pitcher (1931–1946) Hal Schumacher said to me, "You'll excuse a man for not remembering things exactly after fifty years." For example, a player may remember hitting a grand slam that was actually a three-run home run. Or he may misremember the actual final score of a memorable game or who the opposing pitcher was in an at-bat he is reliving or the batter he struck out with the bases loaded.

The ballplayers we will be visiting—whose playing days range from 1912 to 1981—may have misremembered some of the events they describe, but, as prize-winning oral historian Studs Terkel put it, "In their rememberings are their truths."

You are invited on a journey into the galleries of memory of these Hall of Famers and bit players of the past. Whether we are entering a museum or the twilight zone, what we will hear are the truths that resided in their minds when they talked with me in their later years. If you wish to do the research to verify or question their facts or versions of events, do so. I didn't. Perhaps you will find among these storytellers your answer to the question: If you could spend three days with any ballplayer of the past, who would you choose?

Memories are not stored on reels of film but in collections of photographs and sound bites that pop up randomly when one is reminiscing. I have done some editing and rearranging for clarity of the sequence of events. Otherwise what you read is what they said.

ACKNOWLEDGMENTS

THIS COLLECTION OF BASEBALL memories is all that it is because of the countless hours of research, suggestions, vetting, and encouragement by Steve and Annette Braccini. Thanks also to Ed Morton of SABR and Cassidy Lent of the Hall of Fame for their research; to Cynthia Franco of the DeGolyer Library at Southern Methodist University, where the original recordings of these interviews are housed; to Rob Taylor of the University of Nebraska Press, whose idea it was; and to the best copy editor in the world, Bojana Ristich, keeper of the flame of good writing.

1.

Joe Adcock

. . . .

The 6-foot-4 right-handed-batting first baseman hit 336 home runs in his seventeen-year career (1950–1966). He broke in with Cincinnati, but his biggest years were in 1953–1962 with the Milwaukee Braves, pennant winners in 1957–1958.

Before we sat down to talk, we drove around Adcock's 640-acre Red River thoroughbred ranch. During my visit he fielded phone calls for some horse trading. Visiting small grandchildren popped into the den occasionally from the adjoining kitchen.

. . . .

MY GRANDFATHER OWNED THIS farm originally and sold it in 1927. I began buying it back in 1951. I had owned some Black Angus cattle and some Appaloosa horses I was showing and selling and financed the purchase from that. I had as many as ten English pointer hunting dogs at one time. Still, the best dog I ever owned was a setter. He's buried out there.

[Adcock pointed to a tall reddish horse.] I named him Touch 'Em All. That's what the first base coach would say to me every time I passed him after I hit a home run. [Then we drove to a small country eatery, where he was greeted as "Joe Bill," for some genuine chicken gumbo.] It's not pure if it's got sausage in it. [We returned to the farm and settled in the den to talk.]

Our high school basketball team won the state championship, and I went to LSU on a basketball scholarship. Didn't play much baseball when I was young.

If anybody had offered me a contract with the Cardinals, I would have signed it. That's all we knew around here on the radio. In 1934 my dad borrowed $100 and with two other men went in a Model A Ford to the World Series in St. Louis. I was seven. He brought me back a little souvenir bat with Paul Dean's name on it. I still have it. He told me it was not a Dizzy Dean bat 'cause

1

they'd already sold them out. Turned out Sportsman's Park was my favorite place to hit in.

Cincinnati scout Paul Florence signed me. The New York Knicks wanted me to play pro basketball, and the Reds paid me not to play. I wasn't going to play no way, but I took the check when they handed it to me after my rookie year at Cincinnati.

The Reds sent me to Columbia, South Carolina, then to Tulsa. I was never in a hurry to leave the ballpark after a game; never in much hurry to get there either, to tell you the truth. The Tulsa manager, Al Vincent, often came over and sat and talked to me after games. One night he says to me, "You're the only guy on the club can make the major leagues. You got what it takes." He taught me how to run the bases. They could outrun me on a straightaway but not running the bases. One day in Ebbets Field I was in the passageway between the dugout and clubhouse and met Brooklyn GM Branch Rickey. "Joe," he says, "the first time I saw you, I recognized you as being a ballplayer. You had spring in your legs. You could jump like a deer." That was what he said made a ballplayer.

Bill Terry made a first baseman out of me. He came to the Reds' spring training in Tampa my first year there in 1950 and did nothing but work with me every day for a month, throwing the ball at me every which way. Since I was a right-handed first baseman, the 3-6-3 double play was tough, but that's tough for anybody to make. I had good hands, wouldn't trade with anybody.

One day I cheated on a double play throw to me. The umpire was near second base; we didn't have four umps. The runner had it beat, but I caught the ball and threw it up in the air a little like I had caught it in plenty of time, and the umpire calls him out. My foot had been off the base. Later that ump was behind the plate in a game; I came up to bat, and he said, "Joe, you better swing at anything that comes close because you showed me up." I said, "I didn't show you up. You showed yourself up. You made the call."

I learned in sports you win some and lose some, and there's nothing you can do about it. In '56 with Milwaukee we had a one-game lead over Brooklyn with three games left. We finished 1-2 in St. Louis while they won three against the Pirates, and that cost us the pennant by one game. We came back in '57 and '58 and won it.

Red Schoendienst was a great second baseman—smart, did things that don't ever show up in the box scores. Game 5, '57 World Series, Burdette versus Ford in Milwaukee. Red's looking in at the signs the catcher is giving and hollers over to me at first base, "Take three steps to the line, Joe." And on my third step the batter hit a shot toward the right field corner, and I jumped and got it. That turned the game; it was 1–0 for us. People sitting in the ballpark had no idea that went on. My dad was sitting there, and I told him how Red won that game, not my catch.

I drove in the only run in the game. I was a dead pull hitter, but Al Vincent had told me I had to learn to hit to right. He taught me how to put my hands out in front of my body and push it yonder a way. He had me out there forty-five minutes every afternoon the last two weeks of the season. "But don't ever use it unless you have a chance to win a game," he told me. "Keep it as your best shot to break up a game." Whitey Ford had me out twice with that slider coming in on me between the letters and the belt. I had hit ground balls to third and short. Now I'm up [with Eddie Mathews on third]. I knew he was coming back with that slider, and when he jammed me again, I just pushed a dying quail out there to right.

That ability to hit to right field came in handy when I broke up Harvey Haddix's twelve-inning perfect game. [Haddix, then with the Pirates, had pitched twelve perfect innings before the leadoff hitter in the thirteenth reached on an error, was sacrificed to second, and Aaron was intentionally walked.] Haddix was throwing his slider on the outside of the plate, hitting the outside corner with it, and getting me out all night. Struck me out twice with that pitch. I knew I was going to get it in that thirteenth inning. I was going to right field with it and hit it on the nose out of the ballpark. I didn't get a home run on it because Aaron passed somebody on the base paths, but it won the game for us.

The better the pitcher, the better a hitter I was. The pitchers who didn't have the real good stuff, they got me out. I didn't bear down hard enough on them. Bob Gibson was as fine a pitcher as you'll ever see. One night in St. Louis, Eddie Stanky was the manager. Bases loaded. Aaron's the hitter ahead of me. Gibson shakes the catcher off, again, and a third time. Here comes a changeup.

Aaron pops it up to second base. I walked up to the plate, and I said to myself, "I don't know when I'm going to get it, but he's going to throw that changeup sure as two and two is four." Before the second pitch he shook his head, started to shake it again, and went into his windup, and I said, here comes that change, so help me God. I hit the top of the center field wall with it with the bases loaded, and he had us beat 2–0. Three runs score and I'm standing on second base, and here comes Stanky, just shaking on the mound, and I hear him yelling at Gibson, "Goddamn, you get the best hitter in baseball out, and you come along with this guy here who's a guess hitter, and he's beaten you."

The next trip into St. Louis we run into about the same situation. Close ball game, and Gibson threw one right behind my shoulder, right back to the screen. I was looking for that knockdown off of him, the way he was moving his glove and all. Otherwise he would have nailed me. I get up out of the dirt, determined to hit one right back and knock him off that mound. I was muttering to myself. He threw a slider away from me, and if I didn't hit a line shot right between his legs, I'm not standing here right now. I touched first base and called for time, claiming I got a bug in my eye. I walked toward the mound and got within ten feet of Gibson and I said to him, "I'll tell you one thing, you son of a bitch; you ever come close to me again, I'm gonna kill you. But I'm gonna break your arm before I kill you, so you can have something to remember me by." First baseman Bill White came running over. "Hey, you are mad," he said. I said, "You son of a bitch, I'll break your neck now." He went back to first base.

Gibson was a fine pitcher, so fine that why did he have to lower himself to do what he did? When you see him, ask him. [**NM**: Not me.] About ten years ago I went to a card show in Oklahoma City. I don't go to those things, but I wanted to see Warren Spahn and Allie Reynolds, and Gibson was there. I didn't know he'd be there or I probably wouldn't have gone. I wasn't uncomfortable with the man. We met in the airport, and I shook hands with him.

The night Ruben Gomez drilled me was the first game my wife ever saw in her life. We were not married. I'd been telling her, "Joan [pronounced Jo Ann], when you going to come to the ball game?"

One night, after we'd beaten the Giants, she and I were out eating, and I said, "Why don't you come to the ball game tomorrow night? Gomez is pitching, and he can't get me out." She said, "What do you mean, he can't get you out?" I said, "I hit him real good. Come to the game." She said, "Well, I might come. You think you'll get a hit?" I said, "Look, I hit this guy."

So I picked her up at four o'clock, and she took me to the ballpark, and I showed her where my parking space was, [so she could park there when she came back at game time], and would you believe I hit a home run off Gomez with two on the first time I'm up, and the next time up I think I doubled, and we're leading 5-0, although we wound up getting beat 6-5. My next time up Gomez shook off catcher Bill Sarni five-six times. I stepped out of the box, stooped down and got a little dirt on my hands, and said to Sarni, "Say, Bill, you tell that son of a bitch to throw one of his two pitches. Let's get this game going." Gomez heard me I know, and he drilled me right in the ribs. I dropped my bat and went down to first base and stood on the bag and hollered at him, "You son of a bitch, I'll break your arm," and I'm running at him, and I got a few feet from him, and he had another ball, and he rears back and he nailed me on the right thigh and ran for the dugout.

I jumped in the dugout behind him and then it got tough. He came out of the clubhouse with an ice pick in one hand and a butcher knife in the other. He's standing no farther than from me to you. "I'll kill you." But there's plainclothes detectives all over that ballpark, and there's a little fellow in a blue suit, shirt, and tie, and he reached in between me and Gomez and pulled out a snub-nosed .38 pistol and pushed it right in Gomez's stomach, right there in the dugout. I'm out of the game. I go up to the clubhouse and [general manager] John Quinn is sitting in my locker.

"Joe," he said, "I wish you'd have caught him. What would you have done?"

I said, "I wanted to grab his arm and break it over my knee."

He said, "Go on and get out of the ballpark."

I thought Joan would be waiting in the car. I went downstairs, through the tunnel and back out to the car, and she wasn't there. I looked around and didn't see her. I went back inside and asked a coach to go out and take a look in the wives' section for her. He looked and said she's not sitting with the wives. I went back out to the car and looked closer and there she was with her face down on the seat. She said, "You take me home now, and I won't be back. I didn't come out here to see you fight." She never went back to a regular season game that year, but she went to the World Series in '57.

For days after the incident our club was swamped with hate mail out of New York. So when we go into New York next time and we get off the plane, they tell me I'm going to have two FBI men in front of me and one behind. They had adjoining rooms to me and my roommate, ate with us, and went everywhere with us.

I could always hit the Dodgers pitchers. I can still see the pitches I hit for the four home runs and a double at Ebbets Field. I hit a home run off Don Newcombe first time up—a line shot down the left-field foul line. He tried to jam me, and there isn't a man made can jam me.

I can still see the pitch I hit into the Polo Grounds center-field bleachers [475 feet] off Jim Hearn. He had jammed me before too. The next spring we traded for Giants catcher Sam Calderone, and he told me that in the clubhouse after that game Hearn said to him, "No SOB is gonna hit a ball that far off me." The next time I faced him he had hit me and broke my wrist, put me out the rest of the year. And that's how I met my wife, an X-ray technician. It was a bad break, and the doctor would not guarantee I would ever swing a bat again. Every day for two, three weeks I had to go in there for new X-rays. After a month I went home to Coushatta. I fished every day, casting, using my wrist; never did tell the doctor. I had to change my batting grip. I took a twelve-pound weight with a bat handle stuck through it, and I worked with that twenty times twice a morning and the same in the afternoon. After that I held the bat with my fingers, and it made me a better hitter

I had an idea what I was doing at that plate. I looked for pitches. I'd deliberately swing at a bad curve ball and look for that same curve, knowing I'm going to get it again. I've swung at balls in the dirt, knowing I'm going to get that pitch back within the next two.

I studied pitchers. Made it a habit to try to find out everything I could about each one. It was all in my head. No computers. On a 1-1 count you got this pitch before. Maybe you won't see a 1-1 count the next time, but in trouble you'll see that guy come back with the same thing. Sal Maglie, a great pitcher, got beat by me on a home run, 1-0, when he tried to jam me. He never jammed me again. He stayed on that outside corner, short-armed it right on that black every time. Perfect control.

If I had one fault, I didn't bear down against the weaker clubs like I did the good ones.

I played with a lot of great ballplayers.

Henry Aaron was a natural born hitter as far as I was concerned and one of the best I laid eyes on, but he did what I was taught not to do with a bat. He held it up there, and he buggy-whipped it and popped it like a whip. If I had been moving that bat up there, I don't know what I would have done. Couldn't even foul the ball probably. I kept the bat still.

Eddie Mathews was the best third baseman I ever laid eyes on. Red Schoendienst is my second baseman. Roy McMillan was the only shortstop I saw who could go in the hole twice in one game and throw out Richie Ashburn, and nobody else in the league could do that to Ashburn. No bat, but in the field he was superb. Johnny Logan didn't have a good arm, but he played the hitters. He stood in front of more line drives and one-hoppers than anybody you ever saw. I kept telling him, "Someday I'm going to reach up and catch your throw with my bare hand." He would say, "You do, and I'll bite you."

We got Enos "Country" Slaughter one year, and I'm rooming with him, and he's sitting up till 4 in the a.m. talking about turkey hunting, and I'm saying, "Hey, Eno, let's get a little sleep before the sun comes up." They called him the bald eagle.

If I had to win one game, I'd go to Lew Burdette. You had to beat him. He didn't beat himself. Spitter and all. He had a good one. Unless it was Ernie Banks up there with the game on the line. Banks was a low-ball upper-cut hitter, and he could jump on that spitter. Keep the ball from the waist up, Banks couldn't hit Molly Potts.

Reds pitcher Ewell Blackwell was as tough to face in batting practice as in a game. That ball was sinking, dipping, diving, and everything else. He was all arms and legs. Sometimes his knuckles scraped the ground on the mound, and other times he would come at you from the side. I could see he wouldn't last.

The best manager I ever played for was Bill Rigney with the California Angels expansion team. We didn't have a team. Look at that roster. Over the hill. We were 82-80 and didn't have a ball club. Rigney got a lot of mileage out of not much. Couldn't hit their way out of a wet sack. We had two great pitchers, Dean Chance and Bo Belinsky, but those boys couldn't handle it. They had great ability but [were] a pair of wild horses. Chance struck out Mantle four times one night. Afterward Mantle said, "I'd rather hit at a rattlesnake than that guy."

I would not trade my career with anybody I played with or against. I accomplished some things that nobody else ever did.

Two days before the [1966] season ended, Bill Rigney told me [Indians GM] Gabe Paul wanted to talk to me about managing Cleveland. I met him at his hotel and told him I would sign only if he got rid of a few players on his team I didn't want. He promised me he would, and I signed. He tried to get rid of them all spring training and all through the season and couldn't get anything for them; I knew we couldn't win with them and I'd get the heat, and we didn't win and I got the heat.

[As thrice-fired manager Pat Corrales said, "Honesty has gotten more managers fired than incompetence."]

2.

Richie Ashburn

PHILADELPHIA, NOVEMBER 3, 1991

• •

Richie Ashburn's fifteen-year career (1948–1962) included twelve with the Phillies, two with the Cubs, and a final year with the Mets. Rookie of the Year in 1948, the speedy left-handed batter perfected the art of bunting, averaged 185 hits a year as the Phillies leadoff man, and was only the second major leaguer (after Rogers Hornsby) to lead the league in both hits and walks since 1900. He led in hits three times, walks four times, and triples twice. Early in his career the Phillies urged him to avoid swinging up on the ball and hit everything on the ground. As a result, 82 percent of his 2,574 hits were singles. After his playing days, he was part of the Phillies' broadcasting team for thirty-seven years.

We met at the otherwise empty press box at Veterans Stadium.

• •

I WAS BORN IN 1927 in Tilden, Nebraska, population 1,000. My given name was Don Richard, but my birth certificate got it wrong; it just says Rich. I've been Rich or Richie ever since.

It was all farming and ranching around there. My grandfather was a blacksmith. I used to spend a lot of time with him, helping shoe horses, grinding plow blades. Then they went into the farm machinery business when tractors replaced horses. Later my dad went into the monuments business.

My dad was on the semipro town team. Every Saturday and Sunday we watched him play. I became a left-hand batter because my dad put the bat on my left shoulder when he threw to me. He said that would put me a step or two closer to first base.

We were a captive audience for the Cubs; that was the only broadcast we could get. Stan Hack was my favorite player. When I was seventeen, I went to Chicago for a tryout. I was taking batting practice at Wrigley Field, and I remember Hack ran me out of the batting cage: "Hey, bush, let the big leaguers in there." Later Hack was managing the Cubs, and I said to him one day, "I guess you don't remember kicking this young kid out of the batting cage." He didn't.

I was a fast runner. In high school I ran sprints, but we had no track coach. When I got to Philadelphia, the Temple track coach, Bill Ogden, said to me, "Boy, you can really fly, but you don't know how to run. You run like you're carrying a baby in your arms." He showed me the technique of using your arms like pistons and probably put a foot or two on my speed to first base.

I was a catcher as a kid and played American Legion ball. At one time I was scouted by twelve of the then sixteen major league clubs.

My first contract was with Cy Slapnicka of the Cleveland Indians. He offered me a minor league contract with a percentage of my sale to a major league club. But that was illegal. I'm not even sure I was out of high school, which was also illegal. I'm seventeen and I got a call from Commissioner Kenesaw Mountain Landis. I took the train to Chicago and met with him and minor league president William Bramham. Landis was an awesome looking character with that flowing white hair. He looked like God to me. I told them everything I knew. I remember Landis asking me as I left his office, "Do you think you can become a major league player?" I said, "I hope so." He said, "Good luck," and that was it. I was released from that contract.

I then signed with the Phillies for a $3,500 bonus. The reason we picked the Phillies was that they had a terrible team. We figured if I had what it took to get there, I'd get there sooner with them. I think I could have made the Phillies in six different positions because they really didn't have that much at all. It turned out that way because I only spent two years in the minor leagues.

In 1945 I went to Utica in the Eastern League as a catcher. The manager was Eddie Sawyer, and that was a good break. He was the best manager I ever had. He let us play. We made mistakes, and he'd talk to us. Catchers back up plays at first base a lot. I used to beat the runners down to first, catcher's gear and all. I could fly. One day a guy hit a ball wide of the first baseman and he went to get it, but the second baseman caught it. The pitcher didn't cover first, so I made the putout. I've never seen another 4–2 play at first base. Sawyer said, "Son, if you can make that play, we're going to move you to the outfield." I started in left field because it's an easier position, then moved to center.

After the '45 season I was drafted into the army the day the Japanese surrendered and was in only fourteen months. I was stationed in Alaska a summer and winter and played some baseball and basketball. On July 4 we played a traditional midnight game without lights.

I went to North Fork College on a basketball scholarship and got an education degree. In the off season I did some substitute teaching and coached junior high basketball. If I hadn't played ball, I probably would have gone into teaching, like my brother and twin sister did.

When I came back in '47, Sawyer was still at Utica. We'd won the pennant in '45, and we won again in '47 with a lot of the future Whiz Kids.

In my rookie year with the Phillies in '48 I slid headfirst into second base and jammed my finger and broke it. I always liked the headfirst slide because I could pick my spot better to slide. You're a lot tougher to tag 'cause you're using your arm to pick a spot and the fielder can't just swipe. He's got to put a tag on you somewhere and you can use your arm to evade him, and I always felt on close plays I got the benefit of the doubt from the umpire. But I never slid headfirst into first base. That slows you down. Or home plate; there's too much there to hit.

Until now I had never seen a left-handed pitcher with a good breaking ball. The guy who really helped me was Johnny Hopp, from Hastings, Nebraska. He was a veteran with Pittsburgh, and they had a sidearm lefty who was tough. I said to Johnny, "This guy is really giving me a lot of problems." Hopp said, "Two things you gotta do. Don't bail out. Don't give him an inch of ground. Stay there, even if he hits you between the eyes. And concentrate on picking up the ball as quickly as you can out of his hand." It takes some courage to do what I'm talking about. I made up my mind to do that, and when I saw how much easier it was, that's all I needed to know. It was that simple. And it worked.

One thing that surprised me was that there were players who didn't want to play every game. There are still some who want to play three or four a week instead of six or seven. We kids wanted to play every day. One old-timer I remember was Schoolboy Rowe, the pitcher. I loved to sit and listen to stories he told of the old days. One thing I remember about this big, strong, strapping guy: on the days he pitched he would throw up after every inning. Go into the walkway to the clubhouse, gagging. There was a nervousness he had. But a great competitor.

That first year we lived a few blocks from Shibe Park in a boarding house. Then my parents came to Philadelphia and rented a house for a few months during the season, and I and some of the others stayed there.

Eddie Sawyer took over as the Phillies' manager in mid-1948. He was very patient, but he could be firm. At first Robin Roberts didn't like him because Eddie never said much to the players. I asked him one time, "Eddie, how come you never say anything to us?" He said, "I don't have to. You guys like to play, and I put you out there to play." Later Robin admitted to me that he thought Sawyer was a great manager.

Shibe Park was a great park to play in. Good vision, good range in the outfield. Grounds were always perfect. I only hit twenty-nine home runs, but I hit two in a game three different times. I was a singles hitter, and when I hit one out of the park, it kind of worried me that I was doing something wrong. My whole game was getting on base.

In terms of emotion, that last game in Brooklyn in 1950 was a highlight. We had a one-game lead, and if we lost, it would force a playoff. We were beat up. We'd lost Curt Simmons to the army in August, lost Bob Miller and Bubba Church. Andy Seminick broke a bone in his ankle; they would shoot him up with Novocain, and he played. The Dodgers were in much better shape than we were.

We were tied in the last of the ninth. Brooklyn had Cal Abrams on second and Pee Wee Reese on first with nobody out. Duke Snider hit a hard line-drive one-hopper base hit right at me. The third base coach waved Abrams around third. I had a decent arm and worked hard at getting rid of the ball quickly and throwing accurately. I made a perfect throw, and Abrams didn't have a chance. The catcher, Stan Lopata, had so much time he caught my throw and went up the line to meet Abrams. I've made a lot better plays in the outfield, but this was at a crucial time. When you get thrown out at home plate with nobody out and Jackie Robinson coming up, that's a mistake. Snider went to second on the play, so it's still second and third with one out. They walked Robinson, then got Carl Furillo and Gil Hodges. [Dick Sisler hit a home run in the tenth to win it for the Phillies.]

One day Cal Abrams, a card show promoter, said to me, "I never did get a chance to thank you for what you did for me." I said, "What do you mean?" He said, "People have never forgotten that play, and they wonder how I could have gotten thrown out at home plate."

The Sunday night before that game, four of us were on the Ed Sullivan TV show. Granny Hamner, Puddin Head Jones, Dick Sisler, and me. We were a pretty good quartet. I was the tenor. We'd sing together a lot in the shower, around the clubhouse. We had a song, "The Fightin' Phillies," that a fan had written for us. We're ready to go on, and suddenly some guy jumps up out of the audience onto the stage and starts talking about some charity. Before they could get him out of there, he took up our time, and we never got to sing on TV. I saw a film clip of that show in 1976, and what surprised me was how young we all looked.

Being in the 1950 World Series was a career highlight even though we lost in four games. It was a major disappointment that we didn't hit, but the Yankees didn't either. I thought we would get there again because most of us were very young.

In the 1950s Brooklyn and New York dominated the National League. They had added those great black players, and the Phillies had none. That was probably the one big reason we didn't win more in that decade. We didn't need much more to contend. Roy Campanella told me that in '46 or '47 he came to a tryout at Shibe Park, and they wouldn't let him in. He wanted to play with the Phillies. Project that: Campy catching for us. But Bob Carpenter didn't want it.

The fifties, with the coming of the black players and only eight teams in the league, was the strongest, best baseball decade I've ever seen, and I've now seen quite a few decades.

As a rule pitchers didn't throw at me. They didn't want to hit me and put me on base. I was hit some because I crowded the plate. One day I was fouling off a lot of pitches from Russ Meyer and he was getting frustrated, and finally he yelled, "Okay you little so-and-so, if you want to get on base, here," and he hit me in the back.

Jackie Robinson was the best base runner I ever saw. We didn't steal as many bases as they do today. I led the league one year with 32. But every base we stole was an important one. Were we wrong? I was on so often, I could have stolen 100 bases. That's one thing that has definitely changed. In those days, if we had a 3–1 lead and I stole a base, somewhere down the line I was going to pay for it. The attitude was that you were showing them up. A pitcher was going to stick one in my neck, or a shortstop or second baseman would put a tag between my eyes, or they'd spike me. You paid for it then, and you knew you'd pay for it. Home run hitters don't stop trying to hit home runs when they get a three-run lead. And you might need five or six runs to win the game. But managers didn't want you running and showing them up. I don't think that's right, but that's the way it was.

Maury Wills and Lou Brock told me when they started stealing bases, they'd get drilled with a pitch or spiked for a while. Then when the press made such a deal about their stolen base totals and breaking records, the thinking became, "Maybe this isn't such a bad thing."

The Carpenters paid well, and we were like a family, but in 1958, when I led the league in hitting and we didn't have much of a ball club, John Quinn was the general manager. The first contract he sent to me called for a $2,500 cut. I was not only disappointed and hurt, I was mad. I had a figure I was going to sign for, but now I decided I'm going to get more. I called him. "Why did you do that?" He said, "You don't hit your singles far enough."

I'd never heard that one in my life. I said, "Well, if I hit them any further, they'd be outs." Outfielders played me shallow, and if I hit a single, it was easier for them to throw out a runner ahead of me. Quinn was tough. He wouldn't be able to operate in today's baseball.

I finished up with the Mets in 1962. Casey Stengel was the manager. They said he was slipping, but his memory of long ago was still there. I remember one day before a game a guy looked in the dugout and said, "Casey, do you remember me?" Casey looked at him, and he remembered the guy's name, the game way back in Kansas City they had been in maybe forty-five years earlier.

The Mets were losing 120 games. To the older players, if you're not on a contender, you're flogging a dead horse. If I had been with a contender, it might have been different. At thirty-five, I had a shot at three thousand hits and sometimes regret not trying for it. [GM] George Weiss offered me a $10,000 raise, but I wanted to quit baseball before it quit me.

In November the Phillies offered me a broadcasting job. I said no. They said think about it. I was very active in Republican politics in Nebraska. They asked me to be a candidate for Congress. Our congressman was a good friend of mine, and the party wanted to defeat him. They asked me to run against him in the primary. But I didn't want any part of that. He lost the election. So my wife and I talked about the broadcasting job, and I said why not give it a shot. Twenty-nine years later here I am, still giving it a shot.

I've seen two things disappear in baseball: the ability to slide and to bunt. We used to work hard on perfecting slides in spring training. We had sliding pits, and you had to practice different kinds of slides. Sliding pits are gone. Nobody teaches it. Bunting is a lost art. Nobody works on it. The best bunter I ever saw was me. Thirty-five of my 225 hits one year were bunts, most of them push bunts toward third. Dragging a bunt takes it toward two players. Pushing it toward third is at one guy.

Of all the outfielders I saw, Richie Allen could have had a Hall of Fame career. When he came to the major leagues, you could not have found a better kid. All he wanted to do was play ball. No BS about him. He was all baseball. I think the incident that probably started him downhill here was when he and Frank Thomas had a fight right on the field in 1965. As a result of that fight, the Phillies sold Thomas, or at least they used that as the reason. It was the time they were having race riots in north Philadelphia. People were really uptight about this stuff. Now you get a black guy and a white guy in a fight, and they get rid of the white guy. Thomas was popular here, didn't play here long, but fans liked him. Then they put a gag on Allen, wouldn't let him talk to the press under duress—I think a $500 fine or something. Thomas was free to be on every radio and TV show in the city and said he tried to apologize to Allen, but Allen wouldn't accept it, which is true. I think that was the start of it. Allen wasn't blameless. He started isolating himself in the clubhouse.

The two outfielders I would want playing alongside me—defense only—would be Willie Mays and Roberto Clemente. Clemente had a better, more accurate arm and quicker release, getting to the ball, getting rid of it, and throwing right on the money.

Mays and I played shallow. I always hated to see balls drop in front of me, and I could go back for one. Mays was the same way. He really played in shallow. I hit one over his head one time in San Francisco, but he took a lot of hits from me.

I played in the shadow of great center fielders: Duke Snider, Mickey Mantle, and Willie Mays. That might have affected my consideration for the Hall of Fame. In fact, one voter told me that was the reason he didn't vote for me. They hit home runs and I didn't. My job as a leadoff man was getting on base, and I did that as good as anybody I've ever seen.

[Ashburn was elected by the Veterans Committee in 1995.]

3.

Elden Auker

VERO BEACH, FLORIDA, DECEMBER 20, 1991

• •

Elden Auker succeeded Carl Mays as the only truly underhand pitcher in baseball. He won 130 games in his ten years with the Tigers (1933–1938), Red Sox (1939), and St. Louis Browns (1940–1942) and pitched in two World Series (1934–1935). His wife of fifty-six years, Mildred, joined us at their waterfront home, a short drive from a golf course.

• •

I WAS BORN IN Norcatur, population 250, in northwest Kansas, in 1910. My father was a rural mail carrier for forty-five years, starting on horseback with a wagon, later on a motorcycle, and eventually in a Model T Ford. My mother's father had received a land grant from President Ulysses S. Grant and built what they called a soddie—a sod house made out of blocks of soil and buffalo grass, like an igloo. He was a bronco buster, catching and taming wild horses that he sold to people going west on the Oregon Trail.

Growing up, we had no interest in major league baseball. The first major league game I ever saw, I pitched in it. There were twelve of us in my high school graduating class. We had a football team of twelve boys altogether and a basketball team. Basketball was a different game in those days. In my senior year we won a tournament final game, 10–9. I scored nine points. We had no baseball team, so I pitched some for our town team.

Football was my game. I played in the backfield until I had to quit when I got banged up with a neck injury. I was set to go to the University of Nebraska and play basketball. They had a job lined up for me. A coach at Kansas State said to me, "You're a Kansas boy. You should go to school here." He got me a job to pay my way, so I went to the state school in Manhattan. I was going to be a doctor and took pre-med courses.

I was talked into playing football by accident in the fall of my freshman year. I was standing near the practice field, and the varsity punters were practicing kicking. I'm standing there in street clothes and caught a few of the punts and kicked them back, and I was kicking it farther than the punters were. The coach, Bo McMillin, came over to me and asked why I wasn't out for football. I said, "I got my neck hurt in high school and was told not to play football."

He said, "Do you like to play football?"

"More than anything in the world."

He took me to the doctors, and they gave me some exercises to do until they said I was okay to play. In practice a week before the first game I suffered a shoulder separation. Couldn't raise my arm. I could kick and played with a steel brace and padding on my shoulder. The next year I hurt it again.

When the baseball season came, I had to throw sidearm. I had a good fastball—a natural sinker—and curve, and I pitched that way the last two years. I lost only two games in college. I was All-Big Six conference in three sports and the first college athlete to be named *College Humor* magazine All-American in three sports.

Mildred: I never did see him pitch in college. Football and basketball, yes, but baseball wasn't a major sport in college then.

During the summer of 1931 we formed a team from school plus some local players. The Kansas City Monarchs came to Manhattan, and I pitched against Satchel Paige and won, 1–0. First game Paige had lost in one and a half years and the Monarchs' first loss in thirty-three games. Later I pitched against them under the name Leroy for $75 at the Arapahoe County Fair in Oxford, Nebraska, and beat them, 2–1.

When I graduated in 1932, the Chicago Bears offered me a twelve-game contract at $500 a game. That was big money in those days; my father was making $60 a month. I really wanted to play football, but that would interfere with my going back to school to become a doctor. Playing baseball wouldn't prevent me from going to school. Five big league teams scouted me. Brooklyn offered me $500 a month. Steve O'Rourke, a Detroit scout, offered me $450. I chose Detroit because they were building with a young club. The Dodgers were mostly veterans.

They sent me to Decatur in the Three-I League. Bob Coleman, a former catcher, was the manager. He watched me throwing sidearm and said, "The mechanics of throwing that way is a tough deal. You're hitting home plate from an angle. Most sidearmers are wild; they just can't get the ball over the plate. There was a guy named Carl Mays, used to pitch. Built about like you. He threw directly underhand. Did you ever try it?"

"No."

He showed me and I tried it, and it became natural for me. No strain on my arm. If my arm got a little to the side, I lost my stuff. I never scraped my knuckles on the dirt. My hand came down about six inches off the ground, my arm alongside my leg. My follow-through came up over my left shoulder. I was a good fielder. My fastball was a sinker. My curve broke up a little, not down, defied gravity a little. At least it didn't sink. I threw a screwball that broke down and in to a right-handed batter.

I never saw anybody pitch the same way. Later I watched Dan Quisenberry on TV. Sometimes he'd get more sidearm and get into trouble with wildness. If he'd stayed down there all the time, he'd have been a lot more effective than he was.

So I'm now throwing underhand at Decatur. When I threw batting practice, the guys said, "Gee, he's upside down." They had just started night games, and the lights were pitiful. One day first-place Quincy was in town. Coleman said to me, "I'm going to start you, and you're going to pitch the complete game. I don't care if they get a hundred runs off you and you walk the ballpark; you're going to pitch nine innings."

I shut them out, one hit, one walk. From that day on, that's the only way I threw.

The Three-I League went broke. They kept me and Claude Passeau and two others and sent us to Moline in the Mississippi Valley League.

Mildred and I were married in February 1933. She was teaching school in Hutchinson, Kansas. I was pitching in Beaumont and had an apartment with Passeau. When my folks drove Mildred down in June, he had to get out. I came home one day and said, "We can't stay here anymore."

"Why not?"

"We're going to Detroit." And she started crying. We drove to

Springfield, where her brother lived, and I flew on the Bee Line, the original Braniff, to Chicago in a five-passenger plane and met the team there. I remember we took off, and the pilot and copilot pulled out a box of popcorn and were eating popcorn while we flew.

When I got to Detroit, the club owner, Frank Navin, told me his philosophy. "We want you to be a starting pitcher. When you go out there, we expect you to pitch the entire game, whether it's nine or ten or twelve innings. I can't afford to pay some guy to start the game and another guy to finish it. I don't have that kind of money. Just one pitcher for each game."

We spent that winter in Manhattan, Kansas, and I went to spring training with the Tigers in 1934 and opened the season in Chicago.

Mildred: I was to drive the car from Kansas and meet him in Chicago. I had the car loaded with all our worldly belongings. I took the car to Detroit, and he went to Cleveland for a three-day series, and then they were to be met by the fans at the railroad station and be welcomed home. So I was to meet him there. I got to Detroit and went to the hotel, and there was a message there for me to call a number out in Grosse Point, and it was the assistant prosecuting attorney's number; he knew Elden's father from way back, so he wanted me to come right on out to his place. I drove out there and I still had the car packed full; we had dinner, and he didn't want me to go back downtown to the hotel at night, so he said, "We'll put your car in a commercial garage." So we went out to my car, and the window was broken out. There wasn't a thing left in the car, and I had exactly what I had on my back, and Elden had a weekend bag in Cleveland. We had sixty-four dollars between us. Everything we owned was in that Chevrolet. Now we didn't have anything. That wasn't a very good welcome to Detroit.

They had about five thousand people at the Fourth Street station when we came in. Everybody was celebrating, carrying banners, band playing. We got off the train, wives came around, greeted their husbands, laughing and joking. Mildred came toward me, and she's crying. I thought: something's wrong. I said, "What's the matter?" She said, "We've been robbed. We don't have anything."

She had arranged an apartment out on Chicago Avenue. We

didn't have money for a down payment, but they took us in. Payday was a ways off. I went down to the ballpark the next morning, and Frank Navin wanted to see me. He said, "I understand you had a little problem."

"Yeah."

"Did you find anything?"

"No."

"Did they get all your clothes?"

"Yeah."

"Mrs. Auker have any clothes?"

"Nothing."

"How much money do you have?"

"Sixty-four dollars."

He went out and came back and handed me a check for $500. Most money I ever saw in my life. After a couple months they gave me a bonus of $1,500. Then we got in the World Series and got a little check for that.

Navin was a wonderful person, like a dad to me. He didn't have much money. That's why he brought Walter Briggs and Mr. Kelsey of Kelsey Wheels in as partners. Harry Heilmann once told us that after he led the league in hitting in 1927, he thought, "I'm going to get some real money next year." He went to see Navin, and Navin said, "Harry, you had a great year. Here's a contract. Take it home, fill in what you want, and bring it back." Harry told us, "I couldn't sleep for a week. I didn't know what to do with it." He didn't have guts enough and gave himself a very slight increase.

That was Mr. Navin.

Mildred: Being with the players' wives was sort of like being back in school, a fraternity or something. We did everything together. Players all real young. Except Charlie Gehringer, the most popular bachelor in the American League. I was in awe of him. You spoke to him only if he spoke to you first, which wasn't often. If one of our players made an error, you didn't say a thing when fans got on him. You kept very quiet. You wanted to bat 'em over the head sometimes, but you just pretended that they weren't there.

[Mickey Cochrane had come from the Philadelphia Athletics as a player-manager in 1934.] Cochrane was a leader. Everybody respected him. There was a lot of pepper on the bench, encouraging our guys all the time. He had an eleven o'clock curfew. He wanted us to be in our rooms by then. Be gentlemen. Shirt and tie and jacket in the hotels. Concerned about the image of the club and us.

Mickey had some crazy ones to handle. We had a pitcher, Boots Poffenberger. Never left the hills of Pennsylvania. Once in Philadelphia he went someplace, came in about two. A writer saw him in the lobby. Cochrane found out and called a pregame meeting. He said, "A rule was broken last night by Boots. Word came to me that you didn't get in until two this morning. Where were you and what the hell were you doing?"

Boots sat there all innocence. He says, "Mr. Cochrane, I refuse to reveal the identity of my whereabouts."

Cochrane sent him home for a week.

Boots was pitching one hot, humid afternoon. About the third inning he gets the first guy out and walks toward our third base dugout, comes in, sits down, wipes off his face. Cochrane comes over, thought he was sick or something. "What's the matter, Boots?" Boots says, "Too hot for me. Ain't pitching anymore."

Gee Walker was an outfielder who loved to run. He got caught off base a few times. Once in St. Louis he gets picked off. Cochrane called a meeting. "I'm tired talking about this. From here on it's an automatic fifty-dollar fine if anyone's caught off base. Second time, a hundred dollars. Third time, suspended."

Next day Jack Knott is pitching against us. Hell of a move to first base. Cochrane gets a single. He gets talking to the first baseman, takes a step off first base, and Knott nails him. First to get caught after the meeting. He said, "That walk back to the dugout was the worst I ever had." He was so mad you coulda struck a match off his face, it was so red.

Cochrane worked each pitcher a little differently. He handled me completely differently from Schoolboy Rowe, who was just a kid out of high school, not mature, could not take too much criticism. Mickey had to handle him gently. Tommy Bridges was a professorial kind of guy, businesslike. General Crowder was a veteran; he had ulcers, drank milk during the games. Mickey left him alone.

With me, Cochrane never complimented me on a game I pitched. It used to bother me, make me mad 'cause he was always praising Rowe. I worked a game against Cleveland—hot day in August in old League Park—and we were in a pennant race. Indians outfielder Sam Rice was hard for me to pitch to. He stood flatfooted and hit the ball through the infield. I shut 'em out; they got maybe five hits off me, and Rice got three of them. Game over. In the clubhouse guys are going, "Nice game," to me. Cochrane's locker is right next to mine. He comes in—always wore his mask on top of his head—sweating, threw his mask in his locker, jerked off his chest protector, looked at me, said, "When in the hell are you ever going to learn how to pitch to Sam Rice, for Christ's sakes?" That's the only thing he said to me. Made me so goddamn mad, I could fight him, but that was what he wanted me to do. I found out later: he wanted me in a fighting mood all the time.

If a batter got a hit on an 0-2 pitch, it was a fine. The whole league knew about it. I was pitching against Boston one day. Jimmie Foxx at bat. Cal Hubbard the umpire. Cochrane is catching. It's like a fraternity at home plate, those guys always talking, laughing, and joking, and you're out there in the hot sun working your ass off, and you want to get off the mound as soon as you can. I had two strikes and no balls on Foxx. Cochrane called for a fastball. Normally I'd try to back a hitter off the plate. Lou Gehrig, I'd always throw at his feet. He'd dig that left foot in and rack it. I'd try to keep that left foot loose on him. Broke his toe once.

So I throw a fastball right down the middle of the plate and Foxx was just frozen, couldn't turn it loose, and Mickey yelled, "Jesus Christ," and Hubbard, a big guy, said, "Ball one," and before he got his hand down, he took his mask off and took about three strides out toward the mound to me and said, "Look, you big-eared bastard, that ball was right down the middle and I just blew it, and don't you say one thing."

What made Mickey Cochrane a great catcher? He gave you a good target. He worked with you. He was with you all the time, keeping you on your toes. If he thought you were letting down a little bit, he'd wake you up, pretty near knock you off the mound. He was always talking to you. I could hear him in Yankee Stadium with fifty thousand fans yelling.

Cochrane told us young pitchers right from the start: "I'm the manager and I'm the catcher, but you're pitching the ball game. I never want you to throw a pitch that you don't want to throw. If you don't have confidence in that pitch, don't throw it. It's not what I think, it's what you think will get the guy out. Your thoughts are a hell of a lot better than my thoughts."

I shook him off many times. I had a reason for doing it, and he never questioned it. Sometimes I was wrong, and sometimes I was right.

Our pitching philosophy was to let 'em hit the ball. Cochrane said, "Keep throwing it till they start hitting it." In a game against Cleveland one day I never threw a curve. With a three- or four-run lead, you pitched differently: let 'em hit it. Not concerned with strikeouts. I threw a lot of sinkers that were hit on the ground. At home the groundskeeper would see that the infield grass was a little damp. Earned run average didn't mean much to me. Winning was all. If we had a big lead, I didn't care if they scored some runs.

Funny thing—on a team in those days we never looked at each other as stars or anything. You had a particular job to do on the club, and you are part of the organization. I had no idea what the other players were making and didn't care. Tommy Bridges and I were very close, roomed together on the road. I never knew what Tommy made. Never inquired. It wasn't any of my business. There was no publicity about it. Later, when salaries were all over the newspapers, that all changed.

We knew Charlie Gehringer was a great ballplayer, but he was on our club and he was our second baseman, and we just felt he was the best in the business. We had Billy Rogell at shortstop, and we thought he was the same way. [Future Hall of Fame outfielder] Goose Goslin came over from Washington in '34. So did Al Simmons, who didn't come through for us like Goose. Simmons had an air about him like he was above the rest of us. But Goose was a good guy, always trying to help the younger guys. Everybody loved him. A bachelor, he won the title of ugliest guy on the club.

Only one I ever saw who smoked a cigar in the shower. He liked to come over to the apartment after a game and eat onion sandwiches and drink Stroh's beer and play bridge.

Pete Fox was an underrated ballplayer, good base runner, covered a lot of ground in the outfield. One year he got into a slump and wound up talking to a Chicago psychiatrist who told him, "Your problem is your mental attitude. You're down on yourself. You have to change that. You should be the sparkplug of the club." Pete comes out to the ballpark after the session. He says, "From here on in, just call me Sparky." It changed his whole personality. He was hitting around .260 in June and finished at .321.

Jo-Jo White was a fast, smooth outfielder, covered more ground than anybody but DiMaggio. Always going with the pitch, like he knew where the ball was going to be hit. Great leadoff man till he hit a home run. For the next three weeks he was trying to hit the ball out of the park and couldn't get a hit.

We had Hank Greenberg at first base, and Hank was a big, gawky guy when he first came up, awkward at first, couldn't catch a fly ball—he'd get dizzy. Hank had flat feet, could hardly make it through a doubleheader. His feet were killing him. He needed a foot rub after a game. We didn't look at him as anything special, even with the Jewish element. We never looked at Hank as a Jew. He was just a teammate. I didn't know what a Jew was when I came out of Kansas.

Mildred: We had an apartment in a restricted building, and I had to ask Elden, "What does 'restricted' mean?"

I had to ask somebody else because I didn't know. The White Sox were the worst jockeys. In Comiskey one day somebody called Greenberg a yellow Jew son of a bitch. After the game he went in, took off his shirt and shoes, and walked out of our clubhouse, never said a word, walked over to theirs, opened their clubhouse door, and went in and said, "I want that guy who called me a yellow Jew son of a bitch on his feet." Not a guy moved. He walked around the room. Nobody said a word. He walked out.

I think I was more effective the way I pitched because it was different. Some hitters didn't like unorthodox pitchers. Babe Ruth was one who didn't like 'em. We had a left-handed sidearmer, Chief Hogsett. Ruth couldn't hit Hogsett with a handful of sand. The Yankees had a third base coach named Art Fletcher, a real jockey. I didn't know who he was. The first time I faced Ruth, I struck him out. When I went out to start the next inning, here's this guy yelling at me, "Hey, bush." I didn't pay much attention to him. Then he says, "You really got the Bam upset. He just said he's struck out a lot of times, but it's the first time a goddamn woman ever struck him out." I coulda killed him, but I didn't dare say anything.

[Yankees manager] Joe McCarthy said, "Elden Auker is a good pitcher, but I wouldn't have him on my ball club because he's unorthodox, and I don't go for unorthodox ballplayers."

I knew I was going to have trouble with some of the shorter umpires. In the American League they worked directly behind the catcher and couldn't see the low pitches. John Quinn couldn't see over our catchers, especially Ray Hayworth.

I didn't feel any nervousness before the 1934 World Series against the Cardinals. We'd played 154 games, maybe 30 more exhibition games before and during the season. In a pennant drive every game is important. We didn't care what the writers wrote, sometimes didn't even read the papers. A pennant drive was a big deal, especially for us because we were a bunch of young kids.

I pitched Game 4 in St. Louis, won 10–4. My sinker ball broke more bats than they got base hits. That's the game when Dizzy Dean went in as a pinch runner. Rogell's throw hit the bill of his cap, which helped save him from injury. It went straight up in the air, and Diz went down like somebody shot him.

There might not have been a Game 7, but the day before umpire Brick Owens had called Cochrane out on a play at third base and he was in there safe. The ball was this far from Pepper Martin's glove, and the ump's hand was already up in the air. We lost, 4–3.

So it was me and Diz in Game 7. I was ready. We were home, where the groundskeeper always soaked the area in front of home plate pretty good for me. I thought I had better stuff there than I had in St. Louis. I thought I was faster, but the ball wasn't moving. Later Dean told me, "In the first inning the guys said, 'He doesn't have it. We're gonna get him.'"

The game blew up in the third. They had the bases loaded and two outs when Frankie Frisch hit one over first base. Greenberg jumped a little too soon, and it hit off his glove toward the right-field stands. Pete Fox went after it, his spikes slipped in the rain gutter, and he kicked the ball toward the dugout; Cochrane ended up fielding it, and they scored seven runs. For the rest of the game Dean was laughing at us and we were all sore. I took a shower and went home. [St. Louis won, 11–0.]

In 1935 we had eight regulars hitting .300. [Detroit won the pennant and met the Cubs in the World Series.]

Ernie Quigley was umpiring at third base in the third game. He used to officiate football and basketball in the Big Six when I was in college. I knew that he hated to be called Quig. We had a volatile third base coach, Del Baker. I warned him, "If you get any close plays at third base, don't ever call Mr. Quigley 'Quig.' If you do, you're in trouble." In the sixth inning there's a play at third base and it goes against us. Baker starts on him: "Goddamn it, Quig . . . er, Mr. Quigley." The ump said, "Don't 'Mr. Quigley' me. You're out of here." Baker came into the dugout, stopped at me, said, "Mr. Quigley, my ass."

[The Tigers led the Series, 3–2. Game 6, at Detroit, was tied, 3–3, in the last of the ninth.]

I'm sitting on the steps, due to start Game 7, and Goose Goslin sat down beside me and said, "I got a hunch. I'm going to drive in the winning run if I get up there with a man on base, and we're going to win this game." And he did. Drove in Mickey Cochrane with a single and then ran right for me. "What'd I tell you . . . ? What'd I tell you . . . ?"

Our World Series share was $6,500. Tommy Bridges bought a Cadillac Coupe Deville, all black, loaded with a radio and heater, paid $1,000, and we thought he'd gone crazy. What a waste of money that was. I had a deal with Pontiac. I gave them $100 and got a new car every year. Tommy had the same deal, and here he was spending a thousand dollars for a car. That was terrible.

Shortly after the World Series, Frank Navin died. We were upset by his loss. Walter Briggs was now the owner. I'd made $8,500 or $9,000 the year before. Won eighteen games. We were world champions. We're in Lakeland, Florida, and I get a letter from the Detroit Baseball Club with a 1936 contract for $10,000. I sent it back unsigned. I got another one, for maybe $10,500. I sent it back. I'm out playing golf, and I get a call from Mr. Briggs's secretary, Joe.

"Elden, Mr. Briggs is at his home in Miami Beach, and he'd like to talk to you."

We drove down there, and his son, Spike, was there. Joe said, "The old man's on the phone. He's got a strike on at the Mack Avenue plant, and he's in a hell of a mood. All night. They set some building on fire."

Mr. Briggs was a paraplegic, had Locomotor Ataxia, hadn't walked in ten years. Mean, tough, had a violent temper, swore like nobody else. His wife had to make an appointment through Joe to talk to him. I go into this plush office. He's sitting behind this twelve-foot desk, papers all over the place. A gruff "Sit down. Why didn't you sign those contracts we sent you?" He barked at me like he was going to bite me.

"I don't think it's enough money."

"How much do you think you're worth?"

"Well, there's two things here: how much I think I'm worth and how much I'm gonna get paid. I don't think you have enough money to pay me what I think I'm worth. But if you want to know how much money I want to sign a contract, I want $15,000."

He was furious. "Fifteen thousand dollars!" He started swearing. "What am I going to pay the rest of the club?" He went berserk. I got up and started to leave. He says, "Where you going? Sit down."

I said, "This doesn't look like much of a conversation to me."

I got the $15,000. He really didn't like me after that, and he let it be known. Hated my guts.

[In 1937 Mickey Cochrane was hit in the head by a pitch that ended his playing career.] I was on the bench when Bump Hadley threw a slider high and it moved in on Mickey; he turned his head, took his eye off the ball, pulled back, and the ball followed him—slid—right in, and he didn't get out of the way in time. Hit him solid. Sounded like a board cracked. Went down just like he was shot. I thought he was dead. He was lying on the ground shaking. After a few minutes, our trainer, Denny Carroll, said, "Let's get him upstairs. We'll call a doctor." The Yankees' trainer agreed. Rowe and I and a few others got him by his arms and legs and head and picked him up and carried him upstairs. He was in and out, groaning. The doctors came, and they took him to the hospital. We knew that he'd been hit hard, but we didn't know then that it had fractured his skull in eight places. We just thought he'd been knocked down. I'd seen guys hit in the head before. We went back to the bench, and the game went on. Nobody knew then how serious it was.

Bump Hadley felt worse about it than anybody.

I think it bothered Mickey's eyes. He could still catch, but he couldn't hit. As a manager, he was different because he wasn't playing. He was happy when he was playing but like a caged lion when he wasn't. Couldn't sit still on the bench. Talking it up, smoking, nervous as a long-tailed cat in a room full of rocking chairs. Everything changed. We no longer had the leadership on the field. Ray Hayworth and Rudy York and Birdie Tebbetts were good catchers but not leaders.

George "Birdie" Tebbetts was a kid out of Providence. When he came to New York to try out with us, Tommy Bridges had gone home, and they asked me to share my room with him. I was in bed reading the paper when this redheaded kid came in. I asked him about his family, his team in Providence. Very devout Catholic. He was fooling around, lights on. I'm ready to go to sleep. Finally I said, "George, ready to go to sleep?"

"Mr. Auker, I'm kinda embarrassed."

"What about?"

"I always say my prayers before I go to bed. I don't know whether to say 'em or not."

I said, "Sure you can. I'll get down on my knees too."

So we did. That was the start of our relationship. I pitched his first game as our catcher. Whenever we were in Boston, his mother would bring us a cake or apple pie. Nice people.

Third baseman Marv Owen had stomach problems, sometimes got sick in the dugout. He retired, and that's how I wound up in Boston in 1939, traded for third baseman Pinky Higgins. That was one of the worst seasons I had. Won nine, lost ten. When that season was over, I was ready to quit. The manager, Joe Cronin, was a nice guy, but he had problems handling a pitching staff. He was very nervous, and when he was playing shortstop, before just about every pitch he'd run to the mound and say, "Keep the ball down on this guy . . . keep it away . . . don't give him anything good to hit but don't walk him . . ."—that kind of stuff, kicking the dirt around. Back and forth. Every time you make a pitch, you turn around and he's on the mound. He made you nervous just to watch him.

In Detroit I was used to pitching my own game. In Boston I found out I couldn't. One day I'm pitching, and Gene Desautels is catching. I'm shaking him off two or three times, and finally I called him out to the mound. "What's the matter with you? When I shake you off, I mean it. I'm pitching. I know these hitters."

He said, "You can't shake me off because Cronin is calling the pitches."

"Cronin is calling them? Jesus Christ, I never heard of such a thing, telling the pitcher how to pitch."

I never did get used to it. So one day I'm working a game against Lefty Gomez and the Yankees. When you're working a ball game, it's just like golf. You're concentrating. Can't hear the people in the stands or anything. You're concentrating on what you're doing. It's the same as if a golfer is playing in a tournament and is just ready to putt and some guy comes over and says, "Look, Arnie, get this hand a little lower. You gotta make this putt." It disrupts your concentration. You get into a rhythm in pitching, and that can get upset by small things, and Joe kept you upset constantly.

So I'm working this ball game against the Yankees, and Joe is out there every pitch, nervous as hell, telling me how to pitch to every hitter I've been pitching against for six years. Finally, about the third inning, I got so frustrated, the next time he approached, I walked off the mound and handed him the ball and said, "Here, Joe; why don't you pitch the goddamn ball game and I'll play shortstop?"

I didn't pitch again for twenty-one days.

The only pitcher he didn't bother was Lefty Grove. When Grove was due to pitch, the press got on Joe because he couldn't tell them who was going to pitch. Because if Lefty felt like pitching, he would, and if he didn't, he wouldn't. And Lefty wouldn't tell him.

Cronin drove the other pitchers crazy too. We got so screwed up, in the middle of the year [Red Sox owner] Tom Yawkey turned the pitching staff over to Jimmie Foxx to handle.

This was Ted Williams's rookie year. He was just a kid, about nine years younger than I was, but we became good friends. He lived by himself in a hotel and came out to our house often. Loved Mildred's fried chicken. From his first day of spring training, he was one of the great students of the game. Constantly asking questions about pitchers. By the time the season started, he knew as much about every pitching staff in the league as somebody who'd been in the league for years. Had his head in the game all the time. He'd be sitting on the bench and we're watching the game, and Ted would say, "He started the last nine guys off with a curve ball." Constantly studying the pitchers, and the hitters when he was in the outfield. He knew how the pitchers would pitch to batters and would position himself. When I was pitching, he'd play hitters one way, and another way when someone else was pitching. Like Joe DiMaggio—always in the right place; when a line drive was hit, he was right there waiting for it. Made it look easy. No spectacular plays. Some guys would be out of position and had to keep moving, making diving catches. Williams and DiMaggio moved themselves.

[Auker was with the St. Louis Browns 1940–1942.]

One day I'm pitching against the Red Sox. Bob Swift is the catcher. I have a one-run lead in the ninth inning. The leadoff man beats out a bunt. Ted Williams is up next. Swift came out to me and said, "What do you think he'll be doing?" I said, "I don't know. You think they'll be moving him over, playing for a tie? Or let him hit? Let's just waste a ball on him, keep it away from him, and see what he does." I was going to throw one outside and see if Williams turns to bunt or what. So I threw the ball low, about six inches off the ground, and outside. And Ted reached out and hit that ball into the center-field bleachers like a two iron shot, and it wasn't over the plate at all.

Game's over and I'm burned up, and I walk down the runway toward the clubhouse—both teams used the same runway—and he's down there in the runway waiting for me, laughing like hell.

He put out his hand. I said, "Get away from me, you bastard. You just killed me." He said, "I saw you and Swift talking. I knew what you were talking about. You were saying, 'We'll just waste one outside and see what he's going to do with it.' I knew right where you were gonna pitch it. I could see it all the way." He knew how I pitched, and he was thinking right with me, and that's what made Ted Williams a great hitter.

I had been working for an abrasives company during the winters, and they got into making anti-aircraft guns during the war, and I was frozen in that job until the war ended. I became president of the company, which became part of Dresser Industries, and retired in 1975.

4.

Dick Bartell

ALAMEDA, CALIFORNIA, 1985–1987

· ·

Dick "Rowdy Richard" Bartell was the premier NL shortstop of the 1930s. A holler guy, he was the sparkplug for three pennant winners: the 1936–1937 New York Giants and 1940 Detroit Tigers. He was the starting shortstop in the first All-Star Game in 1933. His .284 lifetime batting average ranks with other shortstops in the Hall of Fame. I interviewed him many times at his home while collaborating on his biography, *Rowdy Richard*, published in 1987. In one session he talked about his least favorite year.

· ·

IN 1939 I WAS traded to the Cubs. It didn't take me long to get into trouble with my mouth. In those days a common way to ride an overweight player was to yell at him, "What time does the balloon go up?" We trained at Catalina Island. The clubhouse was down by the shore, and from there we walked up a path to the ballpark. There was a wire fence with a little gate to go through.

One day I was walking up the path with Dizzy Dean and Woody English. A large, heavyset man was ahead of us. He had to turn sideways to get through the little gate. I didn't know who he was. I yelled out, "Hey, what time does the balloon go up?"

Diz said, "You know who that is?"

I said, "No."

"That's Ed Burns, the baseball writer for the *Chicago Tribune*."

Burns turned and pointed a finger at me. "You'll hear from me all summer."

And I did. The season started, and I was getting charged with errors where none had occurred, by the official scorer—Ed Burns. And infield hits I beat out were being charged as errors to the other team. Headlines in the *Trib* might read: "Cubs Win—Bartell Makes Error." When a ball was hit to me, the whole press box would sing out, "Error, Bartell."

I heard this: "If you want a souvenir at Wrigley Field, sit behind first base and Bartell will throw you one." That kind of stuff.

That winter the Chicago Baseball Writers had their annual dinner and show. Early in the proceedings a man walked out on stage holding a tiny baby bootie and announced, "A boot for Bartell." Later he came out with a bigger one: "Another boot for Bartell." This went on all night, the little shoe getting bigger each time.

Despite it all, I didn't lead the league in errors. But I didn't lead in anything else either. It was my worst year in baseball.

5.

Ray Berres

TWIN LAKES, WISCONSIN, MARCH 8, 1997

· ·

A light-hitting catcher, Ray Berres rode his glove and ability to get inside the heads of pitchers to an eleven-year playing career with four NL teams in the 1930s and '40s and nineteen years as the pitching coach for the Chicago White Sox—ten of them for manager Al Lopez—in the 1950s and '60s. Fellow old-timers visitor Jim Kreuz and I spent an evening with the eighty-nine-year-old Berres in the den of his lakeside home.

· ·

MY FIRST THRILL IN baseball was signing a pro contract with Oklahoma City in 1929. I'd have signed for anything. My dad had died when I was young. My mother didn't understand the situation, but my brothers and sisters encouraged me to give it a shot.

Like so many eager beaver kids, I was going to show how much I could do on the first day of spring training and hurt my arm and couldn't throw the rest of spring training. The manager liked me and I hit okay, but the owner was going to send me to the Cotton States League and he didn't know if I was worth my $1,000 salary for the year, so he released me on opening day. They had paid my one-way fare. Now I had to hitchhike home. I went through Waterloo, Iowa, and when I got there, I remembered there was a kid from home who was with them. I found out what hotel they were living in and went there and met him and tried out with them. I started throwing better and signed for $75 a month. Your money had to stretch. There was an old restaurant there and the owner was a fan, and he'd give us a meal ticket worth so much for the week, and he'd punch it every time we came in. I never ate so many hot roast beef sandwiches, mashed potatoes and gravy. No dessert though.

Birmingham bought me with a broken leg. I was playing with my right ankle in a cast—you played or went home in those days. Paid $750 for me. The owner wanted me to go out dancing all winter to build it up. He would call me and ask me if I was dancing, and I'd say, "Yeah, I'm dancing."

This was during the Depression, and it was tough for everybody. All the players took pay cuts. It was hot and all day games. I came home one year weighing 127 pounds. My mother got scared something was wrong with me.

The manager, Clyde Milan, was a tutor and father to me. I was relatively small, and I asked him if he thought I had a chance to get to the big leagues. He said, "Your enthusiasm and ability and hard work will take you there, but you'll never be a good big league hitter. You're observant and cooperative, and you'll always have a job. You don't have the offensive drive, but your defensive work will keep you there."

And that's the way it was.

My second biggest thrill was getting to the major leagues. In my first big league spring training, with Brooklyn in 1934, the manager, Casey Stengel, was surprised at my size. He thought I'd be bigger. Stengel was vociferous in the dugout during games. He'd bawl you out for something right then and there. As a catcher I was responsible for every home run hit off us. He'd let me know it sometimes. He could get grossly animated if we gave up a home run on an 0-2 pitch. We were playing one Saturday in Brooklyn against the Giants. Full ballpark. Van Mungo the pitcher, fastball pitcher. A good fastball hitter was up. The guy hit one up in the seats to beat us. Stengel was furious. In the clubhouse he started chewing me out, said I'd kept 10,000–15,000 people out of the ballpark the next day, and he kept on and on and said, "I want you to sit there and think about it, and I'll tell you when you can take that uniform off." I got irritated and said to him, "Case, I just read in this morning's paper where you haven't won a ball game in Brooklyn on a Saturday in two years. How come you never jumped on your catcher, Al Lopez?" That was the wrong thing to say.

Zack Taylor, a former catcher who was a coach, was in the locker next to me. He said, "Keep quiet. You'll get him more stirred up than ever."

I learned how to block the plate real quick. Pepper Martin nailed me one time. The ball and he arrived at the plate at the same time. He dove in there head first and got his hand under my chest protector and ripped that strap, and the buckle parted my hair coming off; I thought, "Boy, there's got to be a better way than this." After that, I stood just off the plate, gave the runner all the plate to see, but as soon as he went into his slide, then I moved to block the plate. They couldn't bowl me over 'cause they couldn't get at me. I had to be quick because I was small. Gabby Hartnett says to me one day, "Ray, you'll never make a penny. Everything you do looks so easy, nobody appreciates it. While we roll around and block the ball, you just catch it."

"Thanks for the compliment," I says.

I subscribe to going with a pitcher's strength when it's also the hitter's strength—to a degree. A lot of times you'll see a hitter take a called third strike right down the middle. That's because he's looking for another pitch. So you can sometimes cross them up by going away from your own strength. You can't be mechanical all the time because they have a book on you too.

As a pitching coach, I was usually in the bullpen, not on the bench. Over the years I spent more time on my haunches in the pen getting guys ready than I ever did as a player. I'd lean on the fence and watch, and when a pitcher started making a glitch in his delivery, I would whistle to the center fielder, who would whistle to the shortstop and get the pitcher's attention when he started dropping down or slipping into a bad habit. Then I'd use sign language to remind him. Sometimes they knew they were doing something wrong when they started feeling it in their arms. Then they'd turn and look at me themselves. After the inning I might talk to them on the phone. I never went out to the mound.

One day in Cleveland I warmed up Billy Pierce, and he had good stuff. The game started and they were creaming him. I couldn't understand it, so I started looking for something. I noticed he was bringing his arm up and turning his hand differently for a curve from his fastball. The hitters picked it up.

We had a knuckleball pitcher, and everybody knew when it was coming. I had to have a kid show me how they knew. When he had to get his fist around a knuckleball, he spread the fingers out in his glove.

When Tom Seaver was a kid with the Mets, I could call his pitches, especially when he had a sore arm. Every time he was going to throw a real good fastball, he'd rear back just a little bit more than for a curve.

I started the practice of keeping charts on pitchers. But I did it as a convincer—if I had trouble convincing a guy to make a change in his delivery. Whenever he made a mistake, I'd mark that pitch, and I could show him what happened as a result of his mistake. Some young kids were hard to get through to. The easiest were the guys that were borderline, getting sent down time after time.

When I couldn't get across to somebody I was trying to help, it just drove me nuts. I commuted seventy miles each way from Twin Lakes to Comiskey Park, so I could let it wear off by the time I got home. I might take a swim or go out and catch some fish before turning in. I'd fall asleep, but about 2 a.m. I'd wake up, thinking, "What can I do to get through to this guy?" And I'd start walking the floor.

In addition to game charts of where each pitch was hit, I had charts on each pitcher: days of rest, how he did, number of pitches. We did not go by pitch count. You can hurt your arm in the first inning or any inning. It's more what you threw and how you threw it than how many pitches you threw.

Years ago, you took a pitcher out when you saw him getting the ball in bad spots, or you saw his velocity drop, or he lost control of his curve ball. If a guy was going well, we left him in there. You could tell when he started losing his stuff or started straining or moving his head to try to pump some more velocity. Al Lopez and Paul Richards were very good at seeing when things were slipping. They didn't need a gun on the pitchers.

I made my living by my ability to look at a young pitcher and know what kind of pitches he should *not* throw. You need the right kind of wrist to throw a curve. Some don't have it. The slider was around then—they called it a nickel curve—but it wasn't used as much as today. Some young pitchers are working on sliders today who shouldn't be. It's a strain on some arms because it's not correctly delivered. A lot of deliveries aren't conducive to throwing good curves or sliders. Many times a guy trying to develop a slider will do something wrong in snapping that thing off and come up with a bad elbow. So many operations on elbows and rotator cuffs are the result of bad deliveries.

I took the slider away from Tommy John because it affected his sinker. I told him he'd come up with a bad elbow if he threw the slider too much. It took a different delivery. Later I watched him on TV and I kept telling him he was throwing too many sliders. Ultimately he had to have surgery and a new arm.

Bob Locker had a good sinker, and he wanted to throw a curve. I said he'd never be able to throw a curve because he didn't have the delivery or the wrist. He'd have to change his whole pitching style. I would demonstrate to these guys how they would wind up with sore arms and elbows if they tried to throw certain pitches with their deliveries. I did it so much I wound up needing an operation on my own elbow.

It's true that some guys can pitch the eighth but not the ninth, or when they're behind but not with a lead. The first time I learned that was when I heard a manager say, "We're down on pitching and in a tough situation. I hope they score a run off this guy in the first inning. He'll coast another eight innings for us if he's behind. But if we tie it or go one run ahead, he'll find some way to get out of there."

Then there was Saul Rogovin. He'd do anything to win, but you had to ride herd on him early in a game because he would coast, try to get by so he'd have his stuff for the eighth and ninth. You could see him start to crank it up when he got to the eighth. If he saw somebody getting up in the bullpen, God almighty! He'd get mad. Lots of times we'd get somebody up, not to use him but just to get Rogovin fired up. He didn't want to come out of there and have somebody else lose the game for him.

In the bullpen I saw guys whose behavior changed when it got to their stage of the game. But a lot of them loved the challenge. They'd go in and pitch two or three innings, eighth, ninth, didn't matter. Gerry Staley was a happy-go-lucky guy, didn't care what the situation was. It's a matter of knowledge, control, and guts.

And there were pitchers who could win on losing teams but not on winning teams, but I'm not going to mention their names.

Your delivery dictates where a pitch will go. Some, like Johnny Sain, had a smooth delivery conducive to throwing every day, which he did. Warren Spahn was smooth. Pitchers like Greg Maddux and

Carl Hubbell had good control because they had good deliveries. I see pitchers now, and it bugs me. They get out of rhythm; their delivery is such that they can't get the ball down.

We picked up Juan Pizzaro one year. He arched his back so much that everything came in high. A lot of pitchers do that. It was also a tipoff to a base runner. I kept trying to get him to change. One day in the bullpen he got so disgusted with me, he just took the ball and threw it back to the catcher without arching his back. I said, "Hey, that's the very thing I'm trying to get through to you." He said, "You mean I'm that dumb?" We were getting beat that day. I called the bench and said to Lopez, "Hey, Al, let's run Pizzaro in there. I think he's gotten what we've been trying to get into his head." We sent him in, and he breezed through them. From '61 to '64 he won 61 and lost 38.

In 1958 I was watching a Detroit pitcher, Bob Shaw, warming up. He had a live arm, but I didn't like his delivery. But the last pitch he threw, I liked and I remembered it. When Detroit wanted to send him down, he quit and went home. We picked him up and I told him what I had seen. He said he'd do anything to stick. So I changed his delivery and he went with it. One day I was riding down Michigan Avenue with Lopez; we passed the Stevens Hotel with the big store windows, and we saw Shaw looking at himself in the window and practicing his delivery. In '59 he won eighteen games, helped us win the pennant.

When Early Wynn started slipping at Cleveland, we got him, and he wasn't winning for us. I didn't want to say anything because he was a star. Finally he came to me and said, "Ray, can you tell me what I'm doing wrong?" Remember, he'd been pitching for seventeen years. I said, "I can tell you right quick. You're changing your delivery when you get mad out there." He'd get mad often, and then he'd be ball one, ball two, ball three. I showed him how he changed when he got mad and he said, "You mean it's as simple as that?" I said, "Yeah, it's as simple as that." I called it doing a nice figure 8 in his delivery. When he'd get mad and get in that wrong groove and couldn't get out of it, I'd holler, "No, Early."

He was 22–10 for us the next year.

I hated having to release a player or send him down. We had

meetings every year in spring training to decide who goes where. Oh, to have to tell somebody that you can't use him. You know they have a family and they didn't have the ability; the thing that bothered me was the guy who gave it the most, but you knew he just couldn't make it, and it literally broke my heart to have to tell him. The managers did most of it, but I had to give my opinion.

When Paul Richards took over the White Sox in 1951, he didn't care for Nellie Fox. He wasn't a classic second baseman, didn't make the double play that well, didn't have the arm, had hit about .250 the year before. We had a dispersal meeting: [general manager] Frank Lane, Richards, all the coaches. It had to be unanimous to let somebody go. When it came to Nellie, one of the coaches said, "He's a ping hitter." I said, "Yeah, but he doesn't strike out. And he's a gamester; he'll play every day for you and you can't hurt him, and you haven't got a replacement for him as good as he is."

Richards got mad as hell at me; he had arranged to trade him to Portland. He said, "Why do you like him so much?" I said, "He'll play for you hurt, and you'll never know it. But if, by the end of spring training, you still dislike him and want to make the deal, okay, but you've got to see this guy every day. He'll play for you if he has to use crutches."

The first exhibition game, first ball hit to Fox took a bad hop and hit him right in the mouth. Nellie spit out some broken teeth, shifted his wad of chewing tobacco, and stayed in there. He kept turning and spitting blood. I told Paul, "You have to get him out of there." "Oh," he says, "it's only the first inning." "Yeah," I said, "but he's spitting blood." So we took him out, and even then Nellie was kicking up a fuss about coming out. Richards brought in Joe Gordon to tutor him on the double play and how to pivot and cheat, and we had the infield throw to him on the inside of the bag so he had a better chance to cheat and make the throw to first. He became good at it.

In another spring meeting [pitcher] Harry Dorish's name came up. I said, "I'll keep him." Frank Lane had a deal set for him. He cussed me out—he was good at that—and said, "What do you like about him?" One of the coaches kidded, "Ray likes Polacks," just to get a smile, but Lane didn't smile. I said, "I like him if he's the tenth pitcher on the club. He's very cooperative. Whatever you ask of him, he'll do and never mumble. I like him because he's got his glove ready if you call on him. He'll go in in a tight spot or to mop up." Some guys have to start hunting for their glove with a "Who me?" attitude. We kept him, and he became a good close-out man.

My last year with the White Sox was 1969; then I went into the farm system, and that drove me nuts. Those kids wanted to do something their own way, and I'd say, "You can't do it that way." And they'd say, "Well, how come I was successful in high school (or college)?" And I'd say, "You weren't facing the same people you'll see up here."

I'm not good at remembering names, but I can recall how pitchers looked in every game I saw them pitch.

6.

Bill Bruton
MARSHALLTOWN, DELAWARE, MARCH 19, 1990

A speedy outfielder and leadoff man for the Milwaukee Braves (1953–1960) and Detroit Tigers (1961–1964), Bill Bruton led the NL in steals in his first three years and averaged more than one hit per game in his career. He proudly wore his 1957 World Series ring—rubies for bases and a diamond in the middle—while we visited in the living room of his home, formerly owned by his late father-in-law, Negro Leagues Hall of Famer Judy Johnson.

I WAS PLAYING SANDLOT ball in Wilmington, and a man who lived here had a connection with the Boston Braves. In 1950 they invited me to spring training in Waycross, Georgia, an ideal training spot. We had our own dorms, and there was nothing else to do there.

They sent me to Eau Claire, Wisconsin, in the Northern League. Andy Cohen was the manager. A good teacher. He wanted to get the most out of you and build your confidence, so he turned me loose. I stole 66 bases. In 1951 I was assigned to Hagerstown, Maryland, but there were racial problems there at the time, so I went to Denver and played for Cohen again. I had no problems in Denver or the other cities we played in.

When I got to the majors in 1953, Charlie Grimm was the manager. Grimm was easy to play for. If he could have picked his own players, he would have had a winner then. He would have picked players he respected and who respected him, who would not embarrass him or the team or themselves on the field. He felt we were playing a boys' game, but we were grown men and had responsibilities. You should know how to act. He seldom if ever fined anybody. We put on our own hit and run. He told us we knew how the pitchers would throw to us better than he did, and we should get our signals worked out between us players. "I'll figure out what's going on," he said.

Grimm told me, "You're in the majors. You should know when

to attempt to steal a base and when not to. Don't wait for me for a signal. You know the pitchers better than I do. If you get a jump, go ahead." He gave me a green light all the time. I led the league my first three years with 26, 34, and 25 stolen bases. You didn't run then just to steal a base. You ran because you represented the tying or go-ahead run. We didn't run for personal records. When you steal 100 or more bases, that's a guy running just because he's on base. If we're leading by 6–1, why should I run into second base and take a chance on breaking a leg? What good is it going to do? Even if you score from there, now it's 7–1. So what? We had enough confidence in our pitchers to hold the lead.

If I led off and got on base, I wouldn't go right away. If the number two hitter failed to advance me, I might even debate then. In Milwaukee our number three hitter was a left-handed pull hitter, Eddie Mathews. If the first baseman is holding me on, that gives him a bigger hole to aim at. If I'm on second, that hole's not there anymore. I was more valuable to the team and to Mathews being on first than second in that situation. Now if Mathews goes out, the number four man is a right-hander, Andy Pafko or Adcock or, later, Aaron. I'm not going to take the bat out of his hands. I'm going to give him a chance for a swing. If he gets two strikes on him, then I might go. If I get thrown out, he starts off with a clean slate. If I make it, I'm in scoring position for a single.

That was the general strategy throughout the league. Not everybody had a green light. I was fast, could run, knew what I was doing.

You steal off the pitcher. If you get a walking lead off second, it's easier to steal third than second. Lefties are tougher to steal on from first because they get away with murder. Righties will have one little thing to indicate they are going to throw home. You have to spot that one indicator. Left-handers are facing you, and they cheat anyhow, so they were tougher.

I never used a head-first slide. I was always afraid of it, and it doesn't get you there any faster. The thing I didn't like about it was: who says that second baseman or shortstop won't have to go up in the air to get a bad throw, and when he comes down, your face could be right under his spikes. If I go in feet first, he can come down on my leg. He might break my leg but not my head.

I hit the first home run ever hit in Milwaukee County Stadium on opening day in 1953, won the game in the tenth inning. It was the only home run I hit all year.

In 1956 we went into a losing streak, and they thought we needed to make a change. In a midseason change, you always wonder what style of ball the new manager will play. I was concerned about it. There were many things that [the new manager] Fred Haney brought to the club that I thought were detrimental, against the kind of baseball that you had learned how to play. My green light was turned off. We always waited for a sign. But we had a good ball club and went on to win the pennant in '57 and '58.

[**NM:** It sounds like you won more in spite of than because of Haney.]

You said it, I didn't [laughs].

I played a shallow outfield and could go back to the fence. I felt if you hit a line drive to the fence in center field, you deserved a hit. But if you hit a fly ball back there, I was going to catch it. I played the position as good as anybody.

When the batter got fooled and held up and then blooped the ball over the infield, I had to play shallow to try to cut it off. It used to gall me to see those little bloopers fall in there, like the one I got hurt on when I collided with shortstop Felix Mantilla in July 1957; it put me out of the lineup and the World Series. It was a little bloop Texas Leaguer, no height to it. The standard thing to yell was "I've got it" or "I'll take it," and the other would say, "Take it." Neither one of us waved the other off. You don't do that. The ball was hit in one of those spots where you did not know if anyone was going to be able to reach it. Looking up at the ball, you don't see each other. The second baseman couldn't come out to warn us; he had to stay and cover second. We both reached for it at the same time. My knee hit his knee. His was swollen but had no torn ligaments. My right knee had torn ligaments. We tried treatment until September 1, but I couldn't run on it. It took surgery to correct it. Even today I can only bend the knee so far, but I had enough mobility to run.

If there was any one leader on the '57–'58 Braves, it was Red Schoendienst. The infield gelled when he came there. Logan and

Mathews and Burdette and Spahn were the fun-makers, kept you loose.

Just being in the 1958 World Series was a thrill. There's a difference in how you feel before that first game than others. But once the ball is pitched, it's just another game. In Game 2 I led off and hit a home run, but that was not my biggest moment in baseball. Home runs were an accident as far as I was concerned. It meant I had hit in the air and I was aiming to hit it on the ground or on a line. That doesn't use my speed. I can intimidate the pitchers more if I'm on base. I wasn't sorry I hit it, but if I had my druthers, I'd have hit a single. Just being on base, they knew I would run, but they didn't know when. That kept them guessing, kept them from total concentration on the hitter.

We had a three games to one lead that disappeared against the Yankees. We came back to Milwaukee with Burdette and Spahn ready to go. We felt good. It wasn't overconfidence. The harder we tried, the less we produced. Mathews hit poorly—four hits. I hit .412 and was always on base when he came up.

I wasn't surprised when I was traded to Detroit in 1961. What surprised me was that the Braves management started breaking up that team a couple years too soon. I would like to have stayed with the same club throughout my career, but I was still in the big leagues. I had to learn all the pitchers and hitters in the new league; new ballparks too.

[Detroit manager] Chuck Dressen was a good teacher, but he wanted to change you from the way that you had been successful. This set well with the youngsters but not with the veterans. He was more valuable in AAA than teaching me his way to run the bases.

One of the best outfielders I saw was Carl Furillo because of his arm. He was more effective in Ebbets Field than elsewhere. He was pretty accurate when you gave him time to throw. In my rookie year we were in Brooklyn and I was on second; a ground single went to Furillo, and I'm going to score on a ground ball to right field. I knew how to make my swing before I got to third, not go home by way of the dugout. I didn't even look at the coach, just rounded third and scored. The coach liked to had a fit, said, "Don't you know he has the best arm in the business?" I said, "I got the best legs. I'm going to make him make a perfect throw to get me, and he can't do that every time when he's hurrying."

Mays, Vada Pinson, Richie Ashburn were good center fielders. If I could pick two outfielders to play alongside me on their fielding ability, I'd pick Mays and Aaron. Nobody talks about Aaron's fielding. He had good hands, good speed, could make the plays, strong arm, instinct to put his head down and get to where the ball was going. He didn't look so graceful doing it, but he got there. He learned to become more graceful as he played, but he could get a jump on the ball.

In 1964 there were no jobs open to black players to stay in the game, except maybe as a scout. I went to work for Chrysler in Detroit and stayed until I retired.

7.

Ralph "Putsy" Caballero
NEW ORLEANS, JANUARY 24, 1993

• •

Ralph "Putsy" Caballero had a brief, undistinguished five-year big league career with the Phillies and would be little noted nor long remembered outside of his hometown but for one fact: at sixteen years, ten months, and nine days, he was the youngest ever major league third baseman. It was September 14, 1944; World War II had stripped baseball of all but the over- and under-aged and 4-F. His wife, Clare, joined us in their home in New Orleans.

• •

I WAS BORN NOVEMBER 5, 1927. My father, a pharmacist, was Spanish; my mother, French and Irish. I had three brothers. Everybody in the family had a nickname. Mom and Dad just started calling me Putsy. That's what I grew up with.

We'd always been an athletic family. I got interested in baseball in grammar school. A young priest, Fr. Dolan, gave us a bat and ball, and we wore it out.

> **Clare:** The Caballero boys were well known in Sacred Heart Grammar School. Everybody used to talk about Putsy. We met in the sixth grade. My daddy owned a couple night clubs on Bourbon Street. He gave Al Hirt and Pete Fountain their starts.

We played in Catholic leagues as kids. I was an infielder. We were taught how to bunt, how to run bases. I read the box scores, followed Bill "Swish" Nicholson with the Cubs. In the summer of 1944 I was playing American Legion ball. Scouts for the Giants, Cubs, and Phillies were trailing us. When the Legion season ended, I became eligible to sign. Ted McGrew of the Phils [then called the Blue Jays] offered me an $8,000 bonus. I had a scholarship to LSU, but my father worked sixteen hours a day and that was a lot of money, so I took it. I signed on September 9, and my father and I rode the bus to Philadelphia. Took twenty-four hours.

I can still remember walking in the clubhouse at Shibe Park for the first time. All these veteran players—guys on their way out—started riding me: "Man, I wish I had your money" and stuff like that. They were probably making half what I signed for to play a whole season.

In 1945 I went to spring training with Utica in the Class A Eastern League. That was the Phils' highest farm club. Eddie Sawyer was the manager. Granny Hamner, Richie Ashburn—we called him Ricky then—were there. In the minors we had to know how to bunt or we got sent to a lower league. I had learned when I was twelve.

We were all seventeen-year-olds, living in a hotel. I roomed with Ashburn. I said to him, "If I ever have a son, I'll name him after you," and I did. And when he had a boy, he named him Ralph—not Putsy. We were roommates eight years, three in the minors and five in Philadelphia.

At the end of the '47 season we got called up to the Phils. That's when I got my first big league base hit. Ben Chapman was the manager. Chapman was a good manager, but he had it in for Jackie Robinson. Robinson was playing second base, and if you went into second and had a chance to knock him down and didn't do it, you were fined $500. If you get your check and there's $500 missing, you'll know why. But the more we tried to hurt Robinson, the more he hurt us. The catcher, Andy Seminick, tried to roll into him and fractured his own ankle. Another guy hurt his shoulder. I remember Schoolboy Rowe saying, "If I get two strikes on him, I'm going to hit him in the ribs." And he did it. Jackie would drop his bat down and head to first base, and before you knew it, he'd steal second. And he'd beat us. Trying to hurt him was losing us games. It got so bad Chapman called a meeting and said, "Let's play everybody the same way."

Throwing at hitters was part of the game. If you hit a home run, you knew the next time up, you'd be brushed back or the next batter would be, but not to be hit. That was baseball. Everybody brushed somebody back. I've seen guys lean over the plate, and the next pitch was at his chin. I remember Puddin Head Jones hitting a home run against Pittsburgh and the pitcher saying to the next batter, Hamner, "All right, let's see you hit a home run. I'm going to stick it in your ear." And that's what he did. The bat went one way and Hamner hit the ground. The umpire said nothing. Now if you do that, they want to start a free-for-all.

Sawyer replaced Chapman in the middle of the '48 season. A lot of us had played for him in Utica. One day he wasn't there. All the brass had gone to Trenton to see Robin Roberts pitch, and they brought him up.

Harry "The Hat" Walker was there. One time we counted: he touched his hat more than twenty times between pitches. A nonstop talker from Alabama, he sorta took us under his wing. In '47 he led the league in batting, but in '48 he was out of a job. Ashburn took over center field. The Philadelphia scouts wanted Ricky to hit everything into the ground, he was so fast. Not up in the air. I remember our scouts telling him that all the time. Marty Marion was the only shortstop I saw go in the hole and throw him out at first base. The other infielders had to come in a step and a half to throw him out.

Rex Barney was a young Dodgers pitcher who could fire that ball. August 18, night game in Philadelphia. He was always wild but not that night. I broke up a no-hitter in the fifth inning, hit a shoulder-high pitch line drive to center. Only hit of the game off him. Me, a .245 hitter. Later Barney said Duke Snider should have caught it. I don't remember my first big league hit, but I can still see that one.

And I can still see the pitch I hit for my only home run, a curve, off Giants reliever George Spencer, down the left-field line in the Polo Grounds in 1951. Leo Durocher was the Giants' manager then. Big bench-jockeying target. He was married to actress Larraine Day and she would be sitting behind the dugout with some other Hollywood stars, and we would call Leo "Mr. Larraine Day."

I cut a hole in the top layer of leather in my glove, so when a ground ball hit in there, it stopped the spin. In those days we left our gloves on the field back of second base. I remember once Eddie Stanky picking it up and looking at it, thinking about doing it to his glove.

[**NM:** What was the life of a baseball wife like?]

Clare: I loved it. Didn't miss a game. The team was like family; the players were close, the wives were close. We were all young. I was nineteen. Schoolboy Rowe was the old man of the team. When fans got on the team, Nettie Vergez and Dusty Cooke's wife would get indignant, but we laughed it off. When they went on the road, five or six of the wives would stay together at the house we rented. Other clubs would say they had never seen the companionship they saw among the Phillies.

I knew the game, but once my sister, Jackie, came up to visit. We were sitting there looking at the scorecard, and she said to me, "Do you understand all this?" I said, "Yes, Jackie." She said, "Beside this guy's name it says 'if.' What does that mean?" I said, "Oh, that means if this guy can play." She said, "What does 'of' mean beside this name?" I said, "That means of a certain pitcher."

In spring training in 1948 I met this older couple. They were always drinking, always loaded. One day they said, "Clare, we'll see you at the game today. We want you to meet our friend, Happy." So at the game I see the couple sitting in one of the boxes. The lady came over to me and said, "Come on, I want you to meet my friend." I said okay. One of the wives said, "Where you going, Clare?" I told her, "I don't know these people. They're always drinking. But they want me to meet their friend." So I go over and they say, "Clare, we want you to meet our friend, Happy Chandler." I said, "Hi, Happy. How you doing?" A perfect gentleman. Wonderful. Asked who my husband was. I'm sitting and I'm talking, and before I left, I patted him on the back and said, "I had a good time. Really enjoyed it." I get up and go back to my seat.

When the game is over, I'm standing with Ben Chapman. As Chandler and his friends walk by, Happy says, "Clare, nice meeting you." I said, "See you around, Happy. I enjoyed it too."

Chapman says, "Do you know him?" I said, "I just met him." That's when Chapman told me he was the commissioner of baseball. I said, "What do you mean, commissioner of baseball?"

Chandler went into the clubhouse and somebody mentioned Putsy Caballero, and Chandler said, "You know, I'll never forget his wife." He knew I was a young rookie wife. He liked the idea of me being natural about it.

In 1949 I had our first baby in Philadelphia when the team was on the road in St. Louis. I called and told him we had a son, and Granny

Hamner got on the phone and said, "Congratulations. But don't ask Putsy to come home. He's doing good." And I said, "Oh no, Granny. I would never do that."

In 1950 we won ahead of schedule. The Dodgers had a better team than we did. But everybody had a good year, no injuries. We had a seven or eight game lead on September 15. By the end we had a two-game lead with two to play in Brooklyn. Saturday they beat us. Sunday we're ahead, 1–0, and Reese hits one into the right-field screen. We're waiting for the ball to fall down, and he went all the way around for a home run. It's 1–1 in the ninth. Snider hit a line drive base hit to center with Abrams on second base, and Ashburn threw him out at home plate. In the tenth Dick Sisler hit a three-run home run. We went back to Philadelphia, and people mobbed the train there. That was the high point of my career.

In the World Series I pinch-hit against Whitey Ford. We're behind, 3–1. My job was to get on base. I went up to work him for a walk. I can still see that first pitch, right down the middle, but I took it. I struck out. My World Series share was about $5,000. That was big money. All my cousins wanted to borrow money from me.

Clare: I missed the Dodgers series and the World Series getting ready to have my second child. I listened to the last Dodgers game on the radio at my friend's house, and when Sisler hit that home run, I was on the floor crying. That night Walter Winchell on the radio says, "Putsy Caballero's wife is at home in New Orleans expecting their second child." My father in the next room is calling me, "Walter Winchell is talking about you." That was big time.

Twenty-five years later the Phillies had a reunion of that team and gave us World Series rings. We hadn't earned them in 1950 'cause we lost. I still have mine. I have this book, *One Hundred Years of Baseball*, and there's one line in it about the 1950 Phils' nicknames: Granny Hamner, Puddin' Head Jones, Swish Nicholson; and—it says—the immortal Putsy Caballero.

In 1951 we were going bad. We couldn't do anything right. We blew games making mistakes. In St. Louis and Cincinnati it was so hot, that's all you heard on the bench—complaints about the heat. Sawyer called a meeting in St. Louis. "Anybody I hear say anything about the weather will be fined $1,000. If anybody says how hot it is, remember the other team has to play in the same weather. I don't want to hear about it."

Ken "Cuckoo" Johnson is pitching. Along about the seventh inning he comes into the dugout, puts a towel on his head, says, "Boy, it's hot." Sawyer starts toward him and Johnson says, "But that's the way I like it." We're all rolling on the floor laughing.

In 1953 I went to Baltimore in the International League, then two years with Syracuse. I'm twenty-seven with three kids. I quit and started a pest control business in New Orleans.

It was hard when that first spring training time came after twelve years of going and I knew I could still do the job, but there was no money in the minors. I'm on the voluntarily retired list. I never got an official release. I'm sixty-five and I still belong to the Philadelphia Phillies.

8.

Jimmy Cooney

. . . .

Jimmy Cooney was a shortstop who played parts or all of seven seasons with the Red Sox, Giants, Cardinals, Cubs, Phillies, and Boston Braves between 1917 and 1928, when he and his brother, Johnny, were teammates. He is the only player to be involved in two unassisted triple plays. We visited on the front porch at his home in Cranston.

. . . .

BRANCH RICKEY WAS THE Cardinals' manager 1919–1925. He had too many signs. Players got crossed up trying to follow them. He had a team meeting every morning at 10:30. Lasted an hour and a half. He used such big words, players didn't know what he was talking about. If you had a good day today, Rickey would bring up some mistake you made four or five days ago.

Rickey handled the contracts. One guy went into his office one morning looking for a raise and came out hours later with no raise. He could talk you out of anything. But he didn't talk much on the bench during a game. "Judas Priest" was the strongest language he used. He didn't manage on Sundays. Burt Shotton took his place.

Rogers Hornsby and Rickey didn't get along. Hornsby would be reading the racing form during the meetings. Stud poker and horses were his gambling interests. When I was called up from Milwaukee, Rickey told me and first baseman Jim Bottomley to take all the pop flies on the right side no matter where they were. He didn't trust Hornsby catching them.

The St. Louis official scorer helped Hornsby, giving him hits on balls that if I was the batter, they'd be errors.

I heard Branch Rickey tell this story about outfielder Heinie Mueller: Mueller was acquired by the Cardinals in 1920. He came up to Rickey's office to sign a contract. Rickey said, "Can you hit?"

"I can hit as good as Tris Speaker."

"Can you run?"

"I'm as fast as Ty Cobb."

"Can you steal bases?"

"Yeah, I can steal as good as Max Carey."

"Judas Priest!"

"I don't know him, but I'm just as good as he is."

Rickey always reminded Heinie, "When you get the sign for a slow ball, move in. For a fastball, move out." Eventually the fans in the bleachers caught on to Heinie's movements. One day with three on, the catcher called for a fastball; Heinie moved in, the ball was hit over his head, and they lost the game. When Rickey asked him why he did that, he said, "I knew it was gonna be a fastball, but the crowd in the bleachers was getting on me and I wanted to cross them up."

Later, when Heinie Mueller and I were both in Buffalo, he told me this story about playing for Giants' manager John McGraw. In a close game, the Cubs had a man on third and one out. A spitball pitcher was pitching for the Giants. The batter hit a fly ball to Mueller in left field. He went to throw it home and the ball slipped out of his hand and wound up in center field. After the inning he comes in, and McGraw cusses him out: "Don't you know we've got a spitball pitcher out there? Put some dirt on your hands." Heinie says, "You goddamn Irishman; there ain't no dirt out there. It's all grass."

I was involved in two similar unassisted triple plays. I was on second base when Jim Bottomley hit into one made by Pittsburgh shortstop Glenn Wright. The other was one I made in 1927, when Paul Waner lined out to me and I caught Lloyd Waner off second and tagged Clyde Barnhart coming down from first.

9.

Johnny Cooney

A career .286-hitting left-handed pitcher whose arm problems forced him to become an outfielder, Johnny Cooney had a twenty-year big league career as a player with the Boston Braves and Brooklyn Dodgers between 1921 and 1944, followed by eighteen more years as a coach with Boston/ Milwaukee and the White Sox (1946–1964). He and his brother, Jimmy, were together on the 1928 Braves. We were joined by Cooney's wife, Alice.

I WAS BORN IN Cranston, Rhode Island. I'd go on weekends to pitch for a semipro team in Willimantic. The catcher and manager was an old-timer named Ed McGinley. One day in September 1920, I pitched a six-hitter against the Braves in an exhibition game. A Red Sox scout was in the stands, and he asked me to come to Boston and sign. McGinley says, "I'll go with you. I'll be your agent." So we went to the Red Sox office. Ed Barrow was the manager. McGinley and I go into the office, and I said, "I have an agent."

"An agent!" he says. He pulls out a contract and says, "We'll give you $500 to sign and $300 a month."

He starts writing out a check. Mr. McGinley says, "No check. We want cash."

Barrow blew up. "What? You wouldn't take a check from the Red Sox? Get out of this office."

We left and sat on a bench in Boston Common, and McGinley says, "Maybe we shoulda taken that check."

A few days later a Braves player came to see me and asked me to sign with them. This time I went by myself. I got $500 and $400 a month. I still had to give McGinley $250.

I joined the team in New York for the last few weeks of the season. First time I'd ever been out of Cranston. I took the overnight train and arrived about seven o'clock in the morning. I'm standing there looking lost, and along comes the Braves shortstop, Rabbit Maranville.

"What's the matter, kid? You lost?"

"Yeah."

"Come on with us."

We get in a taxi and out comes a whiskey bottle. "Want a drink, kid?"

"No thanks."

Seven in the morning and Rabbit's already drinking. Welcome to the big leagues. I never drank, smoked, or chewed tobacco.

George Stallings was the manager. He didn't wear a uniform, looked like a minister. First day I'm sitting near him. A spitballer, Dana Fillingim, was pitching. He always wore expensive hats. This day he was wild. Stallings said, "Look at him. A ten-dollar hat and a ten cent head." I'd start the game near him, but by the end I'd be down the end of the dugout. I never heard so much cussing in my life.

After a few weeks in 1922, I went down to New Haven, where I was 19-3 when I was recalled in September and stayed through 1930. By 1925 I was among the best left-handers in the league: 14-4 with twenty complete games. Then my arm went bad. Chipped bones in the elbow. My first operation left the arm paralyzed, crooked. For three months they tried to straighten it electrically, put me on a stretching machine in a New York hospital, 250-pound pull. I got out of there, and first thing the arm bends up again. Three months later another X-ray showed a bone block on the inside of the elbow. Locked all the time. Chiseled those off. By that time my arm was two and a half inches shorter. It took my fastball away. I was a utility man 1927–1930, went back to the minors at Toledo in 1931, then Indianapolis for four years, hit .375 in 1935.

Ballplayers make the manager. Rogers Hornsby managed the Braves in 1928. George Sisler was near the end of his Hall of Fame career. One day Hornsby sent me in to run for Sisler, the first time he had ever been taken out of the lineup. He was so mad, he and Hornsby almost came to blows in the clubhouse. But Sisler was a real gentleman, very quiet. We finished seventh with a 60-103 record. The club owner, Judge Emil Fuchs, figured he couldn't do any worse, so he became the manager. He knew nothing about baseball. A genial guy, he'd sit on the bench telling stories. One day a batter had a 3-1 count on him; he looks in to the bench for a hit or take sign, and Fuchs sat there and did nothing. Finally the third base coach called time and came over and asked, "What do you want him to do?" Fuchs looked at him and said, "Tell him to hit a home run."

We had a pitcher, Socks Seibold, didn't like Fuchs. Refused to sit on the bench with him. He sat alongside the dugout. When Fuchs wanted Socks to go in to pitch, he'd tell a coach, "Tell Socks to go down to the bullpen and warm up." Socks would say, "You tell the judge I'm not going down to the bullpen."

We finished last, but with Judge Fuchs managing, we won six more games than we did under Hornsby.

I played for Casey Stengel four different times over seven years, at Toledo and Kansas City in the minors and Brooklyn and Boston in the majors. Casey knew his baseball. In Toledo they didn't have much money. Once, when payday was coming up, Casey had a team meeting. "Boys," he said, "decide what you think you're worth; we'll write it on a card and pin it on your back, and we'll have an auction to meet the payroll."

In 1931 I took my regular turn pitching and played in 113 games for Toledo. I'm in right field one day in St. Paul. The second baseman made two or three errors in a row. Casey pulled him out and brought me—a left-hander—in to play second base. Another time in St. Paul they got seven runs in the first inning. The first two Toledo hitters went after the first pitch, and Casey went wild. "From now on everybody takes two strikes," he yelled. Along about the fifth inning, the St. Paul pitcher caught on and began to throw the first two pitches right over the plate. In the sixth inning Casey put me in to hit and said, "Don't take two strikes." I hit the first pitch on the roof.

Stengel brought me to Brooklyn in '36, and at the end of '37 I was traded to St. Louis with three other players for Leo Durocher. Branch Rickey was the GM at St. Louis. He wanted me to go down to Columbus. I was a ten-year man and said no. Came opening day, Rickey says, "I'll give you $7,500 to go to Columbus and be the manager." I said, "Mr. Rickey, I don't want to manage, and I don't want to go to Columbus." So he gave me my release. I could have collected ten days' pay from him because they didn't give me any notice. But I already had a job with Stengel, who was now the Boston Bees' manager.

Alice: I grew up in baseball. My father managed the Albany team for quite a while. He also umpired. But I never dreamed I'd marry a ballplayer. The wives were not allowed to go to spring training. We got along beautifully. I loved it. We dressed up—hats, gloves, the works—to go to the games. One time in Boston one of the wives wore slacks. She was told by the front office not to wear them again. After a game we'd go for lobster dinners in Boston. When the team was on the road, the wives would go out to dinner, play bridge. I never missed a game. We had one boy and would rent an apartment. We spent the winters in Sarasota. When school was out, we'd pack up the car and away we'd go. It was a nice life. I think it was a wonderful time. I enjoyed every moment of it. I wish we could go back.

I didn't like night baseball. It interrupted your whole living schedule. It was terrible. In the old days you couldn't find an open place to eat after a night game. And if you did, you couldn't go to sleep afterwards. He [Johnny] was almost electrocuted one night in Jersey City.

They had just put the lights in, and they ran the cables inside the fence. It was damp; the grass was wet. A ball was hit along the fence. I came in, and my spikes cut through the wire and gave me a shock. The next day they put the cables outside the fence.

I was with Boston five years, second in the NL in hitting in 1939–1940. End of '42 they released me. Ted McGrew, a Brooklyn scout, called and offered me a job with the Dodgers. And who is the general manager there now? Branch Rickey. They released me in the middle of the 1944 season. Joe McCarthy of the Yankees called me. What was I getting paid? I said, "$9,000."

"Oh, we can't pay you that kind of money. I'll talk to Ed Barrow."

Now, twenty-five years after he had thrown me and McGinley out of his office in Boston, I'm dealing with Ed Barrow again. I said, "You probably don't remember this, but twenty-five years ago you kicked me out of the office in Boston." He laughed. He gave me what I wanted. But they released me in August.

Then I got a call from Burleigh Grimes, who was managing

in Toronto. Grimes had been a tough pitcher who would throw at you, and if you didn't like it, you'd go down again. He wanted me to play for him, so I went with the understanding that I'd get my release at the end of the regular season, before any playoffs. When I got there, I found that he was going to be my roommate.

My son was in the navy, about to ship out, so I left the team as agreed before the playoffs to go see him. I got a notice from the minor league office that I had deserted the team. I wrote them and explained and never heard any more about it.

Now it's 1945 and I'm forty-four, Casey Stengel is managing at Kansas City, and they're at the bottom and need help, so I go with no spring training, and I run into a few doubleheaders and a three-week road trip, hit .343 for them. A pitcher hit me and broke two ribs, and that was the end of my playing days.

Casey went to Oakland and wanted me to go with him as a coach. But Billy Southworth took over the Braves and offered me a three-year contract as a coach, so I took it. Otherwise I would have wound up with the Yankees when Casey took over there in 1949.

Southworth was very strict. In spring training in Bradenton he would put little toothpicks on top of the doors of the players' rooms. He'd come back later, and if the toothpick was gone, he knew you'd gone out or come in late. He'd have the little clubhouse man, Shorty, sit out front of the hotel to see who came in late. We won the pennant in 1948, and I got a World Series check.

I managed briefly, filling in for Southworth for a couple months in 1949. I even umpired once—for two innings in 1941. In those days the umpires took a boat from New York to Boston. We were playing Brooklyn, and the boat the umps were on was fogbound and late arriving. I was designated the home plate umpire, but I stood behind the pitcher and called the balls and strikes. After two innings, the umpires showed up.

10.

Tony Cuccinello
TAMPA, FLORIDA, JULY 20, 1985

· ·

Tony Cuccinello was a baseball lifer: forty-four years (1926–1969) as an infielder with four NL clubs and the Chicago White Sox (1930–1945) and a coach with the Reds, Indians, White Sox, and Tigers—sixteen of the years for Al Lopez at Cleveland and Chicago. We met in the clubhouse at the golf course where he played eighteen holes almost every day with Lopez, his friend of more than fifty years.

· ·

I ORIGINALLY WAS SIGNED by the Cardinals for Syracuse in 1926. They wanted to send me to Topeka, Kansas. I came from Long Island City, just outside New York. I said, "Where the hell is Topeka, Kansas?" At Syracuse I got into a couple games. Burt Shotton was the manager. Pepper Martin was playing there. He said to me, "Do you want to get into a game?" I said, "Sure." So he'd say to Shotton, "I feel a little tired," and Shotton would tell me to get a glove and go in. I'd get a base hit, then a few weeks later would get in again and get a hit. I hit .750 that season, got three hits in four times up.

So they farmed me to Lawrence, Massachusetts, in the New England League. In 1927 I asked them to send me back up there. It was twilight ball, wool mills all over the place. We'd play about four o'clock, when the mill workers got off.

My first big league spring training was in Tampa in 1930 with the Reds. They had all these old-timers. I'm only about twenty-two, and these guys are 35–40 years old, probably playing before I was born.

It was kinda tough, being a young fellow going up to the batting cage, with all those old-timers jumping in there; I was scared to get in there. Finally, one of them pushed me in and said, "Come on, take a couple swings." I finally got into the lineup, usually at second or third. We set a double play record. [Teams with Cuccinello at second base led the NL in double plays five times during the 1930s.] Of course on a bad ball club you had more chances to make double plays. Every time you look around, there's one, two, or three men on base. We finished seventh or last two years in a row.

I played for a lot of second division teams. You worried more about what you did this year because that's how you got paid next year. If you had a good year, maybe you'd get a thousand or two raise. A $20,000 man in the early '30s was pretty good. Sometimes we had pretty good hitting but no pitching. We'd get six or seven runs, but the other club would get eight or nine. Then when we did have the pitching, we didn't have the hitting.

When I was with Brooklyn in 1932, we had pretty good hitting and pitching. Mostly older players on their way out. That's where I met Al Lopez. He and I and Van Mungo were the babies of the club. We were leading the league until the last few weeks of the season, then finished third back of the Cubs and Pirates and got a rare share of the World Series pot.

I was the last batter in the first All-Star Game in 1933. John McGraw was the manager. We were two runs behind in the top of the ninth with two outs. McGraw called me over. He said, "Young man, take a strike." That's all he said.

I thought to myself, "Geez, with Lefty Grove pitching, they ought to give me a strike."

Anyhow, I took the first pitch for a strike. Then he came inside. The next pitch, I got around real good and pulled it into the left-field stands, just foul. I fouled off a few more, then worked him to a 3–2 count. The next pitch was right down the middle. I swung right through it and missed it.

Lopez and I were traded to the Boston Bees in 1936. Bill McKechnie was the manager. McKechnie was like a preacher, but he knew baseball. He played for one run all the time; if we got one run, they'd have to get two to beat us. In that ball park in Boston on the Charles River, the wind used to blow in. You could hit drives out there, and they'd come blowing back in at you.

Opening day was Patriots' Day. We'd play in the morning, then they had this race, then we'd play again in the afternoon. We played the Phillies and they beat us, 1–0 and 2–1, and they were the tail-end team in the league. But they had a good hitting team—in Baker

Bowl. I got 6 for 6 there one day. They had a tin fence out in right field. Broad Street was right behind it. The balls would hit those cars driving by. They had a big Lifebuoy sign there. I used to hit it all the time, and you had to run like hell to get a double because the right fielder could throw you out.

Then Casey Stengel became the manager. He was always for the younger players. He'd rather play them than the older ones.

Ernie Lombardi belongs in the Hall of Fame. I played with him and against him in Boston. For a guy who couldn't run, he sure could hit. I used to play thirty feet back on the grass when he batted. I would let him bunt; the pitcher could throw him out. But he hit shots.

[Lombardi was elected to the Hall of Fame in 1986.]

We got into fights with the Cubs. They were known for throwing at batters. Lon Warneke and Pat Malone and Tex Carleton—those guys could throw like hell, and especially at Wrigley Field with those white shirts out in the stands, it was tough to pick up the ball. I remember Stengel saying, "Who do I have here who can go out there and knock somebody on his fanny?" And Mungo was the one. The only guy I didn't want to see get hit—he was a really good guy, never caused any trouble—was Gabby Hartnett. Mungo hit Hartnett right on the elbow, put him out for a week or two. We had an infielder named Mickey Finn. An inning or two later he slid into second base, and he and Billy Jurges came up swinging and started a real free-for-all. Then I think it happened again in Chicago. It finally got settled because it got to where somebody was going to get hurt.

One day Dizzy Dean threw one right at my face. I stuck my hand up and it hit off my hand and got me in the face. At Cincinnati we had a catcher, Clyde Sukeforth. He had been in a shooting accident while hunting the year before. Got birdshot in his eye. I think he still had a pellet way in the back of his eye. In the spring one day, Dean took the button right off his cap. You could see he was stunned. He went out to the mound and took the bat and said to Dean, "If you ever do that again, I'm going to hit you right over the head with this bat." Dean never threw at him again.

But that's the way things were. You'd hear pitchers say, "When he comes up to bat again, I'll get him."

That's why I'm still having trouble with my knee today. It happened in 1939. I was with the Braves. Dick Bartell was with the Cubs. What happened was one of our guys threw at his head, and, I was told later, he got mad and said, "I'm going to get the first guy in my path." I was the first guy in his path. I didn't know it until they told me later. If I had known it then, I could have protected myself. So he came into second base on a force out. We'd go into each other to break up a double play, not to hurt one another. There was no chance for a double play, and when I reached out to get the ball, he gave me a football block across the knees. I was in the hospital for a week and came back on crutches and was out for two months. That's when they told me what he had said. I never played in over a hundred games any year after that until 1945. That was during the war, and everybody was away. I was thirty-eight and signed with the White Sox on a month-to-month basis for $1,000 a month.

On opening day in Cleveland I pulled the hidden ball trick on Indians' manager Lou Boudreau. Was he ever embarrassed. The night before they'd had a big father and son dinner, and Lou was the speaker. Somebody asked him about the hidden ball trick. He said, "Oh, they don't use that any more. That's obsolete."

So I'm playing third, and we've got a three-run lead. The Indians get a few men on, then Boudreau gets a hit, and the next guy up gets another hit, and Boudreau comes around and slides into third. And I tag him.

The umpire calls him safe. I argue a little bit, and the pitcher comes over. I tell him, "Stay off the rubber," and I keep the ball. So he goes near the mound while I'm pounding my fist into my glove like it's empty and sure enough Lou takes a few steps off the bag. I dive for him as he dives for the bag. The umpire yells, "He's out if you got the ball." I had the ball, all right.

Jimmy Dykes was a conservative manager, but he'd gamble with you. In Detroit one day we got a few men on base, a run behind in the seventh inning. I get a 3-0 count. I look around, and he's got me hitting. I didn't believe it. I look again, and by God he's got me hitting. I hit one in the seats. He'd gamble sometimes like that, then he'd sacrifice for a run.

In 1945—my last season—I had a chance to lead the league in batting, and you had to have over 400 at bats to qualify. I had a two-point lead over George Stirnweiss [of the Yankees] going into the last day of the season. We were scheduled to play a double-header and got rained out. I had 402 at bats. The Red Sox were playing in New York. First time up Stirnweiss hit the ball to the third baseman, who booted it, then threw it away. The writer for the *Bronx Home News* was the official scorer. He called it an error. A few plays later, it came over the ticker that our games were rained out. The writer thought, "Now Stirnweiss has a chance to lead the league." He changed the error to a hit. I know that's how it happened because I'd played at Boston and knew all those writers, and they were fighting with him over changing the scoring. Stirnweiss wound up with .30856, and I was .30845. So the records show him with .309 and me at .308.

In those days the league gave you a plaque and you got a $500 bonus. Today that's tip money, but in those days it meant something. Plus getting your name in the record books. But number two is not in the record books.

11.

John Francis Daley
MANSFIELD, OHIO, MAY 25, 1987

A cup-of-coffee player with the St. Louis Browns in 1912 (nine hits in seventeen games), John Francis Daley claimed credit for one of baseball's most memorable one-liners. When he died in 1988 at 101, he was the oldest former big league player. He recalled his cup of coffee at his Ohio home.

I WAS BORN AND raised in Pittsburgh. A bunch of us youngsters would hang around the players' gate at the Pirates' ballpark, waiting for Honus Wagner. When he arrived, he would parcel out parts of his gear to some of us kids to carry, and we would get into the game for "helping him" that way.

In 1912 I was playing shortstop for Mansfield in the Class D Ohio State League. Along about July the St. Louis Browns, who would lose 101 games that year, needed infielders. They bought me for $3,500, and I was suddenly in the big leagues. In my third game, on July 20 in Washington, the score was 3–3 in the top of the ninth. With the bases loaded and two outs, who comes in as the relief pitcher? Walter Johnson. And I'm up.

I worked him to a 3-2 count and fouled off a few. The next pitch I never saw. I heard it smack in the catcher's mitt and the umpire call strike three.

George Stovall, our playing manager, was on deck. I guess I looked sort of dazed. He said to me, "What's the matter, kid?"

I told him, "You can't hit what you can't see."

The next day that quote was in the Washington papers. A couple years ago some other fellow claimed he was the originator of that phrase, but I told him I'm the one who did it and you could look it up.

The Browns had made a small down payment on me and wanted to keep me but didn't want to pay the balance, so they sent me back to Mansfield. I played in the minors until 1916, then worked for the Mansfield Tire & Rubber Company for forty years.

12.

Joe DeMaestri

NOVATO, CALIFORNIA, AUGUST 1995

· ·

After a fourth-place finish in his rookie year with the Chicago White Sox (1951), shortstop Joe DeMaestri dwelt deep in the second division for seven years with the St. Louis Browns and Philadelphia/Kansas City A's. He was ready to quit the game when he was traded to the Yankees and wound up in the 1960 and '61 World Series. For most ballplayers, their most unforgettable moment was a career highlight. For DeMaestri it was an inglorious lowlight, as described by him at his home.

· ·

AFTER FIVE YEARS IN the minor leagues, I was drafted by the Chicago White Sox and went to spring training in 1951 in Pasadena. Paul Richards was the manager. Nellie Fox was on the verge of being shipped out. He fielded every ground ball down on one knee, and he wasn't hitting. In his stance his feet were pointing in different directions. At that time, you couldn't see what he would turn out to be. Doc Cramer was a coach. Cramer said, "We're going to teach Nellie to hit." He sent me to the outfield to field the hits and gave Nellie a bottle bat. He started hitting and used that bottle bat after that.

Paul Richards was the toughest and best manager I played for. He was two or three days ahead of everybody in his thinking. But he never got close to his players. He was a loner. Never smiled. Never a pat on the back. You could not corner him to talk to him. In his office, yes, but don't try to strike up a conversation with him because it wasn't gonna go. I learned how to keep my eyes open and mouth shut.

Staying in shape while riding the bench and never knowing when you might get in a game is the toughest thing in baseball. It's the middle of June and we're in first place, and I hadn't started but once, had made one hit. We're at Fenway Park and Mel Parnell is pitching for the Red Sox. We're a few runs behind in the fifth inning and our pitcher is due to lead off. Richards looks down the bench and says, "DeMaestri, get a bat."

I'm telling you, I felt like I was walking on eggs. Your whole life changes. I'm what—twenty-two years old. I get a bat and Parnell threw me a couple pitches. I swung and I knew I hit the ball. I swear to God, to this day I could never remember where it went when I hit it. But I knew I hit it good. I take off and I'm running and I don't pay any attention to the coach. I'm running for a double. The ball hits the top of the fence in left field, and Ted Williams could play that left field wall like he was in a rocking chair, but I don't know that. He just waited for the ball to come back to him and turns and fires it in to Bobby Doerr at second. I get about a third of the way to second, and all of a sudden my legs don't want to run anymore. I'm starting to go down. Doerr gets the ball, turns around to make the tag, and I'm not there. I ended up flat on my face about from here to that fireplace from second base. I just couldn't move. Doerr sees me and walks over and says, "Are you hurt?" I said, "No." He says, "Well, you're out."

Now I gotta get up and go back in that dugout. Richards is sitting at one end of the bench with nobody near him. They had a restroom at the other end of the dugout; you went through a swinging door and down a short hallway to get to it. There were twenty-four guys pushing and shoving to get in that doorway; they were laughing so hard, and they didn't want Richards to see them.

I went into the dugout and sat down. Richards didn't look at me. Never said a word. His face was like stone. That was typical of him. I knew what was going through his mind. It would have made me feel better if he'd chewed me out. I learned a lesson: watch your coaches. The first base coach knew how Williams played that wall. He'd have held me up.

My wife had flown back to Chicago; she was pregnant with our first child. When I get home, she's waiting for me with this newspaper photo of me flat on my face in Fenway Park.

A few years ago our first baseman, Eddie Robinson, came through here scouting, and we met for dinner. We had just said hello to each other, and Eddie says, "I'll never forget that night in Boston." That's after forty years.

I was originally signed by a Red Sox scout, Charlie Wallgren, a friend of my dad's. I had some high school teammates who got

$10,000 bonuses, but I was ready to sign for nothing, I wanted to play so bad. My mother finally wrung a $600 bonus out of them. I signed for $140 a month, bounced around in Class C, lived at the YMCA, rode a red school bus on the road. I was up to $225 a month in Birmingham when the White Sox drafted me.

After that '51 season they traded me to the Browns. That was a horror story. Rogers Hornsby was the manager, a rough guy for a young player to get involved with. We played an exhibition game in San Francisco, and he wouldn't let me go home and spend the night just across the Golden Gate Bridge. He said the only two people he'd pay to see were Jim Rivera and Clint Courtney. Rivera was a wild man, and Clint was a tough, tough guy, got in fights all the time, and could not throw the ball back to the pitcher. With a man on first, I'd stand between the pitcher and second base in case he threw it over the pitcher's head.

Hornsby hated Satchel Paige. But Satch could handle him 'cause he had the owner, Bill Veeck, behind him. In spring training we were sitting in the bleachers, and Hornsby was going over the day's schedule. No Satch. He's talking to us and here comes Satch, sneaking in behind him. Hornsby got on him: "I'm fining you $250 for this," and on and on; Satch just stood there and said, "I don't think so."

It got to where there were guys who were going to refuse to play for him. We were in Boston, and we all got together. I don't think there was one leader; maybe Marty Marion and Bob Young, who were roommates, were seen as leaders. Veeck came to Boston and fired Hornsby. We all chipped in and gave Veeck a huge trophy.

That winter I was traded to the Philadelphia A's. The A's didn't have any more money than Bill Veeck. One night after a series at home against the Yankees, both teams were at the train station, and I saw how the other half lived. They had dining cars on their train, and we had box lunches.

I'd been making the minimum $5,000 for three years. In '54 I held out for $6,000. After a lot of back and forth, I finally got it.

We were there two years. Didn't have a car, so we rented a row house two blocks from Shibe Park. Italian neighborhood. I'd come home after a night game, and the guy next door would be sitting on his porch waiting for me. Had to sit and drink wine with him before I could get home. But the neighborhood was changing. Some people were trying to incite race riots in the area. That last year was a tough year.

That fall I heard on the radio that the A's were going to Kansas City. That was the first I knew of it. We enjoyed our five years in Kansas City. Didn't win, but it was a nice place for the family to spend the summer after Philadelphia.

[I asked Mrs. DeMaestri what she remembered most about her days as a baseball wife. "I remember driving kids cross country," she laughed.]

After the '59 season I was ready to quit. I had a young family, and my dad and I had a Budweiser distributorship. I'd had nine years in the major leagues, and things didn't look any rosier at that time, so I figured that was enough. Then I got a call from the Yankees: they'd made a trade for Roger Maris and me. In those days it was pretty definite you'd be in the money with New York. Best move I ever made.

The GM, Roy Hamey, asked me how much I wanted. I said, "Twenty-three thousand." He said, "Get out of here." I left, was going to quit. But I got it. I was surprised at how little the players were making in New York.

My first spring training with the Yankees, I'm sitting in my locker, and all of a sudden there's about five guys around me—Bill Skowron, Yogi Berra, Gil McDougald. They had lost to the White Sox in '59, and they weren't used to losing. We were talking and they said, "Just remember, every time you take the field, you're playing with our money." That never left my mind.

Roger Maris was a friendly guy, a team guy who went out with us. He was wary of strangers. He didn't know how to handle the press, but in Kansas City he never had to. We had only two or three writers and got to know them well. In New York there were a lot of young, inexperienced guys from small area newspapers. If somebody asked Roger a dumb question, he'd fire back at them. In 1961 it hit him overnight. I can still see Mantle sitting there laughing while Maris was surrounded by maybe fifty reporters, trapped by his locker, no way to escape.

Mickey Mantle was the best player I ever saw, the only guy who could run on his heels. Casey Stengel was a master psychologist. I saw him do something with Mantle one day that was unbelievable. We were getting into our game uniforms, and Mick had had a rough night. He was hurting pretty good too. He was sitting there, bent over, wrapping his legs, and Casey could see us from his office window. Casey walks up to Mantle, looks down at him, and says, "You're not gonna play today," and walks away. Before Casey got back to his office, Mantle was right there and says, "Don't you ever take me out of that lineup." If there was any thought that Mickey didn't want to play that day, Casey changed it just by looking at him and saying, "You don't want to play today."

In meetings Gil McDougald and I would get back in our lockers as far as we could 'cause we'd start laughing. Casey could talk all day long, and you didn't know what he was talking about.

One night in Cleveland we're getting beat about 5–1, and Casey is dozing on the bench. About the sixth inning he wakes up, looks at the scoreboard, jumps up and says, "Hey, I think it's time we got this guy."

I think we won, 11–5 or something. He didn't miss anything. But everybody was so professional, knew their job, it didn't matter.

Game 7 of the 1960 World Series, I roomed with Yogi Berra. The night before he said, "They're gonna have Elroy Face in there tomorrow. I'm gonna hit one off him." And he did. During the season, when we had a good lead, Casey would move Tony Kubek out to left field to replace Berra, and I'd go in at shortstop. He thought that was his best defense. I was set to do that when a ground ball hit Kubek in the throat, and I had to replace him then. We really lost that game because our pitcher, Jim Coates, didn't cover first on a routine grounder in the eighth inning. The next spring when Coates showed up and greeted Clete Boyer, Boyer said to him, "Yeah, if you'd covered first base, we'd all be a little richer." They never forgot it.

The worst move I made was when I retired after '61. The Yankees wanted me to stay, and they wound up playing the Giants out here in the '62 Series.

13.

Woody English

. . . .

Elwood "Woody" English was the shortstop and captain of the Chicago
Cubs during their series of triennial pennant winners—1929–32–35. He
was there when the Cubs blew an 8–0 lead against the A's in '29, when
Babe Ruth allegedly called his home run in '32, and when the Cubs were
fined by Commissioner Landis for their raucous bench jockeying against
the Tigers in '35. A fleet-footed leadoff man with large hands, he played
alongside second baseman/manager Rogers Hornsby.

English was living alone in the old family home, a two-story white wooden
structure with columns in the front, in Newark, Ohio. Occasionally his cane
thumped the bare wood floor to punctuate a story.

. . . .

I PLAYED SEMIPRO BALL on Sundays around Ohio, and a scout
signed me for Toledo in 1925. I got into the lineup because the regular shortstop drank too much orange juice and his hands broke
out. In 1926 I hit .301. Casey Stengel was our manager. One day
Stengel says to me, "Wood, if you had your choice, which major
league club would you like to go to—the Cubs, the Philadelphia
Athletics, or Cleveland?"

Hack Wilson and Earl Webb had been Toledo outfielders. They
were now with the Cubs. I said, "Cleveland is close to home, but
I guess I'll go where Webb and Wilson are." It was the best decision I ever made.

Headed for spring training in '27. I got on a train in Columbus.
A veteran Cubs pitcher, Percy Lee Jones, got on in Kansas City. I
introduced myself to him, and we sat down and I started talking
to him, and he paid no attention to me. I thought, "What the heck
kind of a guy is this? Is this the way they all are?" Finally, after I
was talking about ten minutes, he says, "I'm hard of hearing in
this ear, Woody. You'll have to talk a little louder."

Playing alongside Rogers Hornsby in the infield was a real challenge. My first spring training we're taking infield practice, and

we're practicing double plays; he fielded the ball and threw to me at second, and that ball just whistled by me. He said, "Listen, lad, if you're going to play shortstop with me, you're going to have to get that kind of throw."

Hornsby could not go back for a pop fly, and he knew it. It might be a cloudy overcast day, but he'd still tell me before the game, "That sun's in my eyes. You come over and cover pop flies." He could field good otherwise and could really run.

I liked Joe McCarthy. He was the kind of manager where everybody was equal with him. But you better hustle. The guys who didn't give 100 percent, he'd boot in the rear end. If you gave your all, he'd pat you on the back. But after we blew the 1929 World Series to the A's, Mr. Wrigley let him go and replaced him with his favorite player, Hornsby.

Under Hornsby there was no reading the papers in the clubhouse. He didn't want players ruining their eyes reading. Hornsby and I became good friends. We had roomed together for a while. Later, when he managed the Browns, he asked me to be a coach, but I didn't. He encouraged me. If I struck out with the bases loaded, he'd say, "You had a helluva cut up there." And he had the guts of a burglar. He'd put himself in to pinch-hit. If he hit a home run, those straw hats would come flying out of the stands. Hornsby liked anybody who could run. But we didn't run much. Didn't have to. With Riggs Stephenson and Kiki Cuyler and Wilson and Hornsby batting behind me, I never got a steal sign. Hornsby had power to all fields. But he aimed every hit back up the middle. I scored 152 runs the year Hack Wilson drove in 190. In those days four teams dominated the league: Chicago, New York, Pittsburgh, and St. Louis. We won 21 in a row in 1935.

I had a room in a hotel near Wrigley Field. Hornsby came up to my room one day and asked to use my telephone to make a call to St. Louis: "Mr. Gray? What's your best bet today?"

In Chicago betting was pretty wide open. We walked down the street toward the ballpark and there was a Florsheim shoe store, and in back of it they had the book. Hornsby went in there. The guy's name was Sonny Stern. Hornsby says, "Sonny, give me $500 to win" on whatever horse Gray had told him. So about the seventh inning I'm at short and he's on second waiting for the throw down from the catcher. Hornsby says to me, "That horse won."

I said, "How do you know?"

He said, "I know."

After the game we went back to the bookie, and Hornsby says to Stern, "Well, that horse won."

Stern says, "I can't pay you off. I didn't get the bet in."

Hornsby says, "You run a book, don't you?"

"I couldn't lay it off anywhere."

Hornsby says, "I'll tell you what we'll do. The first person that walks by this shoe store, we'll call him in and ask him whether you should pay off."

Sonny says, "Oh no, I wouldn't do that; I just can't pay you."

Hornsby bellowed at him, but he never got his money.

He borrowed money from players. We were in Philadelphia in August 1932, in second place, five games back of Pittsburgh. Hornsby had borrowed $1,200 from me, said he wanted to pay something on his income tax. I had no note or anything. Bob Lewis, the traveling secretary, asked me if Hornsby owed me any money. I said no, as he'd just repaid me. Lewis said, "He owes a lot of people, and I'm glad you got yours because he's going to get fired."

And he was. The next day it was raining. We're all sitting around in the lobby. Hornsby comes in and says, "Well, [first baseman Charlie] Grimm's the new manager. That's the bad deal." To me he said, "You're the new captain. That's the good deal." And we all shook hands with him.

That afternoon Grimm had a meeting. He says, "If everybody takes care of himself and we hustle, we still have a chance to win this."

Rollie Hemsley was our catcher. Rollie was a drinker but not a good one. He could take two beers and be drunk as the devil. Rollie gets up and says, "Yeah, all you guys take good care of yourselves. I'm going to now too. We can win this pennant." About three in the morning the traveling secretary, Bob Lewis, and Grimm had to go over to Camden, New Jersey, and get Hemsley out of jail.

Grimm was the easiest manager I played for. He got the best

out of his players in an easy way. He'd say, "You guys take care of yourselves now. I've heard some bad reports about some of you." Then on the way to the dugout he'd say, "That don't go for you . . . that don't go for you . . . ," and before he was done, it didn't go for anybody.

As the Cubs' captain, I took the lineup out to home plate. The commissioner's office was in Chicago, and Judge Landis went to many games at Wrigley Field, sitting in the front row right behind home plate. I always made it a point to go over and shake hands with the judge.

Landis was a great, great man, strict but fair. These were the days of Al Capone and John Dillinger. Capone came to Cubs games, sitting in the box seats with his bodyguards with the big velour hats. One day in 1939 Cubs manager Gabby Hartnett went over to shake hands with Capone. Judge Landis was there. The next day there was a notice in every clubhouse: "There will be no more fraternizing in the stands. Signed: Kenesaw Landis." They put the umpires up in the stands to watch before games. You couldn't even go over and talk to your mother and father or your own wife in the stands.

When we played the Yankees in the 1932 World Series and Ruth is supposed to have called his home run—which is not true—there was bitterness there. The reason was that Mark Koenig, a former Yankee, came to the Cubs late in the season. When we voted on the split of the World Series shares, only the regulars entitled to a full share were in the meeting—no coaches or manager. I was the captain, and I held the meeting. It had to be unanimous on every vote for part shares and for the trainer and batboy and others. Two players held out for half a share for Koenig. "He didn't get here until late in the season," they said. "He didn't play in very many games." The rest thought he should get a full share.

So this came out in the papers before the World Series. That's what started the friction between the two clubs. When Babe Ruth was at bat and had the two strikes on him, our guys were all over him from the dugout. The Yankees had said our guys were cheap and miserly, and, boy, that really burned us up because we didn't really think we could beat 'em anyway, but we wanted to give them a hard time. We were in the third base dugout and Ruth batted left handed, so he was looking right at the guys in our dugout who were calling him all kinds of names when he held two fingers up showing that's only two strikes, and he said, "That's only two." I was playing third base. Hartnett was catching and Charlie Root pitching. And the next ball he hit over the center-field fence. The press box was way up, maybe two hundred feet behind home plate. It made a good story, but we all said that wasn't right; he didn't call that shot, although he hit it hard enough. We liked Babe Ruth; he was a grand man. But we didn't like him in '32.

That's not the end of the story. I'm back home in Ohio later, and I get a call from Judge Landis's office. They said, "Mr. Landis has the flu, but he would like to see you at his apartment in Chicago." I went up the next day, and the judge was lying there in bed. First thing he said was, "Woody, get me one of those pills over there. I'm sicker than a dog." Then he says, "The reason I called you up here is about that controversy in the World Series. Mark Koenig got a half share and that seemed to stir up the antagonism."

I said, "That's the truth."

He said, "Tell me about it."

I told him about the two guys who held out for a half share, and he had me call his secretary to check on when Koenig had joined us. August 14.

"Woody, how many games did you play?"

"Almost all." "And how many did Koenig play?"

I said, "Between 30 and 40." Landis said, "And Mark got a half share? I think that was a very fair decision. Send a bill to my office for your expenses."

My next dealings with Judge Landis came during the 1935 World Series between the Cubs and Tigers. There was bitterness from the dugouts. Hank Greenberg was playing first base for Detroit, and we were pretty noisy and raucous riding him. Both clubs were calling each other names. It was loud. An American League umpire, George Moriarty, had some close plays to call, and he called them all for Detroit. So it got to the point where we thought we were being a little cheated by the umpire. It's Game 3 in Chicago, and Moriarty's umpiring at second base. There was a very close play, and he called it against the Cubs. All the guys in our dugout started yelling at him, led by Charlie Grimm. He was the first to be ejected by Moriarty. The rest of us kept it up—except Tuck Stainback, a kid who wouldn't say "God" even in church, until finally Moriarty calls time and walks all the way over to the Cubs dugout and points at Stainback and says, "You're out of the game."

I said, "What for? You can't put him out."

Moriarty said, "He can't call me what he did."

I jumped up and said, "That guy don't even swear. He didn't do that."

Moriarty said, "And you're out of the game too."

Then I said, "You're just exactly what he called you, a blind so-and-so."

Landis called a meeting for nine o'clock the next morning at his office, with us and our second baseman Billy Herman, who had been jawing at Moriarty out at second base but was not thrown out, and the umpire. We're there waiting. No Moriarty. Landis said to his assistant, "Did you notify Moriarty that this meeting was called for nine o'clock?"

"Yes, sir."

Ten more minutes go by. Finally the umpire shows up. The judge glares at him. "Mr. Moriarty, what time was this meeting called for?"

He says, "Nine o'clock, judge, but I had trouble in the coffee shop at the Drake Hotel. I'm sorry I'm late."

So we all told our stories. Landis came to Billy Herman and says, "What did you call Moriarty?"

"I don't want to say, judge."

"Go ahead, this room has been filled with blue smoke before."

The windup was we got fined $400 each, and Moriarty got fined $500. So it was a little bit of a winner for our side.

I played in the first All-Star Game in 1933. I didn't start. Bill Klem was the first base umpire. John McGraw, who managed the National All-Stars, never got along with him. Klem called a few close plays at first base against the Nationals. McGraw was calling Klem everything you could imagine. Klem never came over to the dugout. After 4½ innings, the umpires changed positions. Klem came into our dugout to put on the gear to work behind the plate. I thought, "Here we go. McGraw's a goner." But Klem never said a word. After the game McGraw came into the clubhouse and shook hands with all of us and said, "We'll get 'em some other time, boys. You can keep your uniforms."

I was traded to Brooklyn in 1937. Burleigh Grimes, a teammate with the Cubs, was the new Dodgers' manager. He was tough, argued with the umpires almost from the first pitch. He had an automatic $50 fine for anybody caught drinking hard liquor. He'd say, "Don't be staggering around drunk anywhere."

One of our pitchers was Van Mungo. He was one tough guy, big arms and hands and didn't give a darn what happened. His pitch was clocked at 113 [m.p.h.] at West Point. He'd strike out a bunch, but eventually he'd blow up when an error or a walk beat him. He got pretty stiff one time in St. Louis. My roommate and I were in the room next to Van's, with a door between his room and ours. There was a knock at the door. I said, "That's Van and he's drunk. We don't want him in here." So we shoved a chair against the door, and it had my good suit on it. Mungo kept knocking and said, "If you don't open this door I'm going to break it down."

"Go to bed, Van."

"I'm coming in there," he said, and wham, here he comes busting through the door. My good suit was on the floor. The house detective and manager came up, and Mungo was fined $1,000. His excuse was that his kid was having an operation and that threw him out of gear. It could have been.

I liked Van. In his next start we had a one-run lead in the ninth, and I started a game-ending double play to win it. In the clubhouse Van thanked me.

In 1938 Johnny Vander Meer pitched two consecutive no-hitters. I pinch-hit in the second one, in Brooklyn, a night game. They had fireworks before the game. It was foggy and all the smoke filled the air. It was pitiful. I'm sitting on the bench in the eighth inning, and Grimes says, "English, pinch-hit." I said to myself, "I'm not going to go up there and spoil this guy's second no-hitter." I struck out.

Dizzy Dean was a good guy. Fun-loving. In Sportsman's Park the clubhouse doors were right next to each other. We'd be having our pregame meeting and Diz would open our door and yell, "Hey, you guys. I'll tell you how to pitch to Medwick. Just throw it right down the middle. He can't hit one down the center." I went to spring training with the Cubs in 1939. Diz and I roomed together, barnstorming home. I'd get to the room and find he'd had my suit pressed and put a few beers on ice.

14.

Ferris Fain

Georgetown, California, February 1998

. . . .

Aggressive, hot-tempered Ferris Fain was the premier first baseman of his time, twice leading the American League in batting during his nine-year career with the Philadelphia Athletics, White Sox, Tigers, and Indians (1947–1955). A five-time All-Star, he led in assists four times (and errors five times) and fights—well, they don't have stats for that. With a walks-to-strikeouts ratio of 4:1, his .424 on-base percentage ranks fourteenth in the record books. He did it all with two bad knees that left him so arthritic he was unable to walk twenty-five years later. In 1985 Fain was living in the gold country town of Georgetown, 150 miles northeast of Oakland, when he was busted for growing and selling marijuana (which he never used). Three years later I set out to find him. I had no phone number, no address. This was before the all-knowing internet. I didn't know that he was on probation, which meant the sheriff and feds could—and did—knock on his door to check on his activities at any time without a warrant. And here I was, a stranger intent on dropping in on him unannounced.

So one morning I stood in the center of town and debated how to locate him. Where to inquire? The Georgetown Hotel? One of the four bars in the town of nine hundred, most of whose residents were probably protective of their most famous—and to the sheriff, infamous—neighbor? The sheriff's office? No, they might suspect I was there to make a buy. I decided the safest place was the post office and found someone who gave me directions.

It was about 10 a.m. Not knowing if I would be greeted by a shotgun or a pack of hungry dogs, I arrived at a country lane lined with hedges that led to a modest one-story house with steps up to a porch and a screen door. The door behind it was open. There was no one in sight. No dogs. I knocked on the screen door.

"Come in," said a voice. I entered into a kitchen that led to a small living room, and there, looking like a Buddha with a buzz cut, sat the 240-pound Ferris Fain on a couch. He was alone. He eyed me warily; later he told me, "In my situation I'm wary about who I talk to until I see they're not here to work me over." I introduced myself and used the magic words that would almost always relax resistance: "Connie Mack. I'm writing a biography of Mr. Mack, and I want to get it right by talking to anyone who played or worked for him."

Pause. Then: "As long as you're here, come on in and sit down."

Six hours later I left, believing that I had not only experienced an unforgettable interview, but had also helped him enjoy a day of reliving his baseball exploits in this beleaguered period of his life.

• •

I BROKE IN WITH the San Francisco Seals, an independent team, in 1939. While I was still in high school in Oakland, they paid me $200 a month—no contract—to work out with them and obligate me to sign with them after I graduated. I was still playing on my high school team. Seven of us went into pro ball.

In the Pacific Coast League they played two weeks at home and two weeks on the road and stayed a week in each city. So when they were at home, I would take the ferry over and work out with them, and when they played a week in Oakland, it was close to home. I used that $200 a month to buy a car, and when I could drive and they went on the road, I drove to where they were and took my girlfriend with me. I was a big spender.

I graduated in June and signed with the Seals, but I didn't get into a game until the last couple weeks of the season, so it wouldn't count toward the four seasons you could play in the PCL before being subject to the major league draft. I played in '40-'41-'42, then three years in the service. My fourth year was 1946.

The Philadelphia Athletics drafted me. They sent me a contract for $6,000, and I was already making $6,500 with the Seals. I didn't see much point in going to the major leagues and taking a $500 cut, and in those days, $500 was $500. I wrote them. They said, "That's it." I said, "I'll stay out here." Then [Connie Mack's son] Earle called me. He said, "Don't ever say anything to Dad," and sent me a contract for $7,000.

I wasn't thrilled with the frugalness of the A's, but getting to the major leagues was a dream. I am not going to say anything to make anybody look good or bad. I'm going to say it like it was. My first impression was the same as when I left the Philadelphia ball club. The organization was headed by Connie Mack, a gracious, kindly, wonderful old man, but I think the key word there was just that: O-L-D. I can't say it any better than that something was screwed up, and I'll interject this before I go any further. I came to the club a twenty-six-year-old rookie, but I was a knowledgeable ballplayer. I couldn't have had a better starting teacher than [Seals manager] Lefty O'Doul, and with my own ability to understand the game, when I go to the Philadelphia club and there's two strikes on me as a hitter and I look up and I am getting the take sign—this is coming from the kindly old gentleman in the white shirt and collar and straw hat—I figure we've got the worst ball club you ever saw or somebody is not with it. [Laughs.] Take your pick. Somebody has to swing the bat and score somebody. So when you're looking at a take sign with two strikes. . . . The signs were being relayed through the third base coach, Al Simmons. Al knew anybody in his right mind isn't going to follow this sign. So he didn't always relay it as he'd been given it. But if the A's coaches gave me a sign, I've got to abide by them. If I was a manager and somebody ignored my signs, we're gonna have something to talk about.

We had a meeting where Mr. Mack was laying the law down, and as part of it he says, "And you, Mr. Simmons, I want you to know I am still running this ball club." Reference being: "You're not giving the signs that I'm giving you."

I had as good an eye as anybody else playing baseball in those days. I watched that ball to the plate. The reason I wasn't hitting was because I was what they called a cripple shooter. I'm not chasing those bad balls, and if I've got you 2-0 or 3-1, I'm gonna look for a pitch, and if I get it, somebody's gonna suffer, hopefully. So my forte was getting that pitcher in a hole. I'm struggling along, not hitting very well, .230 or .240, something like that. Now I'm a rookie, and a rookie's not supposed to be reacting like this. We're playing in New York, and I'm constantly 3-1, look down there, and I'm getting the goddamn take sign. When you take 3-0, 3-1, that ball looks like a basketball and you're taking, and this is not the way you hit. It had rained all night in New York. They had the tarp all over the field. The infield itself was decent, but all around the perimeter of the infield was muck and mire. I go up to the plate, and, if memory serves me correctly, I think I was hitting fourth.

A Punch-and-Judy hitter hitting fourth—hey, that's not bad. They must think this guy might be able to do something in the clinch. There's a man on second base. I get to 2-0, and I look down, and—uh-oh—you're taking, Ferris. They want me to drive that guy in with a base on balls. You think that's all I'm going to get?

The count gets to 3-2. I wasn't one of these players that, with a full count and a pitch that is maybe this way or that way, could be a ball or a strike, but it's close enough, would take it. When you're 3-2, you protect the dish. You hit what's up there. Don't let this guy behind the plate nail you. So now here comes a questionable pitch. I hit a fourteen-hopper to the second baseman. Out. Goodbye.

Next time up, the same situation: 2-0, 3-1, 3-2. This time I chased a pitch that was bad and struck out. Now I am pissed because I had been ordered to let two of those strikes go by, and I'm not liking it one bit. Mind you, I'm just a rook from San Francisco. As I'm walking back to the dugout, I took that bat and threw it, and it hit the ground and quivered like an arrow and stuck in the mud. I get in the dugout and I'm pacing back and forth, and finally I stop in front of Connie Mack and I said, "Take! Take! Take! You take that take sign of yours and stick it in your ass." To Mr. Mack. Mr. Legend. Holy Christ.

Well, this was nice. Had your cup of coffee. See you back in San Francisco, friend. But I didn't care. So after the game Earle Brucker, one of the coaches, said, "Ferris, you better go apologize." I said, "I'm not apologizing to anybody. That guy's taking that bat out of my hands, and I meant just exactly what I said." Earle Mack, Simmons, all of them trying to get me to apologize. No way am I going to apologize to anybody. I did what I had to do for myself: go to the horse's mouth and tell him you're killing me.

All right. We're in New York. Lot of good night life. I'm partaking of it. When I get back to the hotel, though, I'm getting to think, "Ferris, these steaks up here are beautiful. Maybe you better reconsider." I hadn't fully convinced myself the next day when we took a cab to the ballpark. Now Connie Mack never ever got to the dugout before ten minutes before the game, in time to hand the lineup to Earle to take up to the plate. I come out of the runway into the dugout, and I'm going down to the end to get a bat out of the bat rack for BP, and who do I have to go by but Connie Mack? Two hours before game time and there he sits? So I think I'll sneak by him; he won't know who I am, and I'll get my bat and get the hell out of there. And I hear, "Oh, boy. Boy!" And this is the time for me to start pleading.

"Mr. Mack," I said.

"Yes, young man, I know. . . ."

I'm going to cop out at this point. Finally he says, "Now, young man, I just wanted to tell you that you have shown me that you play a decent game of baseball, and from here on, you don't have to look for any signs." That senile old man turned me loose. For the next six years I gave my own signs: take, bunt, everything. It was to his advantage as well as mine. For all we thought was senility, he was there.

He didn't know my name. Most everyone he referred to as "young man" or "boy." Rarely did he call anybody by their actual name. The closest I ever heard him come was "Mr. Majestic" for Hank Majeski and "Mr. McClusky," who was Barney McCosky.

I played all year with the sorriest knee you ever saw—should never have been playing on it—and hit .291. Jackie Robinson beat me out for Rookie of the Year. In those days they named only one for both leagues. I got a token raise with this statement: "When you prove yourself as a major league player, we will take care of you."

When they had acquired me and shortstop Eddie Joost, they picked up two players who filled vital roles. In '48 we now had the makings of a halfway decent club. We weren't contenders, but we were on a roll. We lost two relievers, and that won the pennant for Cleveland.

One of them, Russ Christopher, was a tall, gangly sidearmer with a bad heart condition. Tremendous in relief for short periods. He'd give you two or three innings, and he was tough. Had a good year in '47. That spring I remember vividly the exchange of insults with him trying to negotiate a contract. They wanted him to be a starting pitcher, but they didn't want to give him any more money. He said, "I'll relieve for the same money, but if I'm a starter, I want more money." They couldn't agree. I think the crowning blow was in the clubhouse one day. Earle Mack comes in, and Russ, very unhappy with the situation, looked up and says, "Is it Superman? Is it . . . ?" Some other derogatory remark. "Oh no, it's Earle Mack, coming in on his broom." Two days later Russ is on his broom to Cleveland.

Later in the season we get a veteran reliever, Nelson Potter. He did a tremendous job, but one day we blew a lead, and the old man fired him. That cost us the pennant.

[At this point, Rita, a local woman who cooked and did odd jobs for Fain, set tray tables in front of us and served us large hot lunches with hot tea, later followed by slabs of cherry pie topped with ice cream. We continued to talk while we ate.]

In the years I played with Connie Mack as manager, there was no feeling of leadership in any way, shape, or form. The coaches tried to make up for it. No one wanted to tell it like it was. No one wanted to say the man was over the hump, in respect to his many years. I can understand that. No one was going to say anything derogatory about him. He was an institution, a legend. And he owned the club. I'm not degrading the man. I truly respected and enjoyed him. I just didn't think he was capable of running a ball club.

The players would snicker if a meeting was called: "Oh, here we go again." It was kinda ludicrous. For instance, in 1950 we got Bob Dillinger from the Browns. Hell of a player. Wore those thick glasses. From home plate to the mound he could see like an eagle. Bob was leading the club in hitting, RBIs, and making some plays at third base and throwing his little fourteen-hopper to first base. It was like rolling marbles over there to catch his throws. The only guy in the infield that didn't have a rifle. He was a little nutty but a good ballplayer. Had a reputation for being a little lackadaisi-cal, had a beer or two. When he was with St. Louis and a ball was hit a little too hard to third, Bob liked to go, "Whoo-ee," and give it the howdy-do. With us he was actually getting in front of balls and showing a bruise on his chest once in a while.

I was responsible in a way for them acquiring him. Knowing I had been in the service with him for two or three years, they asked me if I could handle him. I said, "Hell, yes." The halt leading the blind . . . but yeah. "He'll help our ball club." We used to ride to the ballpark together. He lived just a short distance from me. And we'd talk about things. He was doing one tremendous job, battling just as hard as anybody else.

So we have this meeting. One of the things Connie Mack said was, "Our first baseman is the only one who is doing any hustling on this club. And you, Mr. Dillinger, are not worth the money that we spent getting you."

When the meeting was over, Bob says to me, "If that's what he thinks of me, wait'll he sees this." And from that day on, you didn't see Bob getting in front of any hard-hit balls. It was a lot of "Whoo-ees," I'll tell you that, and he whoo-eed himself to Pittsburgh.

[I asked about a play where Fain made a few errors and had words with Mr. Mack.]

I'll go back to what I related earlier. I never dwell on the past. Each day comes and goes. I do the job, good or bad. I remember Bobo Newsom. He could tell you every pitch: what he threw, what inning it was, what the count was, where the hitter hit it— any year. I couldn't tell you fifteen minutes after the game what I did, so if I did in fact make three errors, I'm not disputing it. I could have very easily 'cause I'd get hold of that sonofabitch ball and I'm gonna do something with it, and as long as you keep it going, you got a chance of screwing up. If you know something about it, enlighten me.

[**NM:** The legend is that after you booted a grounder and threw it over the third baseman's head and whatever else, Mr. Mack said something to you.]

Okay, I'll bring you up to date. Now I'm going to give it to you straight from the horse's mouth.

I was endowed with a real good arm. I could throw. In fact, that whole infield, except for Dillinger, was the best-armed infield I ever saw or played with: Majeski, Joost, Pete Suder, and myself. Set the major league double play record. I had a play—man on second, nobody out. If they weren't bunting and the ball was hit to me and I had a shot to knock the runner off going to third, I would go to third with the ball and let the batter get to first and see if he can score on a fly ball from there. I did this on occasion. We play a doubleheader in Boston. The play comes up in the first game, and the ball is hit to me; just as I go to throw it, my spikes get caught in the dirt and I hit the mound with the ball. No way close to third. That took care of that, and that play went to the outhouse. In the second game the same play comes up, and I elevated my sights, scattered people in the fourteenth row, and didn't get anybody. We go to St. Louis, and I nailed a runner on the play at third base.

Now we go to Detroit, and Charlie Keller is on second base with one out [the A's led, 5–4, in the eighth], and the ball is hit to me. I haul off and make the throw to third base. The ball and Keller get to third kinda simultaneously. The third baseman is trying to put up with this nonsense, and they don't call Keller "King Kong" for nothing. The ball bounced off the third baseman's glove down into left field, and Keller scores. At the end of the inning I come into the dugout, and I am fuming. I'm mad because the third baseman— you'll notice I didn't mention any names and I won't—I didn't think he gave it the big college try. He didn't give it his best shot, in my opinion. He could have made a better effort to at least catch the ball. So I'm not happy with that.

In Detroit at that time the runway was right in the center of the dugout, and you went down four-five steps and back in. Well, I just headed right for the thing, knowing that if I stop for one moment and start talking about it, we're going to have a problem. So trying to avert that, I go down in the runway. As I'm going down, Mr. Mack is saying, "Boy! Boy! Boy!" I don't want to listen to Mr. Mack at this point. So I continue down in the runway. He comes up and is standing at the top of the stairway.

"Now, young man, I want you to know that you've tried. . . ." Connie talked haltingly, and it was always "Uh . . . uh . . . uh. . . ." Spit it out. Now I'm getting this, "Now young man, you've tried this play three or four times now, and you've only completed it once." And I said, "Oh, horseshit, Mr. Mack. If the play worked, it was a great play. It didn't, so now it's a lousy play." And he continues with this "Now you've tried it. . . ."

I said, "What are you trying to tell me, Mr. Mack? You don't want me to throw that ball anymore?" And it was, "Well . . . uh . . . uh."

"I'll tell you, Mr. Mack, before I take that ball and throw it for you again, I'll take it and stick it right in my ass."

And he says, "Young man"—now this was a senile old man that

we thought had lost it—"young man, I'd like you to know that that'd probably be the safest place for that ball."

Well, if you didn't think that floored the twenty-two guys in that dugout. Even I could see the humor in that. It was the most apropos response I ever heard in my life, even if I was involved.

When Jimmy Dykes took over in 1951, there was a feeling of relief. In spring training he told us, "I don't want to have to chase you guys around. You want to drink, go into the lounge here in the hotel. Then I know where you are, and I see how much you're drinking. Don't be hiding."

Fine, skipper. It just so happened in the old West Palm Beach hotel they had the greatest smoked swordfish you ever saw in your life. Ain't nothing goes with those suds better than smoked swordfish.

Dykes had another rule: everybody had to be out of the dining room by eight o'clock in the morning. You signed the check for breakfast. After being out all night, I wasn't about to go in and have a big breakfast. I would go outside after I got up, sneak around, and come in through the street door and say to one of the waitresses, "Write me up some ham and eggs, and I'll sign it," and go back into the lobby.

After I led the league in hitting in 1951, I reminded the new general manager, Art Ehlers, that the Macks had promised to make it worth my while when I demonstrated that I was a major leaguer. He urged me to come to Philadelphia and talk. I didn't want to go; you get all that stuff about things you didn't do. Finally I went. I said to Art, "Let's get the record book. You see that four-letter word up there? F-A-I-N, the best hitter in this league. Look down here at Williams," making tons of money, a lot more than I did. So I made $27,500 in 1952.

My drinking buddies were Allie Clark, Sam Zoldak, and Joe Tipton. Dykes called us the "Frightful Foursome." Now we added a Philadelphia sportswriter, Ray Kelly. Most writers—I don't want to go into Boston, where they got ten or twelve different papers and every one is trying to look for you to make a mistake and say something—they don't care what it does to you. Example: Billy Goodman is leading the league in hitting, doing a hell of a job.

A spray hitter like me, he got a lot of those humpty dumpty base hits like we all did, and he beat us a ball game with this. I made a statement like I will do—get my mouth going—that that piss-head bugger beat us with one of those horseshit hits. This guy writes that Fain called this guy a horseshit hitter or something along those lines. I didn't say that. He was a good hitter. He beat us, and I wasn't happy about the way we got beat. That's what we had to contend with.

So when Ray Kelly, who had been on the race track beat, comes up to an old fart like me and says, "I don't know much about this game. The way I can learn it is if you guys help me," that was the start of a tremendous friendship. And he was way ahead of us in the booze league.

So one night in spring training we were in Tipton's room partaking of some white lightning that he had brought with him from Georgia. Ray Kelly got drunk, passed out. We put him on a bed and left. When he came to, he fell in the bathroom and cut his head and dripped blood down the hallway back to his room. Dykes saw it and concluded there must have been a fight.

Next morning Dykes is waiting for me in the lobby.

"Good morning, skipper."

"You out last night?"

"Yeah."

"What time did you get in?"

"Skipper, I don't really know, but I bet you do."

"How about your buddies?"

"Don't know anything about them."

"Who caused the fight last night?"

"What fight?"

So now Dykes says to me, among other things, "You like it on this ball club?"

"Jim, I love it. It's great."

"You keep it up, and you won't be on this ball club. That four-some of yours—I'm gonna get rid of every one of 'em."

Before long Clark and Tipton were gone. I would have been gone too, but the only sonofabitch who was hitting on the club was me. He waited till the season was over to get rid of me.

I led the league the second year in a row, and I'm traded to the White Sox for Eddie Robinson. The White Sox general manager, Frank Lane, calls me.

"We've just acquired your services from the A's. What do we have to do to make you happy?"

One of my less brilliant things I did: I told them. I said, "Forty-five thousand dollars."

That was a mistake. I should have said, "You're the guy. What can you do for me?"

He said, "You'll play for that? The contract is in the mail."

It was my mistake, but $45,000 was pretty good for a kid from Oakland with a fifty-cent allowance.

Twenty-four hours later the phone rings. "Ferris? It's Ty."

"Ty who?"

"Ty Cobb."

I'd never met him or talked to him.

He said, "You signed your contract yet?"

"No, not yet. I haven't signed, but I committed. I told them I would."

The Georgia Peach gave me a terrible going over. Ty saw in me the type of player he was: give no quarter, take none, go for it. He respected that. We played year to year; what you made was predicated on what you did the year before. Big long-term contracts have changed that. Why should they go out and jeopardize that by getting hurt? I played with some of the sorriest hangovers year after year. Why? They couldn't win without me. I wanted up at that plate. My egotism comes through now. I never saw a better first baseman than I was. Keith Hernandez comes close today. Show me a first baseman who could outthink, outthrow, outfield me. Paul Richards said of me, "This guy will beat you any way he can."

Who plays today like I did? Pete Rose.

I didn't lead the league in hitting two years on ability alone. You do a lot of it with your head. I've never seen a dumb champion in anything. When I went up to that plate and I got two strikes on me, at that point you don't look for anything except the ball coming toward you. It could be any pitch. I said to myself, "Look for the fastball, but hit the curve. A curve is gonna be slower. If you're looking for the curve and that fastball gets by you, you're mud." So you look for the fastball. If it changes as it's coming toward you, it's gonna be slower, and you can adjust. If you are thinking that way. These batters today are not thinking anything. Or they're looking for a pitch and nothing else; if it doesn't happen, they're caught with their jeans down.

In Chicago I did the same thing with Paul Richards as I had done with Mr. Mack. Richards was a knowledgeable baseball man, but is that knowledge about every position on the field? He was a catcher and a poor hitter. I don't want to listen to him tell me how to play first base, which he tried to do one day. We got that clarified. I spoke up, and he said I made sense; continue doing what you're doing. But if I hadn't spoken up, I wasn't doing myself any good.

By 1955 I had totally torn up my knee for the third time. Could not run from here to that bowl of flowers. I was done.

I never saw any drug use in baseball but tons of drinking. I was mostly a beer drinker, with an occasional CC. You can sleep away a hangover. I wasn't one who dwelled on how well or badly I did that day. I went out and played all out every day. I gave them my best shot, and now, what's next? My idea was where are the girls? Where's the booze? Let's get it on. You could hear 'em at the ballpark: "Yeah, you pop up, you silly bastard. I saw you last night at the C&R Club, four o'clock in the morning."

I drank too much when I was playing. I warded it off with my youth. I was on the field three or four hours a day. You can only sleep comfortably maybe ten hours. So what do you do with those other hours? But you get hurt mentally; that's the largest part of it. I haven't had a drink for eighteen years. It was messing up my head. But even now I try to look back and have recall on things—was I sober those three days? Now I see on TV a lot of places I should've seen in Philadelphia. I didn't see the Liberty Bell until ten years after I got out of baseball, when I went back for an old-timers game and asked my wife what she would like to see. I never played on a club that had a bed check. It was there: don't let me catch you sneaking on the elevator at one o'clock in the morning, or the fire escape. So you were discreet, tried to do the best you could under the circumstances. If you were staggering, you don't go through the lobby. I never got fined.

Shibe Park was a beautiful hitters' park. I liked Philadelphia people. You could hear the fans out on the field. Their riding never bothered me. I didn't care what anybody thinks of me; didn't then, don't now. I can look in a mirror and say, "Ferris, you suit me." When I joined the A's, Sam Chapman was the star. We would go down to the C&R Club, an after-hours place for dinner and dancing. Sam was the big attraction; he introduced me, but they were all around Sam. Three years later they were all around me, ignoring Sam. I decided to stay away from all of them rather than try to figure out who's who. That's why you see the attitude when you walk in: "Whatta you got to sell, Norm?" You probably saw it, with the apprehensions that I have.

[**NM:** "I knew that. If somebody had met me at the door with a shotgun, I understood that, too."]

It's unfortunate because that's not me. I like people. I like to be friendly, help people.

I got into the kitchen and bath remodeling business with a guy in Oakland, eventually bought him out and moved to Walnut Creek, went bankrupt with ill-advised business operations, ended up here, built a few houses with a little knowledge and a lot of guts, ended up with a contractor's license, and built houses, including this one, for twenty years. My wife and I picked up this fifteen acres and developed it. Retired seven-eight years ago because my knees became so arthritic that I couldn't even drive the truck home.

The VA tells me they'll give me new knees if I get this lard ass off. I weigh 240. They said get down to 200. It's three years, and I'm still trying to get off forty pounds.

I see old timers dying from things like leukemia. I've got it too. My cheeks and jaw are sore. I go for chemo. And these guys are busting me, working me over about growing marijuana. When I was in their local jail, they said, "Hey, you don't look sick to us." I said, "What would convince you? I can't walk. I'll trade you." I'm not saying I'm innocent. I grew some marijuana. I blew it.

One pound of marijuana that comes from one seed sells for $2,500. You get two to three pounds off one plant. Why was it a good gamble for me? 'Cause I'm going to be dead from this leukemia in the not too distant future. I know that. I figure I'm going to be a dead fish before I finish their sentence.

I have no need for money, period. My wife—you haven't met her—is the greatest kid for me. The only reason I'm on this earth right now is that she kept me from getting killed. I contemplated suicide more than once—drunk. She was my savior. When I left this earth, I wanted to leave her where she didn't have to worry about anything. It doesn't take many pounds at $2,500 a pound tax free to make things pretty comfortable.

Somebody sent me a 1953 sports magazine. I'm on the cover. I have copies of it. I'll show it to you. [He pushed himself off the couch, crawled and pulled himself across the floor to the kitchen, searched the cabinets under the sink, and couldn't find it. I helped him get back on the couch, then left. Thirty years later that gesture remains vivid in my memory. Fain was arrested in March 1988, convicted of selling marijuana, and served eighteen months in a state prison. He died at eighty in 2001.]

15.

William "Dutch" Fehring

MENLO PARK, CALIFORNIA, MAY 24, 2004

Dutch Fehring's first and last major league at bat was also his first time at bat at any professional level. The ninety-three-year-old longtime college coach had retired after twenty-two years at Stanford when he relived that experience in the living room of his small brick home.

I WAS BORN ON May 31, 1913, in Columbus, Indiana, a town of about ten thousand, forty miles south of Indianapolis. In high school I played football, basketball, and baseball and was a catcher on the town team.

I went to Purdue in 1930 and played all three sports. In June 1934, between my finals and graduation, I had about a week off. So I went to Chicago to visit a roommate, Jack Brady. He took me to the South Shore Country Club for dinner one night, and who was there but Al Simmons of the White Sox. He invited me to work out with them. Harry Grabiner, the Sox general manager, lived near my friend, whose older brother was dating Grabiner's daughter. Brady took me over to see Grabiner, who okayed my working out.

The team was away on a long eastern trip. Somebody threw me BP, had me catch pop fouls. Grabiner signed me and gave me a $750 bonus and $500 a month, which was good money in the Depression.

I went back to Purdue for commencement and returned to Chicago. Luke Appling, the Sox shortstop, had been left home to be treated for a bad ankle. He and I took the train to Washington to join the team. Luke was a very personable traveling companion. We got in early in the morning and went to the Wardman Park Hotel. There was a group of players sitting on the verandah. Jimmy Dykes was talking about playing golf at a certain course, and he was betting somebody that he could break 100 using just a putter. I don't remember ever formally meeting Dykes. Al Simmons made me feel welcome and introduced me to a few people. Luke

Appling did too. Another person who went out of his way to welcome me was a coach, Muddy Ruel. He was one of the few on that team who had a college degree.

From Washington we went to Philadelphia, Boston, and New York. On the train Simmons studied the stats. He would say, "I think a hitter should do better than one hit out of three. That's considered a good hitter, but a good hitter should be able to go two for five."

My duties were catching BP, warming up pitchers in the bullpen, and spelling Zeke Bonura at first base when he didn't want any more infield practice.

We're in New York on June 25, and I was in the bullpen warming up Slim Kinzy, a TCU graduate who was my roommate. Kinzy had left the pen to start the last of the seventh when the phone rang. Burleigh Grimes answered the phone. He heard a voice say, "Perry?" Burleigh says, "Perry? Nobody hear named Perry," and hung up. Phone rang again. It was Dykes calling for Fehring. I knew then I was going to go into the game.

The dugout looked about twenty miles away from the bullpen. I didn't know whether to go the short way across the field or under the stands. I decided to take the short way and started to run; I got the feeling everybody was looking at me, so I slowed down a little. Finally I got there, and Muddy Ruel helped me on with the shin guards. He said, "Now don't be nervous. You'll do okay." So I go in. [The Yankees led, 10–2.]

First man up is Earle Combs. He hits his first home run of the year. With one out, Ben Chapman comes up. Ben hits a single. At the time he's leading the league in stolen bases. I thought, "Well, I hope he tries to steal. I'll throw him out."

Next batter, Lou Gehrig, hit a foul ball up and back almost in the stands. I remember getting my knees up against the stands so I'd have a measure of whether it was in the stands or not. I never saw a ball do so many flip-flops as that ball did. It was a real high one and the wind took it. I saw it coming down on my left about six feet, and I made a dive for it and didn't get it. I should have caught it but I didn't. The next pitch Gehrig hits over the right-field wall, and he's halfway to second base when the umpire called him back. Foul ball. Lou said some nasty things to the ump, like, "Here I am, going for a record, and you're taking food right off my table, you blind so-and-so." I lost a little respect for Gehrig at the time. I knew it was foul. I think Gehrig did too.

Gehrig then hits a ball to the deepest part of center field. The center fielder goes back and picks up the ball and relays it to Al Simmons, who relays it to the shortstop. I can see Gehrig coming around third base. I know he's going to try for a home run. He was 6-foot-4 and weighed about 220. I was 6-foot-1 and weighed 195. I knew he was going to upset me, especially if I got the ball. I've got my left foot down that baseline, my right foot in front of the plate. I'm waiting for the ball. The shortstop threw a strike right to me, and we had Lou out by at least six to eight feet. He didn't even slide. He knew he was out and wasn't going to take a chance on getting hurt. I thought sure he'd blow his top then. But he didn't. Never said a word. We're behind, 13–2, when I come up to bat with nobody on base in the top of the ninth. I picked up one of Al Simmons's bats—they had a thicker handle than most—and he later gave me hell for it. Bill Dickey is catching for New York, Johnny Broaca pitching. Dickey says to me, "Is this the first time up in the big leagues, son?" I thought, "He's trying to break my concentration." He says, "Right down the pipe. Here comes a fastball right down the pipe." I took it for strike one.

Dickey said, "I'm not kidding you. He's gonna come right down the pipe, same thing." Now I thought for sure it's going to be a curve this time. So I took strike two. Bill says, "You think I'm kidding you. I'm not. I want to see you swing and hit that ball." Even the umpire said, "He's not kidding you, son."

So here it comes, a fastball right down the pipe. I swung and fouled it back. Both of them said, "Good swing. That's what you're up there for."

Bill said, "Same thing," and it was: a fastball, a foot high and a foot outside. And I swung and missed it a foot. That was my only time at bat in the big leagues, and I struck out.

The next day Bill Dickey came over to the White Sox bench and said, "Where's Dutch?" I went over to him. He said, "You thought I was kidding you, didn't you?"

I said, "Yeah, I really did."

He said, "I'd have loved to see you hit that ball right out of the park." He was a class guy to do that.

That was my only appearance in a major league game, my first professional game ever. I had been told when I signed that I would be with the White Sox for the balance of the year. But I didn't have it in writing. When we got back to Chicago, Dykes came to me when I was getting ready to suit up and go out and catch BP. He said, "We lost seventeen out of twenty-two on this trip, and they're after me now to make some changes. Since you're the youngest and the last to sign, I'm going to have to let you go. I'd like you to know you're welcome to go to spring training with us next spring."

I went home. A man from Dallas was looking for players, so I went. There were only four of us northerners on the team. In BP the first day I got hold of one and hit it out of the park. And then I didn't get to see another good pitch. I wasn't going to swing at bad pitches, and the boys waiting to hit behind me got on me. "Come on, rookie, get out of there; let somebody else take their cuts." I look back now, and they were still fighting the Civil War.

They sent me to Longview, Texas, Class D. I didn't have money for a hotel room, so I slept under the grandstand with another player. Hung my clothes on nails. I played in a couple games down there, and that was it.

16.

Dave "Boo" Ferriss
CLEVELAND, MISSISSIPPI, JANUARY 28, 1993

• •

Six-foot-two, 200-pound right-handed pitcher Dave "Boo" Ferriss had one of the most spectacular debuts in baseball history, throwing a record 22⅓ consecutive scoreless innings in his first three games for the Boston Red Sox in 1945. His 8-0 start—beating every team in the league—earned him spreads in national magazines. In four years his record was 65-30. He never had another decision.

After five years as a pitching coach for the Red Sox, Ferriss coached baseball at Delta State University in Cleveland for twenty-six years. A few years before I visited him at his home there, the school baseball field had been named for him.

• •

I WAS BORN IN Shaw, ten miles from here, population 1,500, in 1921. The nickname "Boo" came from when I first began to talk and could not say "brother." It came out "Boo." The family started saying, "Boo yourself." And it stuck. I still use it myself. At one time Shaw was the world's cotton center. My father was a cotton grower and buyer/broker. My mother was the postmaster for twenty-eight years.

There were town teams with good college players all around here in the '20s and '30s, heavy rivalries, plenty of betting on games. My dad played catch with me and took me to those games on Sunday afternoons. He was a player, manager, and umpire in the Delta area, so I got my love for the game from him. The [Southern Association] Memphis Chicks were the big team around here because our daily paper was the *Memphis Commercial Appeal*. My dad took me to my first pro game at old Russwood Park in Memphis. It was a little over a hundred miles, gravel road all the way. We usually had a couple flats along the way. Took more than three hours to get there.

As a kid, I threw a ball against the front steps for hours, drew a strike zone on those steps, imagined batters on either side of it, and would field the balls when they bounced back at me or hit a corner and came back at me in the air. My glove hung on my bike handlebars wherever I went.

We made a diamond in a lot beside my house and played choose-up games. In the seventh grade I was tall and thin and went out for the high school team as a second baseman. My hero was the great second baseman Charlie Gehringer. One of my first games, we were playing Shelby, and I covered the base on an attempted steal; a big boy ran into me, and I fell and broke my right wrist. I was in a cast all summer, so I practiced throwing left-handed. I played second base until mid-sophomore year, when the coach put me on the mound. I pitched and played infield. I would pitch right-handed one day and play first base left-handed the next day, and that would confuse fans. Some guys lost money betting that that left-handed first baseman was not the same guy as the right-hander who had pitched the day before.

My high school coach, James Flack, was a hero to me. He had been a pitching prospect himself. When the town team wanted me to pitch a big game two days after I had pitched another big game, he protected me, kept me from working too much.

The Memphis manager tried to sign me when I finished high school. Other clubs did too. But my dad said I was going to college. I got the first full baseball scholarship given at Mississippi State.

I played semipro after my freshman year, sometimes pitching left-handed, went to the national championships in Wichita. The next summer the Red Sox took an interest in me and arranged for me to play at Brattleboro, Vermont, in a college league.

Then came Pearl Harbor in December 1941. The Alabama coach, Happy Campbell, was a Red Sox scout. They wanted to sign me. My dad and I talked it over. I figured if I didn't sign after that '42 college season, I wouldn't be around long and might never sign. So in the spring of '42 I signed with Boston for $225 a month, a cash bonus of $3,000—which I thought was a ton of money—and a $6,000 incentive bonus once I'd put in thirty days as an active player on the Red Sox. My dad was in on the negotiations and helped me get that bonus put in there. They assigned me to Greensboro in the Piedmont League.

At 3 a.m. on the morning of June 7, my dad put me on a train down in Shelby to go to Greensboro. One year to the day later, he died. He never saw me pitch as a pro.

I was twenty. We lived in a rooming house and ate at a boarding house. I had a 7-7 record, was not the fastest, but I had a live fastball that moved in and sank on right-handed hitters. Pretty good curve. Good control. I knew how to pitch.

In the fall I went back to school, and in December I was drafted, glad to have one year of pro ball behind me. I eventually finished my degree at Delta State in the winters. I was a physical instructor training Air Force cadets at Randolph Field, Texas. They had a fast eight-team league, with some major leaguers on those service teams. It was like playing minor league ball for two years. I was lucky to have Bibb Falk, a former White Sox and Indians outfielder and legendary University of Texas coach, as our manager. He ran it like a pro club. I probably learned more baseball from him than anybody. We talked baseball every waking hour.

I had a history of asthma growing up. In early 1945 it acted up, and they gave me a medical discharge. I was on the Louisville roster, so that's where I went for spring training. I had a couple good outings against Cincinnati. Reds manager Bill McKechnie called the Boston manager, Joe Cronin, and told him, "You got a kid down here who's throwing well, and you're hard-pressed for pitching."

We opened in Toledo, and I was to pitch the second game at night. I was lying around the room that afternoon. About 2:30 there was a knock on the door. The manager came in. "Hey, kid, pack your bag. You're leaving at 5:30." I was on that train to Washington, arrived on a Thursday, and we went that night to Philadelphia. I was working out and watching the games, excited to death just being there. I was riding high.

Joe Cronin had broken his leg, so a coach, Del Baker, was running the team. It was his custom to put a new ball in the locker of the guy who was going to pitch that day. Sunday I showed up to watch another ball game. I look up in my locker, and there's a shiny white ball staring me in the face. I took the ball and went over to Baker.

"Mr. Baker, somebody put this ball up in my locker. I know it's not for me."

He says, "You're it. You're pitching the first game."

My stomach about fell out. I had no book on any of the hitters. We had no meeting. Baker told me, "Aw, kid, just go out there and throw strikes." That was about it. I didn't know their hitters, but when I went to the mound I saw Al Simmons coaching third base. I'd read about him all my life. He was a real jockey. And in the dugout, there sat Connie Mack. I'd read about him all my life too. Pitching against me was Bobo Newsom, one of my boyhood idols. The place was packed, the most people I'd ever seen in my life.

Bob Garbark was the catcher. The first eight pitches I threw were all balls. I was throwing good but just missing. Baker comes out to steady me, and Garbark tells him, "The kid's throwing good, just missing a little bit."

Al Simmons is really letting me have it. Bobby Estalella is the next hitter. Simmons called Estalella down the line and they talked briefly, and Bobby came back to the plate ready to swing. He swung at what was the worst pitch I'd thrown, inside. I figured he'd be taking. He popped it up foul to third base.

Next batter: four pitches, four balls. That's fifteen pitches; I still hadn't thrown a strike. Bases loaded.

Baker comes out again. By this time the bullpen is getting hot. Garbark tells Baker, "Del, he's throwing good. His ball is moving. If he starts getting it in there, he's gonna be all right."

So Del says okay. Dick Siebert comes up. First two pitches— balls. Then finally I threw a strike. I heard it from that crowd. Oh, man, they hollered. I threw another ball. Three and one. Bases loaded. One more ball and I might have been out of there. He took a strike and then hit a two-hopper hard up the middle over my head. I jumped for it but couldn't reach it. I figured: base hit. I'm out of here. The shortstop, Skeeter Newsome, got that ball behind second base, stepped on second and threw to first for a double play. Greatest DP I ever had behind me.

I came in, and they were all patting me on the back, encouraging me.

I went back out in the second inning and walked the first two men. I'd still only thrown three strikes to seven hitters. And suddenly I was throwing strikes. Pitched a shutout, 2–0.

And I was 3 for 3, singles to left, center, and right off Bobo. After the second hit he took a few steps toward first and stood there staring at me. The A's first baseman, Dick Siebert, says to me, "Don't pay any attention to him. He's harmless, just got to let off steam. That's Bobo." So when I hit the third, a shot to right, he came all the way over, and I mean he cussed me out for all I was worth. Boy, I was shaking in my boots.

That was my debut. My record for scoreless innings at the start of a career almost went down the drain in my very first inning.

What kept me from falling apart in that disastrous first few innings of my first major league game, with a crowd ten times as many people as in my own home town? I was always level-headed, had no temper. Errors and such never bothered me. I grew up in a church-going family, and I always had faith and confidence in myself. I had a good stable family life. My mother loved sports; we were a sports-minded family. I often wished my father could have seen me pitch in the major leagues. My mother was a real rock for me, believed in me, always there to give me encouragement. I prayed always before my games, asking the Lord to help me to do my best—not to win—just to give me the strength to do my very best.

I almost fall apart telling about it forty-seven years later.

The Boston papers gave me a big buildup after that, and my next start, on Sunday against the Yankees, the place was full. I shut them out, 5-0. Then we went to Detroit, where they scored a run with one out in the fifth.

I went on to win eight in a row, beat every team the first time I faced them, one team twice. That's still a record. My first loss was in New York, 3-2. *Life* magazine covered that game. It was a big buildup for those days of no television. But Boston had a zillion newspapers in the area. Every time I looked up, there was a mike in front of me.

When I first got to Boston, I didn't have a locker. I had a few nails over in the corner by the bat racks. It was that way until after I had won about five; then somebody got released, and a locker opened up. But the clubhouse guy, Johnny Orlando, wouldn't give it to me as long as I was winning. Before my seventh game, a reporter and photographer came in with a big pair of dice made out of paper and seven dots on them. They said, "You're going for number seven today. If you win, this'll be a great picture for the paper. But you may feel this is a jinx and don't want to do it." So they put those dice on top of the bats where I dressed. I still have that photo; you can see my clothes hanging up on a nail.

Tom Yawkey wanted to meet me. I went up to his office, and he was there with his new wife, Jean. I came to know him and admire him, thought the world of him. They don't make his kind in baseball any more. He got a lot of criticism for caring too much about his players, but he said he would accept that kind of criticism. After everybody'd left the park, he would go out and work out with the clubhouse kids and batboys. He'd swing for that green monster. Did not act like a club owner.

Bill McGowan was a good umpire but a showman. One day at Fenway I had Detroit, 4–2, in the ninth with two out and two on, and Hank Greenberg is up. A home run will beat me. Count is 2-2. I threw one right through there. The game was over. But McGowan says, "Ball." Cronin put up a beef, but McGowan told our catcher, Bob Garbark, "Aw, folks come out to see big Hank hit. Give him another shot at it."

True story. Bob said, "How about that kid out there? He's trying to make his way."

I was making $700 a month. I thought that was big money after being a corporal in the army. I had forgotten all about that $6,000 incentive bonus my dad had helped me negotiate. I was just in seventh heaven being up there playing in the majors. One day in the clubhouse amid my mail was an envelope from the front office. In it was the check for $6,000. At the end of the season Mr. Yawkey wanted to see me. I went in, and he handed me a check for $10,000. I thought that was Fort Knox. The Boston papers had been all over him to tear up my contract and give me a raise, but he did it in his own way. In '46 I got $15,000.

The last day of the season the team gave me a day and a used car—new cars were hard to come by during the war—a black custom-made Lincoln that had belonged to Mrs. Edsel Ford. Had all these gadgets on it, did everything but talk. It was my first car. I drove it home and kept it a few years. It burned a lot of gas.

The Yankees beat me that day, 2–1.

I batted .267 and was never taken out for a pinch hitter that year. I pinch-hit myself 20 times. One day in Chicago I pinch-hit with the winning run on second base, and Jimmy Dykes, the Chicago manager, ordered me walked intentionally. The next guy up got a hit to beat them. Well, the papers gave Jimmy the devil for walking a pitcher and getting beat by a regular hitter. The next day, batting for myself, I hit a home run with a man on to break a 2–2 tie. As I'm going around the bases, there's Dykes up on the dugout steps waving his cap at the press box and pointing to me.

I had a room overlooking the Charles River, near Fenway. Some of the guys I roomed with there were legends in ice hockey, but their names meant nothing to me. All I knew about hockey is they played it on ice.

In '46 they wondered if I could win with all the big boys back from the service. In spring training the writers kept asking Ted Williams about me. He said, "I've never seen him pitch. Wait'll I hit at him." One day I threw BP for him, and afterward he told the writers, "Don't worry about him. He'll win any time. He's got a good live fastball."

I had met Williams in 1941. We had an off day at Brattleboro, and the manager, Bill Barrett, took me and two other kid pitchers from small towns in Oklahoma to Fenway. We had never seen a major league game. It was the day Lefty Grove was going after his three hundredth win. He won, 7–6. After our season was over, I and one of the other pitchers went to Boston to pitch BP, and we made one trip to New York. I saw Lefty Gomez pitch against us. The harder he threw, the harder Ted hit them, three shots. That was Ted's .406 year.

Now I was enthralled to be his teammate. First thing that stood out to me was how hard he worked. Likable guy, always popular among his teammates. Knowledgeable about hitting and never stopped helping anybody who would listen. It was just a few Boston writers who gave him a bad time. But he did not work as hard on his fielding. You'd look out there from the mound before you started pitching, and he'd be standing there taking those imaginary swings.

We got off to a great start, 41-9. But I got off to a bad start, knocked out in my first two games, and right away they started writing, "He's done. The big boys are back." I knew the level of player would be higher. A player who helped boost my confidence the most was Bobby Doerr, a fine fellow and our unofficial captain.

One night in St. Louis rain held up the start of the game. Water everywhere. But they had a big crowd. Our warmup mound by the dugout was in a big puddle of water, so I couldn't warm up. Over on the third base side the Browns' pitcher could warm up okay. Cronin told umpire Cal Hubbard about it, and he said I could warm up on the mound. So the last half of the first inning, I go out and start warming up. Here comes St. Louis manager Luke Sewell. He kept kicking about all the time I was being given and protested the game. Our guys were agitated about playing on a wet field and said, "Aw, let's beat the stew out of them." Well, they beat us, 1-0.

[The Red Sox won the pennant by twelve games.]

On the last day of the season we packed our bags and took them to the ballpark not knowing if we were going to Brooklyn or St. Louis for the World Series. The National League ended in a tie, and we kind of went flat. We had to go back home and unpack and wait for their playoff. Cronin brought some American Leaguers to Boston to play us to keep sharp. But that delay took the edge off us. In one of those games, Ted Williams was hit on the elbow with a pitch. Ted was 5 for 20 in the World Series against the Cardinals, all singles. We felt he was not himself. He was in the whirlpool every day. We didn't think he was swinging his normal swing.

I started Game 3 and had a few more butterflies than usual. Dizzy Dean was out on the field. He was a broadcaster for the Browns then. He was around the batting cage, wearing a big ten-gallon hat and cutting up as usual. After I took my BP swings, he threw an arm around my shoulders and told me, "Kid, just go out and throw the way you been throwing all season. After your first pitch, it's just another game."

He was right. [Ferriss won, 4-0.]

The night before Game 7, my brother and I went to the picture show. He was crossing his legs the whole time, nervous as he could be. I said to him, "Who's pitching tomorrow, you or me?"

That was a real thrill, pitching that seventh game. That's what kids dream about, throwing a ball up against those steps, making up an imaginary setting and game.

They weren't hitting me hard, but I came out trailing, 3-1, in the fifth. Dom DiMaggio tied it in the eighth with a double but pulled a hamstring going into second base and had to come out. Leon Culberson replaced him in center field. Bottom of the eighth, I was in the dugout [when Enos Slaughter singled], but I was out on the steps soon as Harry Walker got a hit and Slaughter took off from first. It was a 3-1 pitch and he was running on the pitch, a run-and-hit situation. He was past second when the ball hit the ground. We never dreamed he was going to try to go all the way. The third base coach tried to hold him up, but Slaughter had his head down.

Johnny Pesky hesitated a second after he took the throw in from Culberson, but he had to. When they saw Slaughter going, Doerr and Higgins are hollering, "Throw it home." But Pesky couldn't hear them. He had to hesitate long enough to see where to throw it and he made a good throw, but it short-hopped, and the catcher had to come out in front of the plate to get it. A throw on a line would have wiped Slaughter out. Pesky got the goat horns, but he did not hold it any longer than he had to, and his throw was hurried.

We had men on first and third with one out in the ninth but didn't score.

In a night game in Cleveland in July of '47 I threw a curve on a 3-2 count with two out and the bases loaded in the seventh inning of a 0-0 game—got on top of it and cracked down on it and struck him out. Doerr won it, 1-0, with a home run in the ninth. Didn't think anything about it at the time. Next day in Chicago I went out to loosen up and couldn't get my arm up. That was the start of my arm trouble. I laid off for two weeks but did not have my good stuff. Finished 12-11.

That winter they worked on it, but X-rays showed nothing. Joe McCarthy had replaced Cronin as our manager. Our relationship with Cronin had been personal. McCarthy held a distance. We all liked Cronin and had to adjust. I was a spot starter and reliever. On the last day of the '48 season we had to win and Detroit had to beat Cleveland for us to finish in a tie with the Indians. We were watching the scoreboard, and Cleveland was losing. I worked the last 3⅔ innings against the Yankees and we won, 10–5.

We all went to Fenway thinking Mel Parnell was going to pitch the playoff game. After the Sunday game we said to him, "We'll get 'em tomorrow." We were all surprised that it was Denny Galehouse who started. The Indians were hot. That was a sad day.

Spring training 1949 my arm went dead. My good fastball was gone. I stayed with the team all year on the disabled list. The next year they sent me to Birmingham. Pinky Higgins was the manager. I did pretty well for him, pinch-hit a lot, but my good fastball was gone. Then he went to Louisville, and I went with him as his pitching coach. When he went to Boston in '55, I went with him.

I can still remember how I pitched to certain big hitters. I can visualize a curveball I threw in the '46 World Series to strike out Enos Slaughter—still see the path of that curve breaking right in there. It fooled him, and you didn't fool him too much. I had pretty good luck against the Yankees. I sidearmed Joe DiMaggio after I got ahead of him and kept it away from him. Curve on the outside. Tommy Henrich and Charlie Keller were lefties. They were tough. I remember this pitch: I had Henrich 3-2 in New York. I threw him a change-up. He was not looking for that from me on that count. He got way out in front of it, and the ball sailed out over the third baseman's head. He just clapped his hands and laughed all the way to first base, saying, "You can't do that."

My choice of a defensive infield behind me would be Joe Kuhel first base, Doerr at second, Phil Rizzuto shortstop, and Ken Keltner third base. When Keltner had time, he always looked at the ball and got his fingers across the seams before he threw. Seems he made a bad throw once as a teenager and his daddy beat him with a stick, and he never made another bad one.

Leaving the Red Sox and Fenway and coming to Delta State, where there was practically no baseball program, no field, not much of anything—it hurt. It took some adjusting. I had an offer to be the Twins' pitching coach. I almost went, but I stayed here and am glad I did. College baseball as a whole has been upgraded. Been to the Division II World Series three times. Had a lot of good kids.

17.

Harry Gumbert

WIMBERLEY, TEXAS, SUMMER 1985

Right-handed pitcher Harry Gumbert was 143-113 in his fifteen-year career (1935–1950) with the New York Giants, Cardinals, Reds, and Pirates. He was with the Giants when they faced the Yankees in the 1937 World Series.

IN THE FIRST GAME of the 1937 World Series, I came in cold off the bench to pitch to Tony Lazzeri with two men on and one out. I wasn't supposed to pitch, but here's what happened. Carl Hubbell wasn't having too good a day, although he was leading, 1–0, going into the last of the sixth. The Yankees started hitting him, and Lazzeri came up. Hub had trouble with Tony. So [manager] Bill Terry wanted Dick Coffman to come in and pitch to Lazzeri. But he didn't go out to the mound. He waved to catcher Gus Mancuso to bring in Coffman. As Coffman started to come in from the bullpen, Gus turns to the umpire and says, "Gumbert" by mistake. So Gumbert gets announced as the new pitcher. Terry jumped up and hit his head on the concrete top of the dugout, and it knocked him down on the ground. He wobbled out and started arguing that it was Coffman. I'm still sitting on the bench. Well, he won the argument, and Coffman takes his warmup pitches. The announcer corrected his announcement. Art Fletcher, the Yankees third base coach, hasn't made a move until then. He comes over to the umpire and says that according to the rules, Gumbert must pitch to one man. The umpire says, "You're right. Bring him out here." So out I go, cold off the bench. I threw Lazzeri two curve balls, and he hit a nice soft ground ball to Burgess Whitehead at second, a perfect double play ball, and Whitey lets it roll between his legs. [Coffman then replaced Gumbert.] They wound up scoring seven runs.

18.

Harvey Haddix

. . . .

Left-hander Harvey Haddix is best known for the twelve-inning perfect game he lost in the thirteenth, 1–0, to Milwaukee in 1959. Less remembered is that he was the winning pitcher when Bill Mazeroski hit his walk-off home run in Game 7 of the 1960 World Series. Haddix won 136 games in his fourteen years (1952–1965) with the Cardinals, Reds, Pirates, and Orioles. He became a pitching coach for five teams (1966–1984.) We met in a hotel coffee shop.

. . . .

I WAS A LEFT-HANDED shortstop in high school, a pretty good hitter, living on the farm and playing semipro ball on Sundays around Springfield, Ohio, in 1943, when a Philadelphia Athletics scout said to me, "I'm going to write to Connie Mack about you."

In the newspaper I saw a St. Louis Cardinals tryout camp at Columbus, and I said, "I'd like to go see what they think of me." St. Louis had twenty-two farm clubs then. There were 350 of us. They put a number on your back and said, "Fill out your dope sheet." I put down pitcher–first base–outfield. They said, "Be a pitcher," and scratched out the other two. This was 9 a.m. I was sent down to the bullpen and stayed there until 4 p.m. They waved me in and said, "Only throw fastballs." I threw about eight, and they said, "That's enough. Can you come back tomorrow?"

I went back at nine the next day, and it was the same thing. Hung around till four again, and the scout said, "Throw what the catcher calls." I threw four or five fastballs and a few curves, and he said, "That's enough. Do you want to sign?"

I said, "No."

Being an honest old country boy, I thought of that scout back home who had gotten me interested in signing. But I never heard from him again, so I went back and signed a Columbus contract for $160 a month.

In 1947 they said, "You're going to Pocatello, Idaho."

I said, "No, I'm not. That's too far from home. You must have someplace else to send me." After a few days they said, "You're going to Winston-Salem, North Carolina," and they gave me a railroad ticket. When I got to the train station, I saw it said "Lynchburg, Virginia," on it—another Cardinal farm. I didn't know if they had messed me up or what, and I had never been away from home on my own. No money in my pocket or nothing. Then I looked in the newspaper and saw those two teams were playing each other a preseason exhibition game.

I went into the seventh inning with a no-hitter several times, never thought about it until I reached that point. In St. Louis I had one into the ninth. First man up, Richie Ashburn, lined a hit to right field. Then I had to struggle to hold my 2–0 lead. Winning is the name of the game, but the no-hitter part started to come into it for me after the seventh. In the perfect game, I only went for the no-hitter in the ninth inning. I thought as long as I've come this close, I'm going to go for it. It was in front of me on the scoreboard the whole time, but I had come that close before. So I went for strikeouts, fanned two in the inning, then said, "Well, I've done it. Now I'll go back to pitching my normal game. I don't care." The difference was not trying to strike guys out any more. My normal way of pitching was: I don't care if guys hit the ball as long as they don't get the good wood on it. I had to have enough in the ninth to stretch those guys out. It's a different mental attitude when you depart from your normal game, at least for me, and that's why so many no-hitters are broken up in the eighth or ninth inning. The mental attitude has a lot to do with it.

In Pittsburgh I was as close to Roberto Clemente as anybody. A fine guy. I liked him. He would not start a conversation, but if you wanted to talk with him, he would. We talked a lot on airplane rides and in spring training. He would not let you get close to him. He wanted his privacy, never went with our groups to dinner. He went by himself. One day he came out and I laughed at him. He was rubbing a white suntan lotion all over him. He said, "You know why? You see so-and-so over there? He too black. You see me? Nice and tan." Was he a hot dog? I haven't seen a guy yet who didn't like to show off his skills. I was called a hot dog a lot of times; I could catch a ball behind my back and other ways. He did not want any attention.

I played with Frank Robinson at Cincinnati and coached for him at Cleveland. A very intense player and student of the game. In this age players want a pat on the back when they do something good. He never wanted it and could not do it in the beginning. He was hardnosed and expected you to do your job. But he adjusted. Star players as managers don't reach down to the little guys to make them happy.

There are no two pitchers alike. You can't just stamp them out. As a pitching coach, you see a lot of guys with great stuff who don't put it all together. Don't have the control or the mental attitude. Guys with lesser stuff but the right mental attitude go farther. Attitude: how they apply themselves to their job, willing to listen and make adjustments.

I did not want to manage. Very few pitchers become managers. Pitchers are concerned with themselves all the time. They think and act different. They don't study the whole game like catchers or infielders.

19.

Carmen Hill
INDIANAPOLIS, SUMMER 1985

. . . .

If you made a bar graph of right-handed pitcher Carmen Hill's record in the ten years he was in the National League between 1915 and 1930—eight of them with the Pirates—it would look like a Kansas wheat field with two tall silos side by side in the middle. He never won more than three games in any year, except for 1927 and 1928, when he was 38-21. In 1915 Hill and Lee Meadows were the first pitchers to wear glasses in the major leagues. We met at his longtime home in Indianapolis.

. . . .

IN 1914 I PITCHED batting practice for the Giants. Their catcher said I'd hear from them. I bragged to my schoolmates about signing with them any day. When I didn't hear from them, I made a promise I'd beat them if I ever got the chance. And I did, in my first big league start for Pittsburgh on September 17, 1915, a 5-0 four-hitter. I had a habit of raising my foot a little before I went into my windup motion. The Giants got on me because of it. This went on for a few innings. The home plate umpire came out to the mound and said, "Boy, you're going to have to stop that."

I said, "What am I doing wrong?"

He said, "That's all right, my boy. Just go ahead," and patted me on the back. The Giants' bench kept whooping it up. The umpire took off his mask, went over and ran John McGraw out of there.

Twelve years later I beat the Giants five times, and the Pirates won the pennant by 1½ games, 2 games over the Giants.

I was up and down between the minors and the Pirates between 1915 and 1919. Casey Stengel was there when I was with them in 1919. There are many versions of this Stengel story. This is the true one.

The Pirates' owner, Barney Dreyfuss, had promised Stengel a raise if he was hitting over .300 on June 1. He was hitting about .320, but when he went up to get his raise, he didn't get it. In the next game, first time up, he kept the bat on his shoulder and took three strikes. The crowd booed him.

One day I was sitting at the end of the dugout and he was next to me. He wasn't in the game. A little sparrow flew into the dugout and I caught it. Casey said, "Give it to me." When the manager called on him to pinch-hit, he took that little sparrow and put it under his hat. He went up to bat, took three called strikes, and the crowd stood up and booed him. He turned toward them and tipped his cap and the little bird flew out. Casey wasn't around long after that. [He was traded to the Phillies that night.] I was out of baseball 1920–1921 with a stomach ailment and had back injuries that plagued me off and on.

In 1922 the Giants were fighting for the pennant. I was with Indianapolis. The club owner called McGraw and said, "I have a pitcher who can help you." McGraw says, "Send him." I don't think I was sold. It was more like a loan. They did things like that back then. Maybe it was on a trial. Anyhow, I arrived in New York for the last month of the season. They were playing Brooklyn a doubleheader. McGraw called me over and sat me down beside him. As each player came up to bat, he'd say, "This is so-and-so, and this is the way I want you to pitch to him," through the whole game.

The next day I'm pitching. Earl Smith is catching. Smitty comes out to the mound and says to me, "Hill, I don't know you, and you don't know me. If I call for something you don't want to throw, just shake me off. But don't look in there at that potbellied sob on the bench or he'll try to pitch your ballgame for you." McGraw used to call the pitches. I said, "Oh, no he won't." Smitty says, "Well, just don't look at him. And neither will I."

Well, McGraw was waving his arms and pacing around during that whole game, but we just ignored him. The score was 1–1 late in the game. They had a man on second base with two out, and Andy High came to bat. He was the only one I remembered McGraw's instructions about. He'd said to me, "Pitch low to High." I got a pitch up a little, and he hit it for a triple. When I came in to the bench, McGraw says to me, "Where did I tell you to pitch to High?"

I says, "Low."

"You didn't do it, did you?"

"No."

"Okay."

That was it. He didn't get on you if you remembered his instructions but failed to execute them. But if you didn't follow orders, watch out. I learned that in a hurry. A few days later Irish Meusel, a good outfielder, comes up to bat with a man on base and the score tied. McGraw says to him, "Irish, take a strike." Well, Irish hits the first pitch into the left-field seats for a home run. Won the game. He circles the bases, comes down with both feet onto home plate, and runs back to the bench feeling pretty good.

McGraw says, "What did I tell you to do?"

Meusel says, "You told me to take one, and I took it right out of the ball park."

McGraw says, "It'll cost you 200."

I never saw a madder Irishman in my life. Irish says, "Make it 400."

McGraw says, "It's 400." And it stuck.

In 1922 the Giants played the Yankees in the World Series. All the Giants players got blocs of three tickets for each game except me. Other players said I was entitled to the same thing. When I asked, the club secretary said I didn't have any coming to me. I said, "I better get them or I'll go to McGraw." He'd sold mine, but the next day he gave me some. The Giants won the Series. The next spring I got a letter from the club secretary: "It is with great pleasure I'm returning your contract to Indianapolis." But I had a World Series ring.

Earl Smith and I became buddies. He was the best catcher I ever saw. Never had a banged-up finger in all his years. He said he could sit in a rocking chair and catch me. He hated McGraw, didn't hesitate to needle him in the clubhouse. Earlier that season McGraw had fined him $2,500 for not being in his room at curfew time.

In 1926 Smitty and I were reunited in Pittsburgh. I won twenty-one games at Indianapolis by the end of August, and the Pirates bought me. I was to join them in Chicago. I took the train and was late getting in. Bill McKechnie was the manager. At Wrigley Field you had to go up a stairway to get to the clubhouse. When I arrived, the players were coming down to go onto the field. Here came McKechnie. He asked me, "Where have you been?"

"Trying to get here."

"Go up and get a suit."

As I got to the top of the steps, he said, "Wait a minute."

He tossed a ball to me. That meant I was pitching that day.

He said, "I'm going to get you in there before you get a chance to get scared."

I beat the Cubs, 3–2, in ten innings. Smitty caught me.

One day in 1927 we're playing the Giants, and McGraw ordered his pitcher to walk Smitty by throwing at him. He was up and down four times. When we went out on the field, Smitty came out to the mound and said, "Bunker"—he'd given me that nickname— "Bunker, are you my friend?"

I said, "You get back there and catch."

The first man up, I turned his cap around. The second one up went down one way and his bat flew the other way. The third man up I did the same. I never threw at another batter. And I had an easy game. It's up to the opposing pitcher to stop a throwing contest. Next day Giants second baseman Rogers Hornsby came out with a newspaper story that a pitcher who threw at a batter should be banned from baseball. He never mentioned that the Giants had started it. Maybe he said it because he couldn't hit me with a paddle. He used to stand way back deep in the batter's box and step into the pitch. I wouldn't let him. I'd pitch him inside first, then outside. If he stepped into the pitch and it was inside, he'd step right into it.

On the other hand, if I broke even with Bill Terry—got him twice and he got two hits—it was a good day. This was a game in New York: two outs and a man on second. He's a left-handed hitter. I was all ready to throw to him when I noticed he'd dropped his left foot back in the batter's box, which meant he was going to shove that ball into left field. So I just opened my fingers, relaxed my grip on the ball, and threw the damnedest slow ball up there that you ever saw, with my usual fastball motion. It went up there slow and slower. He swung at it, and he swung at it again. And he popped it right straight up in the air, and the catcher just stood there and caught it. He grabbed the bat right in the middle and came running out at me—I'll never forget it—he was holding the bat up in the air, and he said to me, "Hill, what in the hell was that? You never threw that before in your life." And I laughed and said, "Bill, that was one I was saving just for you."

Donie Bush took over the Pirates in 1927. We didn't get along. He had managed Indianapolis 1924–1926 when I was there. He had to have a whipping boy, somebody he could pick on. In 1925 I had my only really bad year. I couldn't do anything right for him. I went to the club owner and told him to get Bush off my back or I'd kill him. He called in Bush, and for the rest of the year Bush and I didn't say two words to each other. Bush got on our short-stop instead of me.

The '27 Pirates were a drinking team. Spring training in Paso Robles we had adjoining rooms. You could go from one into the next one on down the building. One evening I came in from a show, and there was pitcher Ray Kremer standing in the middle of the room. They had these chandeliers hanging from the ceiling with lots of little lights in them, and he was throwing glasses at them. Had them all busted out but one. Glass all over the floor.

The newsmen were the same way. Once on a trip to Chicago they went into the baggage car and threw all our trunks off the train. We had to borrow the Cubs' road uniforms for the next game until we got our things back.

One time we were in St. Louis. The mayor and district attorney from Hot Springs, Arkansas, Smitty's home town, had come up to St. Louis to see a game. I had won the first game in the four-game series. Before the third game Smitty says to me, "Bunker, let's you and I take them out on the town tonight. We won't be working again in this series."

So we did. Hit all the high spots in town. Got in about three or four in the morning. We went out to the ballpark the next day, and Bush says, "Hill, you're working." Smitty was all hunched over at the end of the bench, just all bent over. I walked over and said, "Smitty, we're working." He just folded up and fell right over on his head onto the concrete floor.

Well, we started the ball game. I had them beat, 1–0, in the sixth. Somebody hit a pop fly into right field. Paul Waner came running in, and as he caught it, he stumbled and his knee knocked the ball out of his glove. There were two men on at the time, and one of them scored. So it was tied, 1–1. That game went on until the eleventh inning. It's the only ball game I was ever in where I walked up and down in front of our bench begging them to get me just one run. In the eleventh inning their first man up was Jim Bottomley, their big first baseman. He hit the second pitch for a home run up on top of the pavilion. I headed for the clubhouse and got about halfway there, and Bush grabbed me by the shoulder and spun me around.

"Where was that ball?" he yelled. "Where was it?"

I said, "Up on the pavilion roof. Didn't you see it?"

"You did it on purpose," he yelled.

In the clubhouse he came toward me and I said, "Bush, if you don't get away from me, you're going to get hurt." He knew I meant it and walked away. Can you figure that?

That was just one instance of Bush and me. Here's another. We're playing Brooklyn at home on a Saturday. We didn't play Sunday ball at home, so we'd go to Brooklyn for a Sunday game, then come back and play them on Monday. I had beaten the Giants on Friday. After the Saturday game Bush says to me, "I'm taking you to Brooklyn."

I says, "You are like hell."

"You better be on that train."

"Don't hold it for me."

I didn't go. They went to Brooklyn and lost, 11–10. Next day Bush was furious. He said, "You lost me that game. I think I'll fine you."

I said, "What do you have five other pitchers for?" I was taking my regular turn and relieving too, was in forty-four games that year.

Before the 1927 World Series opener, the Yankees were hitting balls out of the park all over in batting practice to intimidate us. They had special baseballs made just for that. When one of those balls came over to our dugout and we tried to get it, one of their men ran over and picked it up before we could get to it.

I never forgave Donie Bush for not using me at home in the Series, where I was 10-2. I started Game 4 at Yankee Stadium, after we'd lost the first three. It was do or die time. Our first baseman had a bad hip. The first three batters hit ground balls that went by him just out of his reach into right field. One run scored. Then I struck out Lou Gehrig, Bob Meusel, and Tony Lazzeri. And those fifty thousand people stood up and gave me a standing ovation.

I had learned how to pitch to Babe Ruth watching Jess Barnes work on him in the 1922 World Series. Barnes stood on the mound and just lifted his leg and threw like a girl and drove Ruth crazy. Ruth had a funny, closed, pigeon-toed stance; he'd see that slow ball coming up, and he'd start hopping and dancing in the batter's box. All four times Barnes pitched to Ruth that way. After the game Ruth had come into our clubhouse and wanted to fight Barnes. It took a few of us to hold him back.

I used to pitch that way to him in exhibition games. He'd say, "Put something on the ball, you four-eyed SOB." I'd laugh and throw him another one.

I remembered all that now. But I almost beaned him his first time up. I didn't mean to throw at him, but the ball went right for his head. He froze. I thought sure it was going to get him. He just sort of pulled his head in a little, like he didn't know what to do. He grabbed that bat in the middle and started out for the mound. Smitty says to him, "Babe, you better not go out there. If you do, the next one will be even closer." That stopped him. That was a close call. It scared me, but I bet it scared him more.

In the fifth inning he hit me for a two-run home run, the cheapest homer he ever hit. He hit that ball right off his fists, pulling away from it, not stepping into it. The ball dropped into the right-field stands 296 feet away, just out of Paul Waner's reach. In most parks it would have been an easy out. That's the one that wound up on the Babe Ruth stamp, which was drawn based on a photo of him hitting that home run. In the photo you can see Ruth, the catcher, and the fans all looking up in the air.

We tied it, 3–3, in the seventh, and I went out for a pinch hitter. Smitty went out for a pinch runner. Johnny Miljus went in to pitch, and Johnny Gooch took over the catching. In the last of the ninth, Combs led off and walked. Koenig beat out a bunt down the third base line. They advanced on a wild pitch. Ruth was walked intentionally. Miljus then struck out Gehrig and Meusel. He had two strikes on Lazzeri when Gooch did something no catcher should ever do. He got down on one knee back where the hitter couldn't see him and signaled for an overhand curve ball. He was sure that would strike out Lazzeri. You know what Miljus did? He didn't know why he did it. He just did it. He came with a way down motion, a sweeping sidearm, almost underarm pitch that rose as it came in. Gooch was down on that one knee and couldn't get up quick enough to do anything but just knock that ball down, just far enough away for Combs to score with the winning run. If Gooch had been on his feet, he could have reached that ball.

Then the funniest thing happened. We left the dugout, crossed two-thirds of the way across the playing field in utter silence. You coulda heard a pin drop. Then the noise broke out. It took that long for the fans to realize that the Series was over. And, you know, the Yankees never talked about that game. Miljus never mentioned it either.

20.

Sid Hudson
WACO, TEXAS, OCTOBER 11, 2007

A 6-foot-4 right-handed pitcher for the Washington Senators and Boston Red Sox (1940–1954), Sid Hudson went directly from Class D to the major leagues. In his first big league start he faced a Boston Red Sox lineup of Dom DiMaggio, Doc Cramer, Jimmie Foxx, Joe Cronin, Ted Williams, and Bobby Doerr. Five years as a scout and fourteen as a pitching coach for Washington and the Texas Rangers completed thirty-eight years in baseball, minus a few years in the air force.

I sat with the ninety-two-year-old Hudson and his wife, Marion, and his scrapbooks and memories, at St. Catherine's Nursing Home.

I WAS BORN IN Coalfield, Tennessee, near Knoxville, on January 3, 1915. I was pitching and playing first base in sandlot ball in 1938, and a fellow from Cleveland, Tennessee, was the manager of the Sanford club in the Class D Florida State League. He saw me play and told me they needed a first baseman. "I'll pay you $100 a month." I said okay, and he signed me. Scouts named as signing me had nothing to do with it. I hit well but we had a terrible team, and they fired him and hired Bill "Rawmeat" Rodgers. They called him that because he liked to eat raw steak. He brought a first baseman with him, so now I'm sitting on the bench.

One night we were getting beat pretty bad, and he says to me, "You ever pitch?" I said, "Yeah, a little." It was the eighth inning. He said, "Go in and see what you can do." I went in and struck out all six I faced, and he said, "From now on you're a pitcher."

Everything I learned was from Rawmeat Rodgers. He'd take me out to the ballpark in the morning; we'd go out to the mound, and he'd talk to me about how to pitch, holding runners on, how to field the position, everything.

In 1939 I was back in Sanford and won twenty-four, pitched twenty-seven complete games. Made $150 a month. Two weeks before the season ended, the owner told me, "I have a chance to sell you to the big leagues. Two teams want you, Cleveland and Washington. Take your choice." Cleveland had Feller, Harder, a lot of good pitchers. I thought I'd never get a chance there. Washington had four knuckleballers. I chose Washington.

In spring training in 1940 I was quite thrilled walking into a major league clubhouse out of Class D. The newspapers said I was twenty-two. I was really twenty-five. I don't recall anyone suggesting I cut three years off my age. Maybe the man who signed me or the Sanford club owner who sold me to Washington did it. It wasn't me.

I was warming up one day and the manager, Bucky Harris, walked up behind me and said, "Let's see you throw a couple." I cut loose two or three pitches. He said, "You'll do," turned, and walked away.

I had a $3,000 salary. The Washington owner, Clark Griffith, was a nice guy. He tried to raise you each year. Next year I got $6,000, then $8,000. Tops I made was $17,000. Mickey Vernon led the American League in hitting making $16,000. The way I understand it, he asked for $20,000. Griffith told him, "I had the best pitcher who ever lived, Walter Johnson. That's the most he ever made. You're not worth that."

On opening day I watched Lefty Grove shut us out. Two days later I started, walked five in the first four innings, then gave up a home run to Foxx in the fifth. We lost, 7–0. But I never lost my poise. I made two plays fielding bunts. The *Washington Post* said I "pounced on ground balls and made brilliant throws to first." That was my fielding style on bunts. I ran full speed and jumped just as I got to the ball, picked it up and threw in the same motion.

I was 2-9 when I got a call from Clark Griffith to come to his office. Harris was there. Griffith says, "Sid, you're having a rough time of it. You aren't throwing like you did back in spring training. You look like you're trying to throw every pitch just as hard as you can throw it and have no idea where it's going. We think you can pitch here. You've got good enough stuff. Go out and show us that you can pitch."

He was right. I threw a two-seam fastball that had a tail on it, curve, changeup. I tried to throw a slider, but it hurt my arm. I won five after that, including two one-hitters. In a night game in St. Louis I knew I had a no-hitter going. I had a 1–0 lead. The *Washington Post* said that in the eighth inning first baseman Zeke Bonura saved a hit diving to his right for a hard-hit ball and threw to first. I never saw Bonura dive for anything in his life. In the ninth Rip Radcliff hit the first pitch two inches fair down the right-field line for a double. I didn't feel a letdown. I was in a 1–0 game. George McQuinn bunts, misses the ball, and the catcher misses it. Now I've got a man on third and nobody out. I struck out McQuinn and got the next two batters.

I threw another one-hitter on August 6, a single in the fifth inning.

One day against Cleveland we were behind one run in the ninth against Bob Feller. Feller had that high kick on the mound, and when he did, he kept twitching his right eye; the hitters would get to watching that, and they wished he'd quit it. I thought he did it deliberately. We had our 3-4-5 hitters coming up. Feller threw nine fastballs and got three strikeouts. Bucky Harris said, "Pretty quick, isn't he?" Harris rated him behind Walter Johnson and Grove. First time I pitched against him, the game was tied with two outs and a man on second. The batter hit a fly to Gee Walker, and he dropped it and I lost.

On September 2, I beat Grove, 1–0, in thirteen innings. They had men in scoring position in seven of those innings. I had a good curve that day.

Mrs. Hudson: The wives sat on the first base side, just beyond the dugout. We had a good time and just laughed off the fans' booing.

The beginning of 1941 Phil Rizzuto said the Yankees were going to trade for me. Washington wanted $100,000 for me, and they wouldn't give it. That year I lost a thirteen-inning game, 2–0, against the White Sox. They pulled a triple steal in the thirteenth. That was embarrassing.

Ted Williams saved me from two losses in my career. In the 1941 All-Star Game, I went in in the seventh, gave up two runs, and was the losing pitcher until Ted hit his ninth-inning home run. Twelve years later I'm with the Red Sox. We're down, 1–0, to the Tigers in the eighth. With Jim Piersall on first and two outs, Ted patted me on the fanny, said, "I'll hit that little slider into the right-field seats for you and win you a game," and he did.

Joe DiMaggio paid me the best compliment I ever had. We finished the 1941 season in New York, and I shut out the Yankees on four hits. We stayed over to see a World Series game between the Yankees and Brooklyn. When the Series was over, reporters asked DiMaggio what he thought of the Dodgers' pitching. He said, "They didn't have a pitcher that showed us the stuff Sid Hudson did in the last game of the season."

In 1942 I got a call from Birdie Tebbetts asking me to come down to Waco Army Air Force Base and enlist and play ball for the base team. That's how I came to settle in Waco. I was 20-1 for the base team; then they sent us and another team to the Pacific. We wound up at Saipan.

One day they chose a team of servicemen to play in New York against the Giants and Yankees at the Polo Grounds. My CO in Waco said I could go if I would bring back Babe Ruth's autograph. I carried an autograph book. Before we got to the clubhouse, there was a little cubbyhole with a desk and a chair, and there sits Babe Ruth. We all stopped, and he shook hands with every one of us. I asked him if he would sign my book. He said, "Sure," and dumb me, I didn't get one for myself.

But I do have four balls signed by presidents. Richard Nixon was sitting behind the dugout one day; I asked him to sign a ball and he said, "Sure," and I tossed it up to him. Dwight Eisenhower came down to the clubhouse. Harry Truman and Gerald Ford threw out first pitches, and I caught them and they signed them.

I came out of the service with a sore arm. I led calisthenics for cadets five times a day five days a week. When I came out, I couldn't throw. I pitched in '46 and '47 with a sore arm. Then they found a spur on my shoulder. Doctors at Johns Hopkins said it came from excessive use from all those calisthenics, plus throwing with a ¾ motion. They told me to throw sidearm. It took me two years to come back.

I was released in the spring of 1955 and scouted for the Red Sox for five years in Texas and New Mexico. Didn't like it, traveling every day, looking for a ball game. Jerry Mallett played at Baylor, good arm, power. Joe Cronin said bring him to Boston. I did, and he hit balls over all the fences. Cronin wanted to see him throw. They hit one to him in the outfield, and he threw it on a line to home plate. They signed him, gave him $70,000. He got into four games with Boston. I figure he didn't have it inside him.

When Mickey Vernon managed the new Washington team, I was his pitching coach. I did the same for four years for Ted Williams in Washington and then the Texas Rangers. Williams was fun to coach for. One day I said to one of our young pitchers, "If you get a first-pitch strike on [Orioles first baseman] Boog Powell, drop down a little and throw from there." He did, and Boog hit that ball over the right-field fence. After the game Williams has the kid in his office reaming him out, wagging a finger in his face about pitching that way. I went in there and said, "Ted, it's not his fault. I told him to throw that way."

He didn't look up or say anything, just kept giving this kid a going over. I turned and walked out. Next day we're at the ballpark early, and he calls me into his office and said, "You got piqued at me yesterday, didn't you?" I said, "Yeah." He said, "Well, that's just the way I like it."

I worked for the Rangers for twenty-five years, scouting, coaching. Fifty-six years in baseball.

21.

Travis Jackson
WALDO, ARKANSAS, JULY 23, 1985

. . . .

Hall of Fame shortstop/third baseman Travis Jackson spent his entire fifteen-year career (1922–1936) with the New York Giants and coached for them 1938–1948, interrupted by a five-year battle with tuberculosis beginning in 1941. A .291 lifetime batter, he played in four World Series. Despite injuries to both knees, he led the NL in assists four times. I visited Jackson, a lifelong resident of Waldo, at his home there.

. . . .

WHEN I WENT UP to the Giants, nobody told me anything. John McGraw didn't teach you anything on the bench. I had to sit and watch and learn and see things I could try in order to improve myself. In 1923, when the third baseman broke his leg, I played third. A few days later the shortstop got pneumonia, and I shifted to short. Now that they knew I had to come through to win the pennant, they paid a little attention to me. Frankie Frisch was the second baseman. He never tagged a man out at second base. He'd get the ball and jump straight up in the air. The umpire would call a man out, but I've seen him miss the tag that far. One day in 1926 he and John McGraw got into an argument in St. Louis. Frisch went home. In December he was traded for Rogers Hornsby. Hornsby didn't get along with the Giants' business manager, so he went the next year. McGraw tried hard to find a good Jewish ballplayer [to attract New York's large Jewish population]. He got Andy Cohen to replace Hornsby, but he wasn't good enough. He had trouble hearing in his right ear. I'd be giving him vocal signs as to who would take the throw at second base, and he'd just stand there kicking his feet together, not hearing a word I said. Finally I gave up and took all the throws at second myself. Then came Hughie Critz, a slick fielder who couldn't hit.

After Frisch was traded, we told our pitchers to bear down on him his first time at bat because if he didn't get a hit his first time up, then he'd drag it for the rest of the game. But if you let him get a hit, especially an extra-base hit, that first time up, then he's going to kill you the rest of the day. So we said, "Give him everything you've got, get him out some way, that first time up." And it worked out that way.

John McGraw was a rough customer to play for. But he knew the ones he could get tough with and the ones he couldn't. High Pockets Kelly was our team spokesman, hardheaded, didn't hold back anything. Catcher Earl Smith and McGraw would go to it, shouting back and forth. Smith would needle him, call him "Muggsy" just to make him madder, and the rest of us would be hiding our laughter.

The hardest thing a manager has to do is handle the pitchers. McGraw could not handle pitchers. That was his weakness—when to take them out. He'd let his Irish temper get the best of him, leave a pitcher out there to take a 10–12 run beating, when he should have been out of there in the second inning and maybe we'd've won the ball game. He'd be mad at a pitcher and make him pitch the whole game.

McGraw called all the pitches. One day Rosy Ryan was pitching. Every time he threw a fastball, somebody hit it good. McGraw had enough. He started calling curve ball, curve ball—18 or 19 straight curve balls. Everybody knew he was doing it for meanness. If a pitcher didn't like it, he'd be in Indianapolis the next day.

I made some mistakes sometimes, but he didn't get on me. Later, when I was the team captain, it was my responsibility to position the fielders. One day at the Polo Grounds a rookie, Jimmy Welsh, was in the outfield. Somebody hit a line drive, he was in the wrong place, and it went for a triple. When we went into the dugout, McGraw was just frothing at the mouth, cussing Jimmy out. And Jimmy said, "Mr. McGraw, Jackson moved me."

McGraw said, "Did you move him?"

I said, "Yep."

McGraw said, "Forget about it, Welsh." And that's all there was to it.

I've seen him get mad at players on other clubs. He'd say to them, "I'll trade for you, and when I get you, I'll send you down to Timbuktu." He was a part owner of the Giants. He paid the newspaper writers' expenses on the road. If he didn't like what they said about him, he'd leave them home. We had a catcher, Shanty Hogan. Six-foot-one, weighed around 240, giant of a man. We used to eat at the Dutchman's, over by Yankee Stadium. We'd pick out our own steaks. When he got through, he'd go back and pick out another one. To look at him you'd wonder how he could be a catcher. You'd think there would be a lot of passed balls. But you couldn't throw one by him. He'd smother it one way or another. He was a tough catcher for the shortstop and second baseman to work with; he had such a hard throw to handle. The ball would come in just as heavy as lead and knock your glove off. That made us move a little closer to the base and leave a bigger space for the hitter. We had to get there to get set for the throw; if you tried to catch it on the move, it'd just eat you up. He was a good hitter, too, batted over .300 for us for five years.

One year in spring training McGraw ordered him to lose some weight or get fined for every pound he was overweight. He worked so hard at it, but when we got to the Polo Grounds, he was still eighteen pounds over. We knew how hard he'd tried, so the players got together and paid his fine for him.

The best all-around, down-to-earth manager in the National League that I followed closely was Bill McKechnie. Everything he did was on the way to being right. When I first started out, I would have liked to play for him.

Bill Terry was the right man to replace McGraw [in 1932]. Newspapermen didn't like him. He was blunt, to the point.

In 1933 I hadn't played much on account of my bad knees. In the fourth game of the World Series against Washington, we were tied in the eleventh inning. I said to Terry, "I'm going to get on base one way or another. But you send in a runner for me."

He said, "You get on down there, and I'll have a runner for you."

I beat out a bunt and made it to first and looked around for my pinch runner.

Nobody. Mancuso sacrificed me down to second. I was hobbling more than running. And I thought sure now somebody would come in to run for me. I got up dusting myself off. Here comes my pinch runner, I thought.

Nobody. Blondy Ryan came up and pulled a hit to left field. The coach waved me home. I gave it all I had and just did make it, but if the ball hadn't been thrown five or six feet up the first base line, I wouldn't have made it. I went into the dugout and said to Terry, "Bill, what is the matter with you? You said I was going to have a pinch runner."

"Yeah," he says, "Bernie James is the fastest man I've got, but he's got no experience. When I told him he was going to pinch-run, he started shaking. I'd rather have you out there. You know what you're doing. He'd have been caught off first base, and that was the winning run."

When my knees got worse, I moved to third, and we got Dick Bartell to play shortstop. I'd just as soon play with him at short as anybody I ever played with. He was aggressive and a fighter. We were both holler guys. He was the first shortstop I ever saw who'd cover third base on a bunt down the third base line with a man on second. They do it nowadays, but he started it as far as I know. He'd start on the pitch and beat the runner to third. We got some putouts that way.

I wasn't supposed to play in 1936. I was going to be a coach. Terry and I went down to Pensacola to a baseball school we held there. Afterward, Terry told me to go home for a few weeks, so I did. When I got to spring training, they were to play an exhibition game, but they didn't have a third baseman on the roster. Terry asked me to fill in. After a few days I said, "I'm not here to get into playing shape. I'm a coach."

"Well," he said, "we're trying to trade for a third baseman. But we want a good one, not just anybody."

That went on for the whole season, and I wound up playing in 126 games.

For about twelve years, the Cards, Cubs, Pirates, and Giants battled it out for the pennant every year. St. Louis pitcher Dizzy Dean was the only man I knew who would make big brags like he did and go through with them. He'd tell you what he was going to throw to strike you out, and he'd do it. When he threw at hitters, it was usually because the guys in the Cardinals' dugout were needling him to do it. When Diz threw at our leadoff man, Joe Moore, Moore's roommate, outfielder Hank Lieber, told Diz to stop throwing at Moore or he'd break every bone in his body. Diz quit throwing at Moore. One hot Sunday Diz threw at one of our hitters. When Diz came up to bat, our catcher, Gus Mancuso, stood on home plate, bouncing the ball off it. He said, "Diz, look down there in the bullpen." There stood Roy Parmelee. He could throw as hard as Dean but was wild, didn't know where it was going. "If you throw at another man, Terry's going to bring in Parmelee, and we're going to start with you, and we're going to knock every one of you flat on your ass." Diz didn't throw at anybody else that day.

St. Louis was the hottest place to play, and the infield was almost all skin, just a little patch of grass here and there. They never had time to work on it because the Browns would play there when the Cards were on the road. It was hard, and the dust would kick up on a ground ball. But it made for good hops on grounders. I usually charged all ground balls—any time you lay back on it, you're going to boot it—but it was too uncertain on that infield.

I saw this happen one day at the Polo Grounds: We're playing the Reds. We had the winning run on second in the ninth inning. Reds manager Chuck Dressen waved Babe Herman to play in close in left field. The next batter hit a single over the shortstop's head. Herman could have thrown out the runner, but he just picked up the ball, stuck it in his pocket, and turned and headed for the clubhouse out in center field. Here come Dressen with those short legs right behind him, trying to catch up with him. He never did.

22.

George "High Pockets" Kelly
BURLINGAME, CALIFORNIA, MAY 1983

. . . .

After several years in the minor leagues, the 6-foot-4 right-handed George "High Pockets" Kelly was brought up to the New York Giants by John McGraw to replace Hal Chase at first base in 1920. In eleven full seasons with the Giants, Reds, Cubs, and Dodgers, he drove in more than a hundred runs five times. In 1930 he built a hacienda on a hilltop that overlooked the San Francisco airport, the bay, and the surrounding mountains. It was there that he talked about playing for John McGraw. Kelly was elected to the Hall of Fame in 1973.

. . . .

HAL CHASE WAS A fancy-fielding first baseman, a tough act to follow. I got off to a slow start, wasn't hitting much. The writers were getting on me. One wrote: "I'm getting ready to retire—I saw Kelly get a hit." Another one wrote a poem: "When Kelly Gets a Hit." The fans picked up on it, and they were on me. McGraw told me, "Don't read the newspapers. You're working for me. I do the hiring and firing."

McGraw never praised anybody, never a pat on the back. Late in August 1921 we're 7½ games back of the first-place Pirates. They came into New York for a five-game series. They say McGraw gave us a big pep talk before the first game. Maybe so, but I don't remember him ever giving any kind of pep talk.

The first game of the series, Babe Adams is pitching for Pittsburgh. We get three men on, and I'm up. The count goes to 3-0. I look down at the third base coach, and he's giving me the hit sign. I didn't believe it. With McGraw, the 3-0 pitch was an automatic take. He'd never given a hit sign before. I step out of the batter's box and look again. Again he flashes the hit sign. If the Pirates had been watching me, I'd have tipped them off for sure. But Adams grooves the next pitch, and I hit a home run. Won the game.

Afterward McGraw comes by my locker and says to me, "If my

brains hold out, we'll win it." Not a word about the homer I hit. [The Giants won the pennant, the first of four in a row.]

We never celebrated a big win or a pennant clinching on the field. Only in the clubhouse. All that stuff today is for television. They play to the cameras.

In the 1921 World Series against the Yankees, we knew Ruth was an overanxious hitter. He chased plenty of bad balls, curves in the dirt. He didn't like to be walked, liked to swing the bat.

McGraw used to change the signs every three innings. You had to look at the card posted in the dugout to see what they were. Nobody told you they were changed. You had to look for yourself. If you missed a sign, it cost you. After a loss, you sat in front of your locker until he was finished talking. There was no food, no beer in the dressing room like they have today.

In a double steal situation, he knew whether the shortstop or second baseman had the stronger arm. He would have the runner on first bluff to see who was going to cover second. If the man with the weaker arm was taking the throw, he'd send the runner in from third. If the guy with the stronger arm took the catcher's throw, he'd have the guy at third base bluff and not try to score.

McGraw called everybody "you big stiff." He'd say to Christy Mathewson, "You big stiff, let's see you get somebody out."

One day he said to me, "You big stiff, why don't you make a play at first base?" So I thought, "What can I do out there? Maybe if I get some dumb base runners, I'll get a chance to trap an infield fly and fool somebody." Sure enough, there were two on and one out and the batter hit an infield fly. Automatic out. I trapped it. The runners went. I threw to second for a double play.

I came into the dugout feeling pretty good. I don't see McGraw on the bench. "Where's the old man?" I asked. Somebody said, "He went out to Belmont when we took the field." He used to go out to the race track sometimes late in the game. It was the only time I made a play like that, and he didn't see it.

One day on the bench McGraw was arguing with a pitcher. We all knew the pitcher was right. The argument went on. Finally McGraw says, "Even if you are right, you're wrong with me."

McGraw wasn't an umpire baiter or showboat out there, but

when he had a beef coming, he let them know. But he never carried anything off the field. The next day it was all over and forgotten.

In those days the chief ump would pull a watch on you. After a few minutes of jawing, that was it. One day the ump—Bob Emslie I think it was—pulled a watch on the old man. McGraw was so mad he knocked the watch out of his hand and stomped on it. Springs were flying all over the place. Of course he was thrown out of the game. The next day, after handing over the lineup card at home plate, he pulled out a new gold watch and gave it to the ump.

I liked him, as a man and a manager. He was tops. He was all business, not much of a sense of humor. He relied on discipline and smart baseball. You were expected to be watching, thinking, learning, all the time.

The players who didn't like him were the same kind of people who don't like to follow the rules and regulations in society. He had his rules, and as long as you stuck to them, he'd back you up. I used to tell young players, "Don't ever lie to him because he knows everything you're doing." He used to have detectives follow some players who were drinkers and carousers. We had a curfew. The trainer came around checking the rooms at 11:30. If you were late coming in, he knew it. And if you lied about it, it cost you double.

They say he hated the nickname "Muggsy." It's true. Once, before one of the World Series games against the Yankees, I'm sitting on the bench with him during batting practice. I look up, and there's a young fellow peering down into the dugout.

"Muggsy?" he calls.

McGraw bellowed like a bull. "Who sent you down here?"

Turns out he was a newspaperman from Iowa or someplace. He wants to know who's the starting pitcher for the next day. McGraw never gave out that information to anybody.

He invites the fellow to sit down. "Those guys up in the press box put you up to this?" The writer nods. "They know I don't give out my pitchers," he says. "But I'll tell you what I'll do. I'll tell you who's going to pitch, and you can scoop them all in your paper. But don't tell them." And he did.

I was traded to Cincinnati in 1927. The fans got on me over there too, even though I drove in a hundred runs.

My last game as a player was with Oakland in the Pacific Coast League. A friend of mine was the manager, and I agreed to play in the outfield for him. We went into Seattle. They had a park there that was like playing in the street. I slid into third base and didn't think I'd ever get up. That was it.

[Kelly coached for Casey Stengel in Boston 1938–1943.]

When Stengel was managing in Toledo, his players weren't talking any baseball. They were all about looking at the stock market in the newspapers. One day he says to them, "I see you're interested in the stock market. I'll give you a tip. Buy railroad stock. A lot of you guys are going to be traveling."

Stengel would never give you a direct answer to a question. If an interviewer asked him one question, he'd get four answers. And if you had four questions to ask, you'd never get past the first one.

23.

Don Kessinger
OXFORD, MISSISSIPPI, AUGUST 1997

Don Kessinger was the shortstop on one of the Chicago Cubs' greatest—and most ignominious—teams, the 1969 club that led the Mets by nine games on August 15 and finished eight games back in second place. A six-time All-Star, he spent twelve of his sixteen years (1964–1979) with the Cubs, the rest with the Cardinals and White Sox, where he was the American League's last playing manager in 1979. He played in the College World Series for the University of Mississippi, where he later coached for six years before becoming associate athletic director. He seemed to be the most popular person in Ole Miss's hometown of Oxford when I visited him in his office; wherever I mentioned my reason for being in town, people responded with, "He's the nicest person; say hello to him for me."

I HAD SEVERAL OFFERS when I graduated in 1964 and chose the Cubs. Some other teams offered more money, but I felt they offered the best opportunity to get to the big leagues. I was right; I spent half the '64 season and the first two months in '65 at Ft. Worth and that's all in the minors.

Leo Durocher became the Cubs' manager in 1966. We all knew about his past, his reputation. He didn't believe in private meetings. If he had something to say, he said it to the radio, TV, newspapers. Open clubhouse meetings. That's the one negative thing I'd say about him. One day in spring training reporters came to me and said, "Leo says he has to find a shortstop. Kessinger can't hit, field, or throw."

Did he say that to challenge me? I don't think so. Leo just said what he thought. I'm just a young kid. Leo runs the show. If I say the wrong thing in response, I could be gone. I said, "Well, I'm glad he thinks I can run." There was a challenge there, but it didn't make me change what I did. I was very happy that it turned out he was wrong.

We had finished eighth in the ten-team league the year before.

Leo announced, "I guarantee you this is no eighth-place ball club." He was right; we finished tenth. Had an awful team. I give Leo credit. He had the courage to play a lot of us young guys, making lots of mistakes.

Leo was in charge. There was never any doubt that he was making all the decisions. I learned a lot of baseball from him. When he went out to the mound, he'd ask the catcher, "Has he lost it?" He'd expect the truth. You don't always get that from the pitcher. He was always an inning ahead, knew what he wanted to do next. Maybe he was harder on me because he had been a shortstop. If he was on you, he was trying to make you better. If he ignored you, you were in trouble. I don't believe his demeanor was always the way his reputation said it was. People think playing for him was so difficult—strict, on you all the time—and it was the opposite. He liked to put the same lineup down every day and let you play. He wasn't concerned with curfews or what you did off the field, wasn't a driver that pushed you during BP. None of that. He was a fierce competitor, hated to lose, and during a game he could get upset, get on you, but that's okay. When people think of him as being tough, hardnosed, it's a little bit misdirected. He was not hard to play for in that sense.

Our personalities were worlds apart. It took some time for Leo to understand that the game was really important to me. I played hard, gave it all I had, even though I didn't have the volatile temperament he had. What made him hard to play for was that he was very open and vocal with his criticisms, and that's somewhat difficult to handle. But that was the only aspect of Leo Durocher that I found tough.

The next year we went from tenth to third. We had more experience, traded for Ferguson Jenkins and Randy Hundley, brought up Joe Niekro. From then on we were always contenders, with Ernie Banks, Billy Williams, Glenn Beckert, Ron Santo.

Do I think we should have won some pennants during Leo's years in Chicago? Absolutely. We had the best talent in baseball, and we didn't win. I don't know why. If we had won in '69, we probably would have won the next two or three years. But there was a stigma attached to not winning that year. There are a lot of different reasons for that. Did we get tired? Maybe. Playing all day games in Wrigley I think contributed. It was a particularly hot summer in Chicago. I always lost about ten pounds playing with the Cubs, and at that time I couldn't afford it. I think it was a contributing factor. Later, when I went to the Cardinals, it was hot in St. Louis, but we played at night, and by September I hadn't lost any weight and still felt strong. The same thing when I came back to Chicago with the White Sox. I was older but still felt strong in September. No, we did not play well down the stretch [9-18 in September], but people forget that the Mets won at a phenomenal pace [38-11 from mid-August]. "Hot" is not the word for it. That may never happen again. Nobody is that great. If they had played normally, we'd have won.

My personal highlights: The 1969 All-Star Game, when four of us Cubs—Banks, Beckert, Santo, and I—were the NL infield. I think Ron Santo belongs in the Hall of Fame. I played alongside him for a number of years, and I didn't realize until the years he wasn't there how much ground he covered at third base. Suddenly I'm trying to throw guys out on balls I never had had to get to. If we'd played in two or three World Series, he'd be in today. I think one day he will. [Santo was elected in 2012.]

Another highlight was my 6 for 6 game in June 1971. I was tired. When I left home that morning, I told my wife, "I need a day off." Steve Carlton was pitching for the Cardinals, and I was like 0 for three years against him. She said, "Why don't you tell Leo?" I said, "Yeah, sure." My first four hits were off Steve. The sixth hit led off the tenth, and I scored the winning run. It was that kind of day.

For a shortstop the toughest play is a ball hit straight at you. No question about it. You have no angle on the ball. You can't tell how hard it's hit. Playing at Wrigley, for about four innings you were fighting that sun on popups. That was tough. As a shortstop, if you're really in the game, you're out there thinking like a manager: "What's the other team going to do?"

I'd been with the White Sox since 1977 when Bill Veeck asked me to manage the club in 1979. We were a fifth-place club in the seven-team division. I enjoyed it, but I did not feel that under the circumstances the White Sox were going to be a contender. Veeck didn't have the money for the free agent market, and that's where you had to be. I thought it was not going to get any better.

I'd learned some things about managing from Durocher and others. One thing was that if you have rules, you have to enforce them for everybody. So you don't want to have too many rules. One manager I had handed out three pages of rules.

I learned the three most important musts for a manager:

1. Know when to take a pitcher out.

2. Never ask a player to do something he can't do, no matter what you think the fans or the GM or the writers think you should do. If the situation calls for a bunt and you know the guy at the plate can't bunt, don't ask him. Let him swing away or put in somebody who can. If you ask him to bunt, you're doing it to protect yourself. You're not giving your team the best chance to win, just giving yourself an excuse for failure.

3. Try to keep the guys who are not playing every day sharp. You can't keep them happy. Play them enough to keep them sharp. If you're calling on a guy to pinch-hit in the eighth inning, bases loaded, score tied, he becomes the most important guy that's going to play in that game that day. And if he hasn't been to the plate in three weeks, you're asking an impossible thing of him. The toughest thing in baseball is to be a defensive replacement. You can only fail. If you make the play, you're expected to. If you miss it, you're the guy that fouled up. Managers have to realize those things.

We had a poor defensive club. My coaches kept telling me, "You need to play." I should have listened to them more. I didn't want the players to think I was playing myself because I was the manager. Another thing made it difficult for us. My weakest part of managing was handling pitchers. I had hired Fred Martin, an experienced coach in the Cubs organization, to be my pitching coach. We found out on opening day that Fred had cancer. He died in June. Veeck paid his salary for the rest of the year but had no money to replace him. So we deactivated one of our pitchers, Ron Schueler, and made him the pitching coach.

People think that when a manager resigns, it's because he was asked to, but that wasn't so with me. I'd been thinking about my future, and in August we are not going anywhere. I decided to not come back the next year. On an off day I told Bill Veeck, "I love you, but I'm not coming back next year. I'm telling you now so you can handle it however you want to." He said, "I want you to come back. You're not being fired. But if you've made up your mind, I will go ahead and bring in Tony LaRussa." LaRussa wanted to be a big league manager. He had been given a choice of coaching in the majors or managing in AAA, and I had advised him to go down and manage.

Today's athletes are bigger, stronger, faster, and better than we ever were. Ballplayers are better than we were. The guy who has the mental toughness will succeed. You can't teach instinct.

24.

Mark Koenig
GLEN ELLEN, CALIFORNIA, 1980S

Born in San Francisco two years before the 1906 earthquake, shortstop Mark Koenig was sixteen when he broke in at Moose Jaw in the Western Canadian League. Bought from St. Paul in 1925, he and Tony Lazzeri came up together to form the middle infield of the 1926–1928 New York Yankees pennant winners. Batting second, Mark often scored ahead of number three hitter Babe Ruth's home runs. In his twelve-year career (1925–1936), Koenig also played for the Tigers, Cubs, Reds, and Giants. He played in five World Series, including that of 1932, when he was the focal point of baseball's most enduring myth, Ruth's so-called "called shot."

I visited Koenig often at his home in a quiet, wooded setting in Glen Ellen, California. Suffering from gout, a jug of Gallo wine on the floor beside his rocking chair, he reminisced about those Yankee teams, carousing with Ruth, and the events leading up to the "called shot."

NOBODY COULD THROW A fastball by me. Two of my "cousins" on the mound were Lefty Grove and Dizzy Dean. They didn't have a good curve ball, so you knew what was coming. Umpires didn't throw out the ball every time it got a grass stain on it. We'd use the same one until it got about as brown as the infield. The spitball was still legal for some pitchers. Then there was the shine ball and the emery ball. The pitchers used all kind of tricks to rough up the ball. Red Faber threw me a spitball once, hit me in the thigh. The trainer used a rolling pin on my leg, rolling it like pie dough. I wound up in the hospital for a week with a bunch of broken blood vessels. That's the kind of trainers we had in those days.

Tony Lazzeri was an epileptic. I roomed with him on the road. He had these fits in the morning but never during a game. He'd come out of it and not even remember it. One day in Philadelphia Al Simmons was on first base and the batter hit a double play ball to me. I threw to Lazzeri at second, and he thought it was the third out and rolled the ball toward the mound. Simmons kept running, and I picked it up and chased him toward third, even though he was already out. The batter went to second. Cost us the game. Next day the papers made a big deal out of it 'cause Lazzeri was considered one of the smartest players.

The Yankees were a great bunch of fellows. There was no feuds, even with all those stars. Ruth was a happy-go-lucky guy. Everybody liked him. He was the big drawing card. During spring training we came north with the Dodgers, playing exhibitions in these small towns. The fans would come with their horse and buggies, and if Ruth hit a home run in the first inning, they'd all get up and go home. That's all they came to see.

On the train we'd play poker in the men's room. One time I bluffed Ruth out of a big pot with a pair of deuces. He got mad, yelling at me that I had no business even being in the game.

One year we stopped in Waco for a game. Dressed at the hotel and walked to the ballpark. Third baseman Gene Robertson and I and Lou Gehrig were sitting on top of the dugout before the game. There was a screen behind us to protect the fans. Robertson looked behind us at the fans and said, "They can really hurl epithets at you." And Gehrig looks and says, "They can't throw 'em through that screen."

We had some country boys on the team. In those days we got four dollars a day for eating money. Some guys would eat a few hot dogs for dinner and pocket the rest of the money. After a while they got so weak they couldn't stand up on the mound. So the front office cut that out and made them sign checks for meals at the hotel.

[Manager] Miller Huggins was a little guy, very quiet, very nervous. He'd sit on the bench late in a tight game, and you could hear him muttering to himself: "This guy has two hits already; we'll pitch to him; he can't get another hit; he won't get another one." He never bawled out a player in front of anybody else. There was one stretch where I was making a lot of errors, and the writers got on me. "The Yankees can't win with Koenig at short," they said.

Huggins called me into his office and said, "I'm managing this ball club. As long as I say you're gonna play, you're my shortstop. Never mind what anybody else says." He gave me confidence. He had the respect of all his players, even Ruth. Once he had a spat with the Babe, and Ruth and Bob Meusel threatened to throw him off the end of a pier. But when he fined Ruth $5,000, it stuck.

[**NM:** How did Huggins deal with the players' partying and drinking till all hours?]

He didn't. There was no curfew. They'd come trailing into the hotel at two or three in the morning after a night on the town. The elevator boy'd say, "Geez, I just took another bunch of you guys up." Huggins didn't care as long as you delivered on the field. If you didn't get the job done, then he'd say something to you.

I went out partying with Ruth plenty of times, but I don't think he knew my name. He called everybody "kid." My locker was next to his for years. But he always said, "Hey, kid" to me and everybody else. Nobody minded.

There were plenty of jokers on the team. We played an exhibition game in St. Paul one day. That night a few of the guys went to a house of assignation. They stole the madam's parrot, brought it to the train, and put it in Ruth's straw hat in the upper berth. By the time we got to New York, the hat was ruined. I shared an apartment with Benny Bengough. He and I bought a cage for the parrot and took it to our apartment. What language it talked! We put it out on the balcony. The things it said to the girls going by—oh boy! I couldn't repeat them.

We all used to go to Lou Gehrig's parents' home for dinner. His mother was a good cook, old-fashioned German cooking. So when we went on the road, we gave the parrot to Gehrig's parents to keep. They already had a parrot that his father used to put on his finger and talk to. He tried that with this parrot, and it almost bit his finger off. He finally gave it to one of our pitchers, Bob Shawkey, and Bob gave it away in Chicago. The madam in St. Paul had a reward out for it, but she never got it back.

[Wilcy Moore was a thirty-one-year-old rookie pitcher who won nineteen games starting and relieving in 1927.] Moore was a terrible hitter. Ruth bet him $500 he wouldn't get three hits all year. He had two hits near the end of the season. We were in Detroit, and he came up and topped a ball down the third base line. The fielders let it go to roll foul, but it stopped on the line. That was his third hit. Moore took the money and bought two mules for his farm. He named one Babe and the other Ruth.

[In 1932 Koenig was with the San Francisco Missions when the second-place Cubs bought him in August. In thirty-three games he batted .353. As a reward the Cubs voted him a half-share of the World Series money. **NM:** How did it feel to be sitting on the Cubs' bench, being the cause of all the riding they were taking from the Yankees?]

The way the Cubs treated me, I was glad the Yankees beat us. I just wasn't accepted by that bunch of players. I had no friends on the team.

Every player could buy sets of tickets for the Series. I bought six sets and gave them to friends. They were the worst seats in the park, way out, and all of them behind posts. Other players got forty or fifty sets, all the best locations.

After we clinched the pennant, I was sitting on the train behind Burleigh Grimes and Pat Malone, two veteran pitchers. They were discussing how to cut up the Series money. I heard them say I should get a full share, but in the meeting to vote the shares they never said a word. Charlie Grimm, the manager, wasn't there. Rogers Hornsby, their manager until August, they voted nothing. With the Yankees, Huggins always ran the meetings, fought for what was fair. So I got a half share. A little over $2,000.

[**NM:** Did Ruth call his shot?]

I don't think so. It'd be ridiculous for anybody with two strikes on him to do something like that, even Ruth. He made a gesture, like he was showing it was only strike two. Charlie Root, the pitcher, emphatically denied it all his life. He said, "If that guy had pointed to the bleachers like that, I'd have knocked him down with the next pitch. But he didn't." If anybody would have known, Root would be the one. I don't believe Ruth did it. But it makes a good story, and it's lasted fifty years now.

25.

Ted Lyons
VINTON, LOUISIANA, JULY 19, 1985

• •

Ted Lyons pitched twenty-one years (between 1923 and 1946) for the Chicago White Sox, won 260 games, and never came close to a World Series. Seventy-four percent of his starts were complete games. He pitched against Ty Cobb and Ted Williams and during the entire career of Jimmie Foxx. Elected to the Hall of Fame in 1955, he was one of the most popular players in baseball and had a lively sense of humor. Lyons managed the White Sox 1946–1948, then coached for five years at Detroit and one in Brooklyn. A bachelor, he lived most of his life in the house where we spent an afternoon. While we were there, a nephew looked in to see how he was doing.

• •

I WAS PITCHING SEMIPRO ball in Louisiana in 1919 when Connie Mack sent a scout to sign me. I told him I was going to Baylor in the fall. Mr. Mack sent another fellow to see me at Baylor who offered to pay part of my schooling and give me a bonus. I liked the Athletics, but I didn't sign. Ten years later Mack asked all our White Sox pitchers to come to Philadelphia and brief his pitchers on the Cubs, who they were going to play in the World Series. We played a city series against the Cubs every year. I walked in, and Mr. Mack said, "See, young fellow. If you'd signed with us, you'd be on a pennant winner." I told him, "Mr. Mack, I could be out in Podunk or somewhere. With all these pitchers you have, I would have had a hard time breaking in there." He said, "I would've found a place for you."

My last spring at Baylor, 1923, the White Sox were training in Seguin, Texas, about thirty miles away. Their catcher, Ray "Cracker" Schalk, came over with three newspapermen just for a story. They said, "Hey, Cracker, why don't you warm up one of the Baylor pitchers?"

My coach called me over. "Hey, Amar"—my middle name—"come over here." He introduced me to Schalk, and that was a big thrill for me. "I want you to throw some to Mr. Schalk." I put all I had on the pitches, popping his mitt. That evening he called his boss and said, "I just warmed up a kid at Baylor. You better sign him. He's going all the way."

The White Sox needed pitchers. They'd lost some good ones from the Black Sox scandal. I signed with them and joined them right after graduation. The first major league game I ever saw I pitched in—one inning. The last week of the season I relieved in the first game of a doubleheader at Cleveland. We scored four in the ninth and won. In the second game, the manager, Kid Gleason, said, "Hey kid, go down and warm up." He never did know my name. I pitched four or five innings and won that game too.

The White Sox and Giants toured Europe in 1924. I got to shake hands with the Duke of York. We played a game in Ireland at noon on a Sunday, and there were twenty-eight people in the stands. The rest were all in church.

You were expected to pitch the whole game in those days. And you fought being taken out. I was pitching against Lefty Grove and the Athletics one day. In the first inning Al Simmons hit a grand slam before I could get anybody out. The manager, Ray Schalk, came out to take me out. I said, "I ain't going."

He said, "You don't want to waste eight good innings of pitching."

"Make that nine innings, skipper. I haven't got anybody out yet. I'm not going. You'll have to get the police out here to get me out. I'm going to stay out here and beat Grove."

I got back up on the mound and wondered what I had committed myself to. Well, they got just two more hits off me; Fats Fothergill and Lew Fonseca hit home runs in the eighth and ninth innings, and we beat them, 6-4.

I don't know how fast Grove was; they never measured it. He was faster than I was, and my fastball was probably in the low 90s.

One day we got two men on base against him in the ninth inning, and Butch Henline was sent up to pinch-hit. Grove got two strikes on him, and Butch was a little afraid of a duster. But Grove just threw the next pitch right by him, and Henline gave it a half-hearted wave. He came back to the bench and I said, "Hey, Butch, that's the first time I ever saw that guy throw a change of pace with two strikes on a hitter."

Butch said, "Change of pace? It looked more like an aspirin tablet to me."

I brushed back hitters by throwing at their feet. Made them skip rope.

Jimmie Foxx was the only one it was bad to pitch to above the belt. Comiskey Park had a big outfield, so throwing the ball up and letting them hit it was usually okay. But not with Foxx. He had those big arms and wore short cut-off sleeves. One day I asked him, "How much air do you put in those arms?" He said, "Thirty-five pounds."

Pitching to Ruth, you had to throw some fastballs—but only where he couldn't reach them—and try to get him out with slow stuff. It didn't always work. When they built the second deck on Comiskey Park, the architect said nobody would ever hit a ball out of there. I told him to wait until the Yankees came to town. First time in, Ruth hit one over the roof.

Babe didn't know you unless you were in your position on the field. One year he picked me on his All-Star team for the newspapers. One day in Yankee Stadium he was in right field shagging flies. I walked out and shook hands with him and thanked him for picking me. He said, "That's okay, kid." Walking back to the bench, he said to somebody, "Who's that number sixteen, anyhow?"

Ted Williams was always learning, watching everything. He was too choosy. We were in the marines together during the war and I told him, "If you'd hit like DiMaggio, be more aggressive and hit those balls just a little off the plate, you'd hit .400 every year." But he wouldn't.

I was rooming with another pitcher, Sloppy Thurston, one year when Johnny Neun came up with Detroit. In a pregame meeting, we asked a couple pitchers who had faced Neun in the minors how they pitched to him. "Low and outside," they said.

Thurston said, "What did he hit?"

".384."

"We'll pitch him high and inside," Sloppy said.

I was a switch hitter. One day in St. Louis I hit two doubles in one inning, one left-handed and one right-handed.

I had one superstition: I would never step across the base line with my right foot, always the left.

In 1935 I was rooming with pitcher George Earnshaw, a night owl. One morning at seven the phone rang. I heard George say, "What for, Jim?" It was the manager, Jimmy Dykes, wanting to see him. When he came back to the room, he said, "I'm going to Brooklyn." The press got hold of him, asked him what he thought about going to the Dodgers. George said, "Just tell 'em I have but one arm to give to the National League."

I would have been happy if Jimmy Dykes had stayed the White Sox manager forever. We finished third five or six times and usually had a good club in the 1930s, but we always seemed to get hurt by key injuries. The press was always putting us down anyhow. The Cubs were the hot team in Chicago.

I played for nine managers, and he was the best. Everybody liked him, even after he cussed them out or fined them for something. Dykes used to smoke cigars between innings during a game. He'd smoke a short one if his pitcher had good control. If his pitcher was wild, he'd light up a long one 'cause it would be a long game.

One day Zeke Bonura was playing first base for us and stole home in the fifteenth inning to win the game. But he pulled a muscle doing it. He couldn't play the next day, so he climbed about thirty-five steps up to the radio booth to watch the game. Dykes went into the clubhouse after a cigar, and he heard a familiar voice on the radio saying, "There goes that train to New Orleans, and I wish I was on it."

Dykes wrote him a note and sent it up to the radio booth: "Listen, Bananas, if you don't get down here and play first base, you're going to be on that train." [White Sox fans had nicknamed Bonura "Banana-Nose."]

When Dykes was fired early in the '46 season, I didn't want the job. I wanted him to stay. He told me the situation got so he wasn't going to stay anyhow. The morning I replaced him he had breakfast with me and told me all he knew about the team. He said, "You've played with these guys, but there's a lot you don't know about them. I don't know whether to congratulate you or sympathize with you."

26.

Mike Marshall

Zephyrhills, Florida, March 2003

. . . .

Over fourteen years (1967–1981) with nine teams, right-handed pitcher Mike Marshall gained his most success with the Los Angeles Dodgers in 1974, winning a Cy Young Award and working in all five games of the World Series. He led in games finished four times and still holds four single-season relief pitching records: 106 games; 208 innings pitched; 13 consecutive games; 84 games finished.

Along the way Marshall alienated so many pitching coaches, managers, teammates, and club owners by his insistence on following his own training and pitching methods and his outspoken player union activities that he never spent more than three full seasons with any team. While playing, he was attending Michigan State University in the fall and winter quarters, earning a BS in 1965, MS in '67, and PhD in physiological psychology in 1978, becoming the only player ever to put a PhD after his name while still playing.

On a rainy Thursday morning, I drove twenty-five miles north from Lakeland on Route 301 to Zephyrhills and turned in at a whitewashed fence with "Pitcher Research and Training Center" painted on it. There, while seated at a picnic table under a cover watching five young men throwing from mounds, Marshall talked about the triumphs and travails of his career and his conclusions after "forty-eight years of thinking about how a baseball should be thrown."

. . . .

WHAT I TEACH HERE is how to increase velocity and avoid arm injuries by bringing the arm straight back toward second base and then throwing straight toward home plate. My goal is to get them to pitch to their ability, whatever that may be. We show them what they have to do to be the best pitcher they can be. That's all.

I was taught wrong myself. Pitching coaches are like the medicine men of the distant past. Some don't have a clue, and they don't have a clue that they don't have a clue, which is worse. The way traditional pitching coaches teach, the pitching motion is the same as they've done it for a hundred years. And it's contrary to all the laws of science. It stresses the inside of the elbow. The result: today I can touch my shoulder with my left hand and stretch the arm all the way out. With my pitching arm, I can't even touch my shoulder. That's because of the traditional pitching motion. I started studying kinesiology in 1964, and it took me till 1971 to put it all together.

My dad was a draftsman in Adrian, Michigan. A thin guy, fast runner, outstanding softball player. I got my speed from him. From my mom's side I got a tendency to put on weight. I have a brother and uncles who weigh 260, 280. I actually was signed out of high school in 1960 as a shortstop by Phillies scout Tony Lucadello. I'm 5-foot-8½, probably weighed 160 back then. I could run very fast, had a good arm, but didn't know how to catch a ball.

I was an all-star shortstop at Chattanooga in 1964, but I had injured my back in a car accident when I was eleven. That caused problems with two adjacent discs in my lower back and led to sciatic pain down my leg. I just couldn't take the bending anymore. I needed the money to finish my master's degree, so I decided I was going to be a pitcher from now on. The Phillies didn't like that. They still wanted me as a shortstop. But they said they'd give me a chance. They sent me to spring training with Chattanooga at Dade City, Florida. I pitched an inning here and there, but when they went on the road, they said I could go as the batboy. Then when we got there, they told me I was starting. Pitchers were going two or three innings at that stage of spring training. I went seven, wondering why they weren't taking me out. They were waiting for me to do poorly, and I didn't. Then I didn't pitch for two weeks. They sent me back to Chattanooga, and I pitched in relief. Then, just before cut-down day, they said I would start the next day. But that day they told me, "You're going to Eugene, Oregon, and you have two days to get there or be fined." I have a wife and two kids. We've rented a place already. So we packed up, drove straight through, got an apartment, settled the family, and I showed up at the ballpark and pitched that night. I played right field and shortstop and came in to pitch from those positions.

Then the Phillies sold me to Detroit. I went back to the Southern League. They wanted me to play shortstop. I said, "I'll play the first month at short, then I'll pitch." This is 1966; I relieved the rest of the year and was 11-7 at Montgomery. The next year I was in Detroit after a month in AAA.

I pitched my own game. The catcher, Bill Freehan, got the manager, Mayo Smith, to order me to throw what he told me to throw. But I didn't. I threw what I wanted to throw. The problem they had was that I was being successful.

After I had a 1.98 ERA [in 1967], I realized I couldn't get out left-handed batters and started working on a screwball. I went to spring training working on it, and Smith told me not to throw it. He said, "You're not even going to pitch to left-handed batters. You don't need it." I was a sinker-slider pitcher, and all he wanted me for was to go in in late innings and get out the right-handed batters.

I said, "That seems rather primitive. I want to be able to pitch to lefties as well."

He said, "Stop throwing it."

"Sorry, sir. Can't do that."

"You're going to the minor leagues." That was his answer. I can't say what I told him.

I used that screwball well against left-handed batters. In 1973 they began having the balls made in Haiti, where they pulled the seams very tight. Surface friction causes a ball to change direction in flight. With low seams, you can't make the ball move. I couldn't throw my screwball as effectively, so I made it into a changeup, and it worked.

[After a 15-9 year at Toledo, Marshall was taken by the Seattle Pilots in the expansion draft.]

Sal Maglie was the pitching coach; didn't like me, called me "that smart-assed college kid" because I wouldn't listen to him.

I didn't listen to anybody. I knew what they were telling me was wrong, contrary to everything I'd learned about physics. They said I was uncoachable, but I didn't care. It was my life, my career. I wouldn't do things in a way I knew was wrong just because they said I should. I listened to Isaac Newton. He never won a game, but he helped me set some pitching records.

But I didn't have everything figured out yet.

I had developed my own way of trying to pick a man off second base. Instead of spinning around 270 degrees, I'd lift my front leg and turn clockwise 90 degrees, facing second, and throw accurately. It was a lot quicker. Once I picked off two guys in one inning. Cut off a lot of potential go-ahead runs that way. The Seattle manager, Joe Schultz, had never seen it, and he didn't want me to do it that way. I did it anyhow. No other pitcher could do it with any velocity or accuracy.

When I was traded to Montreal in 1970, Gene Mauch is the manager. He's observationally smart, not science smart. He has some insight into human behavior, understands what motivates people, what makes a successful person. What I liked about Mauch was he understood that I cared a great deal about what I was doing to become the best pitcher I could be. I worked very hard at what I did, and he understood that and didn't bother me. He and the pitching coach left me alone. When they had meetings with the pitchers, I was not there. They told me to go away: "Go do whatever you want to do."

I sat out the wind sprints the other pitchers did. That made some people mad. I told Mauch it made my back hurt so I couldn't pitch. One year in spring training Mauch didn't think I was in shape. I arrived early one morning, and he's in the dugout. I said, "Hi," and ran to the outfield, ran for thirty minutes, came in, walked by him, said, "Hi, Gene," not breathing hard, and he never said another word about me not being in shape.

They didn't know I was running two and a half miles early every morning at home or on the road. I'd be up at 7:30 after a night game when there's nobody else stirring and I'd jog. One day I was a little bit later and they were up a little bit earlier, and they saw me. Blew my alibi.

I wanted to be a starter. I would make it through five-six-seven innings before I had trouble. Mauch told me, "I'm not sure I want to start you every five days if I can relieve with you three of those five days. Do you mind?"

I had figured out how to throw every day without any stiffness or soreness. I told Mauch, "That'd be fine." And that's how I became a relief pitcher. I give Gene Mauch every credit for the success I had in baseball.

When you can go out and close a game and don't get all nervous or upset about it and are able to do it day in and day out—managers like that. I was averaging two innings pitched a game, not one. It was not middle relief. I'd come in in tie games and pitch till it was over. That's how I got so many decisions [190 plus 188 saves]. In 1974 I'm pitching in 106 games, and other pitchers might want to ask a guy how he's doing that, but most of them didn't. Exceptions: Andy Messersmith asked me a lot of questions, then Tommy John and Don Sutton.

One day I noticed that Messersmith was unable to feed himself with his pitching arm. After the season I asked him to come to Michigan State, where I was going to graduate school. We did a study that showed us the destructive processes of the traditional pitching motion on our pitching arms.

I was the player rep with every team I was on. I was also a league player rep and lead negotiator. While Andy was there, I said to him, "This reserve clause the owners have put in our contracts is open to interpretation. It says that they can renew our contracts for one year. They think they can renew it every year for one year. I think it can be interpreted that they can renew it for only one year and that would be it. You'd be a free agent at the end of that. Tell you what we'll do. You and I will both not sign [1975] contracts. I'll be the lead dog. [Club president Peter] O'Malley will talk with me, and I'll just shine them on till the end of the season."

When I went to the Dodgers in '74 I had said to them, "I'm going to win the Cy Young Award, and I want to be compensated for that. I'll sign for what you want now"—something like $86,000, big money back then—"but next year I want to make a minimum of $130,000, and if I win the Cy Young, I expect a big bonus on top of that. And I'm always going to sign a contract with you that includes a minimum for the following year."

I won the Cy Young, got a $20,000 bonus for that, and they wrote the '75 contract for $150,000. So now, using the strategy Andy and I had planned, I'm holding out on a contract they already have that includes the terms I had earlier agreed to. They took it to the Players Association, who said, in effect, that I had signed a two-year contract. I wasn't thinking about doing that when I'd signed in '74. So I couldn't challenge it, couldn't "not sign" what I'd already agreed to.

That left Andy alone. He went through with it. Dave McNally did too, but he had already decided to retire. Andy was still a star [and became a free agent]. The only way I could deal with my back pain in Los Angeles was to get into the whirlpool every day. Then the assistant trainer, Jack Hommel, would adjust my lower back. I couldn't jog or run hard. After the '76 season I'm playing touch football at MSU. I had to make a quick defensive maneuver and hurt my lower back and had to have surgery. The disc had disintegrated into pieces that moved into the spinal track and was impinging the nerves. They took out all the pieces, and I've had no pain since. I do preventive exercises every day. The operation was in January 1977 and that hampered me, but by 1978 I felt great and could do anything I wanted without pain.

Los Angeles manager Walter Alston was a beautiful human being. I love Gene Mauch for what he did for me. He gave me a chance, let me do it my way, and I certainly respect that. But Alston was by far a better manager and person. He understood more about people and how to get the most out of them. There was nothing duplicitous about this man. He didn't overthink it. If he didn't understand something, he'd come and ask you. Wouldn't make something up about what your motives might have been.

My first day with the Dodgers, he came to me and said, "How do you want me to use you this year?"

I said, "I'll let you know if I'm not able to pitch on a certain day. Otherwise you can pitch me every day if you feel that I can help you win a ball game."

He said, "Sounds good to me." And then he did it.

I called my own pitches. One day Steve Yeager is the catcher. Gives me the fastball sign. I'm looking at him. Does it again, and I'm still looking at him. He calls time and comes out. "What's the matter, can't you see the sign?" "Yeah, I know exactly what you put down. I ain't throwing that. My question to you is, do you want to know what I'm going to throw? But if you don't want to know, I'll just go ahead and throw it."

The problem I had was with my defense behind me. The way

I pitched required a different defense than for whoever started. That was difficult. I told Walt Alston that I needed my kind of defense. I didn't want to look around and point at guys to move them. That's embarrassing to them, and it tells the hitters what I'm going to do with them.

Alston said, "Just tell my third base coach. He'll be on the bench. Tell him where you want the defense, and he'll move them there." So I'd look in at the coach and give him a signal what I wanted him to do. If I wanted an outfielder to move in close or go deeper or whatever, I'd give the coach an appropriate sign.

So one day I'm pitching, and I'm thinking I'd move my left fielder on the line and shallow. I throw a pitch, the batter reaches out and hits a little pop fly shallow near the left-field line. I turn and look and my left fielder is over in left-center field. The ball falls in for a triple. I came in after the inning and said, "Hey, Walt, remember us talking about defense and how I could get the guys to be where I wanted?"

"Yep."

"Just want to let you know: I signaled the coach to move my left fielder over on the line and shallow, where that ball was hit."

He immediately turns and asks the coach, "Why didn't you move him?"

The coach said, "That guy never hits it down the line."

I said, "He did, didn't he? I knew he was going to. I threw the pitch that would make him do that. You're not involved in the decision-making process. If I want him over there, you move him, or I'll turn around and do it myself."

The coach was Tommy Lasorda. After that he no longer set the defense.

[The Dodgers lost the 1974 World Series to Oakland in five games. Marshall worked in every game, giving up one run in nine innings.]

In the winter quarter prior to the 1974 season I was teaching a motor skills class on Saturday mornings at MSU. One of the students, Herb Washington, came to me and told me that Oakland Athletics owner Charlie Finley wanted to sign him as a base runner. What did I think? He was a nice guy, top sixty-yard sprinter, got up to speed quickly, not a baseball player.

I said, "Interesting idea. The only problem is, you're going to have to learn how to read pitchers and how to get a jump. I don't know if you can slide, but you can learn that. Learn how to get a jump because there are some pitchers that will false-cue you, make you think they're doing one thing and they're doing another. I know if I ever face you, I'll pick you off."

And then I did, in the World Series, ninth inning, Game 2. Doug Harvey was the first base umpire. I called him over to the mound and said, "I want you to watch me closely on this. I'm going to pick him off, but I need you not to call me a balk. I'm going to step off and fake him first. So watch me closely."

Harvey said, "You got it, but if you balk, I'll nail you for it."

"I know you will."

I stepped off and looked over there. I threw a pitch. Then I nailed him. I was in the regular set position. He thought that since I wasn't stepping off and I'd already thrown home, it looked like I was going to throw home again. He took a lean toward second base, and that was all that was necessary. My greatest concern was that he would go on my first move and I would have to throw to first base, and if he's moving, Steve Garvey couldn't hit the broad side of a barn with a throw to second, and I don't want him throwing it away and Washington going to third. I had to do it in such a way that he'd try to get back to first. And he did.

I thought the designated runner was a good idea; he stole bases and scored runs that year. If I were coaching him, I'd have told him, "Even if you can't read pitchers' cues, once you start, go like hell. If you're wrong, it'll take two throws to get you at second base."

Joe Rudi was easily the best hitter Oakland had. Not the most powerful, but the best hitter. Right-handed batter. If you pitched him away, he'd hit to right field. He had done this on me earlier in the Series. I tried going away from him, and he just reached out and hit a line drive to right. So in Game 5 he's leading off [the seventh inning, tied 2–2], and I'm thinking, "I've got to get him off the out-side pitch." I'm on the mound ready to pitch, and my left fielder, Bill Buckner, has a little problem with the fans out there throwing something at him. Time's called, and I'm standing there waiting. I don't want to throw any more than I have to, 'cause Alston has told me I'm going to start Game 6 after a day off, and I'm already in my second inning in this game. So I'm waiting, not throwing, and finally things are resolved and Rudi's at the plate. I throw a fastball in under his hands, a little off the plate inside. He opens up—bam, hits it out of the park as if he knew the pitch was coming. He says he was talking with the hitter on deck, Claudell Washington, and they decided the only reason I didn't continue to warm up was because I was going to throw a fastball inside and I didn't have to throw that to warm up, whatever that means. You have to give Rudi and Washington credit. Their reasoning was wrong, but they reached the right conclusion. [Marshall paused to call out encouragement and some direction to one of his students.]

The only way to get fit to throw a baseball is to throw a baseball. That's if you do it correctly. Most pitchers release the ball right beside their ear. My guys release the ball twelve to eighteen inches in front of their head. The ball gets to the plate faster because it doesn't have to go as far. I worked with a kid the Dodgers had released. He threw 88 out of the set position, 94 out of the windup. I showed him how to throw 94 out of the set position and told him, "But I think you can do more." Later he called me from spring training and said, "I hit 103 on the gun today." That was fun.

I had had back surgery when Texas traded for me and asked me to be a starter. One day I went to field a bunt, and I couldn't bend over. I spread my legs to get down, and as I turned to throw, I popped something in my right knee; had to have an operation. That ended my starting days. At the end of the '77 season I was a free agent.

One of the doctorate rules is that you have to be on campus the full year of your final year to earn the PhD. So I stayed at MSU and worked out on my own and in May 1978 received my degree. Some teams showed interest in me. Gene Mauch was at Minnesota now. I got a call from Mauch: "Really could use you." I didn't want to go there. They weren't going anywhere and didn't pay anything. I was getting offers of $250,000–300,000 and I knew Twins owner Cal Griffith pays chicken feed.

Gene said, "Cal will start you at $40,000. If you have a good year, he'll pay you $100,000." I groaned. Then he said, "And he wants you to pitch against our batters in a simulated game." I hadn't had any spring training, but I said okay. I met them in Chicago. I'm on the mound, no defense behind me. No ump. Gene is calling hits and outs. Three times through the lineup. Maybe two hits. Better than ever. But Griffith says no, he can't afford me. I get on a train back to East Lansing. I was going to try out with Pittsburgh. The Pirates are talking $350,000.

Gene calls again. "Rod Carew is complaining that we need you."

I couldn't say no to him. I wound up second in the Cy Young voting. Griffith tried not to pay me the $100,000; said I didn't have a good season.

Now I'm a free agent again. The Mets want me bad. I'd be the top-paid reliever in baseball, four- or five-year contract. Griffith offers me a three-year guaranteed $850,000, with him holding a fourth-year option for $500,000. I know I'll never get that out of him. The Mets offered almost three times as much. I go to Minnesota anyhow and set an AL record with 90 appearances.

From the start of spring training in 1980 Mauch didn't let me work. I knew something was wrong. I asked him. He said, "It's this player rep stuff." Player reps were being traded by anti-union owners. "You gotta stop doing that stuff."

We had a potential mini-strike set for May. We went on strike the last week of spring training, started the season, then were going to go out on Memorial Day. Somebody told the owners it was my idea.

Here's where I had one of my differences with Marvin Miller [head of the Players Association]. We went into negotiation the night of the deadline, May 22. I told Miller I would agree to be the player rep on the negotiating team if he got super seniority for player reps, which means nobody can release you, send you down, or put you on the DL during your term as player rep, which starts in the spring of even years and lasts until the fall of odd years. "That's the only reason I'll help you with this."

He says, "We'll get that, no problem."

The night they settled, he didn't call me. Three a.m. Don Fehr, his assistant, calls me. "It's all done."

"Great. What about super seniority for player reps?"

"Well, we didn't get that."

I was furious. "I'm gone tomorrow."

The Twins released me the next day. They had to pay me through 1981, but I was out of baseball.

I came back in '81 after the strike and finished the season with the Mets, whose manager, Joe Torre, had been a player rep with me. I had a 2.61 ERA in twenty games, but they said I didn't have a good year and released me. I could have pitched another three or four years at that level.

And that's one of the reasons no major league team is asking me to teach their pitchers how to pitch.

I'm still persona non grata in major league baseball, but there's starting to be some nibbles. Some pitching coaches have borrowed a little bit of what I teach. One recently stole my technique; by "stole" I mean it's something I put in my book and copyrighted and somebody writes it like it's theirs. On the other hand, I'm glad he's doing it because he's disavowing how he's been teaching for the past twenty-two years. The point is, I wish he'd steal it all and not just parts. My book can be read on my website, drmikemarshall.com.

I never left baseball. I came down to Florida in 1982. They play baseball here from February 1 to mid-November, and I started at least two games a week for over forty weeks every year from 1982 until I was fifty-six for various teams in over-thirty and over-forty leagues, and we were unbeaten over-fifty champions for five years in Ft. Myers. I was undefeated for over ten years, over eighty games a year. In a tournament I'd pitch four games in two days. I just love to pitch. I'd still be doing it, but I had a household accident, tore up my shoulder. Had an operation, and that terminated my pitching career

I wish I knew thirty years ago when I was pitching what I know now. I did what I did in spite of that. But I was far less than the pitcher I could have been. I'm confident that every pitcher today, no matter how successful he's been, could do better, if they did it my way—applying the laws of physics. All the arm injuries have to do with throwing the ball wrong, not the number of pitches or innings.

Don't get me started on youth sports, or we'll be here another four hours.

27.

Barney McCosky

VENICE, FLORIDA, DECEMBER 1991

. . . .

This left-handed batter's level swing produced over-.300 batting averages in six of his first seven years and a career .312 over eleven seasons (1939–1953) with the Detroit Tigers, Philadelphia Athletics, and Cleveland Indians. He served three years in the navy and missed one year following a crippling back injury in 1948 that limited his playing time and effectiveness for the rest of his career. Sitting on the patio of his canal-front home, we were accompanied by his close friend and 1940 Tigers teammate, catcher Billy Sullivan Jr.

. . . .

I WAS BORN IN Coal Run, Pennsylvania, five miles from Punxsutawney, in 1917. There were nine kids in the family, and I was the baby. My name was William, but I went by my middle name, Barney, all my life. My mother died when I was one, and an older brother and sister raised me. My father was a coal miner. I remember running down to meet him coming out of the hole in the ground with his lunch bucket, just like in the movies. When I was four, my brother moved to Detroit and brought the family there.

My brothers played sandlot ball, and they were all right-handed batters. When I was about eight, they turned me around to bat left-handed, and I did from then on. It doesn't matter if you do everything else right-handed; you can still bat left-handed, and it's a step and a half closer to first base.

> **Sullivan:** And with a man on first, you've got this beautiful big hole to pull the ball through.

I'm sighting the ball with my right eye. I play golf right-handed, but I putt left-handed, sighting the hole with my right eye. There's nothing natural about either way. You can turn anybody into a switch hitter, but in those days they didn't think much of switch-hitters.

When I was twelve or thirteen, we had no money to go to the Tigers' games, so we'd wait until somebody was going in, and

158

when nobody else was looking, we'd double up with a customer and go through the gate, then run off and go find a seat. My favorite player was Charlie Gehringer. I'd go home and try to copy his batting stance and swing. Hung a rope in the barn with a big tire on it and a ball marked on it, and I would swing at that mark trying to get that Gehringer swing down. I could raise and lower the tire to practice swinging at different locations in the strike zone. Later, when I was with the Tigers, a newspaper ran pictures of me and Gehringer, holding bats, with no identification, titled "Which Is Which?" You turned the page, and they showed our numbers—he was 2 and I was 21—and our bats were held exactly the same.

In my junior year of high school I hit .457. In my senior year I hit .727 in fifteen games. I was an outfielder, very fast runner. When I graduated, I had a lot of scholarship offers from big colleges in the Midwest, but I wanted to play ball. My dad knew nothing about baseball. He would say, "Go get a job. Do some work." He didn't come around to accepting it until I had been in the big leagues a few years. Until then it was just having fun to him, not a real job.

Wish Egan, the Detroit head scout, came out to the house. I said, "I'd like to play ball, but I still want to go to college. If I don't make good my first year, then the Detroit club will pay for my college the next four years." He agreed. I went to Charleston, West Virginia, Class C, and hit .400. So I never collected my "college" bonus. This is 1936.

I actually started out in Beaumont in the Texas League and was hitting good, but I made a few mistakes in the outfield. What kind of mistakes? I was playing right field, man on third, one out, batter sliced a foul ball to right. I dove for it and caught it. Guy on third scored the winning run. I went to the bench and on to Charleston.

The pay was $150 a month. We stayed in a boarding house for $7 a week. The longest bus ride took all night and all the next day. Lots of mountains. Night games were like playing by candlelight.

I was at Beaumont the next two years, then went to spring training in Lakeland in 1939. Just before heading north, the manager, Del Baker, told me I was going with them and would play center field. I didn't have a great arm, but I got the ball away quick to the cutoff man. On the train Charlie Gehringer said to me, "I understand you're going to be in the lineup. It's just another ball game. Just keep doing what you've been doing."

Sullivan: I was with the Browns that year in spring training in San Antonio. The Yankees came in for an exhibition game. They dressed at the hotel. After the game I went up to Bill Dickey's room, and he was rooming with Lou Gehrig. Just kidding, I said to Lou, "When are you gonna give up?" It was a completely innocent question. I thought he'd go another ten years without missing a game. Dickey said, "We don't know. Something terrible is happening to him. We hit ground balls to him three-four feet to either side, and he can't reach them." I was flabbergasted.

About two weeks into the season the Yankees came to Detroit. The first day Gehrig took himself out of the lineup [after 2,130 consecutive games]. Before the game a photographer asked him to pose with me. I was uncomfortable. I didn't think they should bother him. But he agreed. He put his arm around my shoulders. It felt like he was leaning on me for support.

I was making $500 a month. In June they raised me to $6,000 for the year; the average salary at that time was about $8,500.

The Tigers were a veteran team, had been together ten or twelve years, been in two World Series. At home I was okay; I stayed with my family. But on the road I was lost. They went together. I was alone. My roommate was Dizzy Trout. He went his own way. Finally it was Gehringer who invited me to go along with them.

We had coaches who could read pitchers and call what they were going to throw. I didn't want to know, didn't want to get fouled up. If you know what's coming, you tend to overswing. In 1940 I was going for my two hundredth hit, and the catcher told me, "You're going to get nothing but fastballs." I popped up, grounded out; just that little bit of difference got my timing off, striding too far or too soon. I was a better hitter with two strikes than none. I would move up in the box for a knuckleball or sinker pitcher.

I hit first or second most of the time. Didn't have much power, but that didn't matter. We had other home run hitters. I was fast, tied for the lead in triples the first year, led the second. We stole bases when we needed it, not when we were two or more runs behind or way ahead. You always steal off the pitcher, not the catcher. The best pitcher I ever saw at holding men on was when I was with the Athletics. The Yankees brought up a left-hander from Newark named Bill Wight. Our first base coach was Earle Mack. I'm about six inches off the bag, and Earle says to me, "They say this guy has a hell of a move to first base. Be careful." I looked at Earle and said, "Too late. He's tagging me out."

Hank Greenberg was a fair first baseman who came out early for extra practice and made himself a good fielder and hitter. In 1940 they tried Rudy York in left field, but he couldn't do the job. So Hank says, "I'll try it." He asked me to come out in the mornings and throw balls against the fence and holler out where to throw them, and we did that for a while. One day he called me to meet him downtown, and he took me up to his tailor and had a suit made for me for helping him.

28.

Gil McDougald

WALL TOWNSHIP, NEW JERSEY, SUMMER 1995

Infielder Gil McDougald played in eight World Series in his 1951–1960 career with the Yankees. Equally adept at second or third, he appeared in three All-Star Games as a shortstop but never played a full season at one position. At his home he talked about what it was like to play for Casey Stengel.

FROM THE START CASEY Stengel was on me constantly, every time we had a team meeting. Nobody on the club could understand it. They told me I got so mad at him there was smoke coming out of my head.

After the 1955 World Series, the team went to Japan. Casey declared the hotel bar off limits. It was a hot night, and I felt like having a beer. I went down, looked around, and didn't see anybody in the bar, so I went in and ordered a beer. Then I looked in the corner, and there was Casey surrounded by Japanese sportswriters. I said to myself, "Well, no use running now. Besides, it's not during the season, so he can't fine me much."

A few minutes later Stengel came over and sat down beside me. I said to him, "Case, I gotta ask you a question. You must hate my guts. For five years there isn't one thing I've ever done that's made you happy. Why don't you just get rid of me and save yourself a lot of aggravation and me a certain ulcer, and we'll both be a lot happier."

He said, "I'm not trading you ever."

"But, Case, why are you always getting on my butt?"

"Very simple. You're a better ballplayer when you're mad. I plan on keeping you mad. What do you think would happen if I got on Phil Rizzuto that way?"

Then I understood. Phil's locker was next to mine. Case was using me to shake up Phil and the others. He knew I would play all the harder. That's what made Case a great manager. He knew his players, who to prod, who to get on, and who to leave alone.

He knew to treat Mickey Mantle with kid gloves because if he said something to Mick, he'd go brood or something.

I always wanted to get out in front of the ball and pull it. The problem was that with a man on first, if I hit a shot to left, he had to stop at second. Casey wanted me to hit to right to move the guy to third so we didn't have to use a bunt to advance the runner. I wouldn't change. He got mad at me, and I got mad at him.

Everybody wrote about how I held the bat [below the belt, pointing at the catcher], but the funny thing is, if they looked at a film, they would see that when the ball was on its way, my hands went up, and when the pitch was coming over the plate, my hands were just like any other hitter's. But once the ball is being thrown to you, everybody watches the ball, not the hitter, so the writers didn't see that.

The year I enjoyed the most was 1957, when I played 120 games at short. Rizzuto had retired, and there was nobody in the farm system that Casey had confidence in, so he asked me if I would try it. I said, "Why not? No big deal." The experts said I was too tall and gangly and I didn't have the good arm, but that just made it a bigger challenge. It was more interesting to me than the other positions. It's easier to see the pitch and position yourself to move either way.

Looking back, it's always better to have memories of winning than losing, and yet the year that stands out for me is 1954, when we lost to Cleveland, even though we played great and won 103 games, more than any other year I was up there. But the Indians won a league-record 111 that year. It teaches you a little humility to lose, knocks a little ego out of you, and makes you try harder the next time.

[McDougald was playing shortstop the day Don Larsen pitched a perfect game in the 1956 World Series against the Dodgers.]

On one play Jackie Robinson hit one that ricocheted off the third baseman's glove; I went into the hole and got it and threw him out, a real bang-bang play. When Dale Mitchell came up in the ninth with two out, I was thinking, "He seldom strikes out. Somebody is going to have to catch the ball and throw him out, and shortstop is where he always hits it." With two strikes on him, he took a borderline high pitch. I was surprised that Babe Pinelli, a National League low-ball umpire, called it a strike.

[On May 7, 1957, McDougald was batting against Cleveland southpaw Herb Score, who had won thirty-six games in his first two years. His line drive struck Score near the right eye, shattering his cheekbone and his career.]

I'll never forget the pitch he threw to me that night. Most of the time he was up around the letters, but he threw one low. I don't know how I hit it or what I did then. I don't remember running to first base because as soon as it hit him, I saw blood fly. I really didn't feel like playing any more. It took a few hitches out of me as a ballplayer, even though I know you can't control where the ball is going to go after you hit it, and everybody, including Herb's mother, tried to tell me it was not my fault.

At the end of the 1959 season I told Casey I was going to play only one more year. When the 1960 season ended, I told him goodbye. But they didn't believe me. Nineteen sixty-one was an expansion year with new teams in California and Washington. The Yankees told me I was protected from the expansion draft, but I wasn't. Washington claimed me. They still didn't believe I was really quitting. They were mad at me because they would have gotten a few hundred thousand dollars for me if somebody drafted me, and I was mad at them for lying to me.

It really bothers me to see the guys who get in the Hall of Fame and the ones who get no consideration. When we went into pro ball, they told us if you can't do three things—hit, run, and throw—forget it. Now they put guys in who are hitters and that's all.

It's a crime Allie Reynolds is not there. He was the right-handed Koufax, relieved as well as started in the toughest situations. Players of our time would rate him number one or two among pitchers. If I had one game to win with a big crowd on hand, I'd choose him.

Roger Maris is an example of sportswriters' thinking, where prejudice comes in because of personality. I couldn't believe the beautiful stroke he had, hitting line drives to all fields. MVP twice, over guys like Mantle and Berra. Played the outfield, ran, hit. He belongs.

29.

Sam Mele

. . . .

Sabath "Sam" Mele was the nephew of fifteen-year major leaguer Tony
Cuccinello and one-year major leaguer Al Cuccinello. An outfielder, Mele
broke in with the Red Sox in 1947 and played for five other teams in a ten-
year career before managing the Minnesota Twins 1961–1967. We met
one afternoon in the deserted press/scouts dining room at Oriole Park.

. . . .

I GOT A GOOD education in baseball from my mother's brothers,
Al and Tony Cuccinello, growing up in Astoria, New York. Tony
used to bring his good buddy Al Lopez to the house, and just listening in, you had to pick up something.

One day I was playing Queens Alliance ball; I was hitting good
and thought I was a big shot. Then, in a doubleheader, I was 0 for
13. I came home and threw my uniform on the kitchen floor and
said, "I quit." My mother chewed me out; then she called Uncle
Tony, and he chewed me out, told me he went 0 for 32 one time
and still played. Then she called Uncle Al, and he chewed me out.
"No way are you going to quit this game."

Uncle Tony was my agent. He knew this Red Sox scout, Neal
Mahoney. They took me to the Hotel Commodore in New York
to see Tom Yawkey. I was about to go into the service, so they
offered me $5,000, half then and the rest when I got out. Tony
was with the Boston Braves then, so I worked out with them. But
they couldn't match the Sox offer, so I signed.

I was in the marines, stationed at Pearl Harbor, and played
against major leaguers in pickup games, which helped me in the
long run.

I got out in '46 and started at Louisville but wound up in Scranton, where I led the league and we won the pennant by eighteen
games. In '47 I was with the Red Sox, playing right field alongside
Dom DiMaggio. He had to cover a lot of ground between me and
Ted Williams. I learned a lot talking baseball on the train rides. I'd

sit and talk hitting with Ted Williams, and when you got up from him, you thought you could be the greatest hitter in the world. Then he'd say, "If you want to know anything about fielding, go over to Dom DiMaggio."

I learned a lot from Dom, not just about fielding. My first road trip we were at the Ben Franklin Hotel in Philadelphia; I'm sitting in a corner, not knowing what to do, and I see all the players at the front desk getting the keys to their rooms. Then DiMaggio came by and said to me, "Okay, rookie, get the bags." I didn't know what he meant. Then I found out I was rooming with him, and in those days the rookies carried the bags. I learned he kept a book on every pitcher in the league—what he threw, when he threw it, and on the catchers too. He was a tremendous player and friend.

In those days we worked on fundamentals in a way you don't see much anymore. We practiced hitting the cutoff man, throwing to bases. They sent me out to right field and hit balls off the fence at Fenway. When Williams was hurt and I had to fill in in left field, they hit balls off the green monster so I could learn to play the caroms. At Yankee Stadium they would roll balls along the fence so I would learn how to play the bounces. You worked at it so you wouldn't look bad out there and maybe get sat down for a few games because you made a silly mistake.

Later, when I managed in Minnesota, I had Billy Martin and Jim Lemon as coaches, and they were excellent guys. If they had a guy practice something 99 times and the guy complained, they'd tell him, "You're going to do it 100 times or 150 until you get it right." They helped me win because they worked to cut down the mistakes in execution.

After hitting .302 in '47, I played only sixty-six games in '48. I don't know why. Joe McCarthy was the manager. He traded me to Washington. Clark Griffith wasn't as cheap a club owner as they say; he paid what he could afford and had no other business behind him. The concessions income paid the players' salaries.

On to Chicago, where I played with Nellie Fox. He was not a .300 hitter until Paul Richards got hold of him and taught him how to bunt toward third base with a backspin so the ball dropped dead before it got to the third baseman. Absolutely Hall of Fame caliber.

Minnie Minoso was one of the best all-around players I ever played with. He did everything a ballplayer could be asked to do: throw guys out, take extra bases, break up double plays, play outfield or third base, get hit by a pitch to get on base.

After my playing days were over, I scouted for Calvin Griffith at Washington until he called me to become a coach. I moved with them to Minnesota in 1961. Cookie Lavagetto was the manager. He had an operation and missed seven games, and I managed the team until he came back. Ten days later I get a call from Griffith to come to his office and wear a shirt and tie. I had no idea what was going on.

He said, "Have you ever thought about managing?"

"I guess every player thinks about it."

"Analyze the players because I may make a change in a couple weeks."

All of a sudden he gets on the phone trying to locate Lavagetto to tell him he's fired that day. He finally finds him and then he opens the door, and in comes the New York press. The Yankees were in town, and he must have told them he was going to make a change. Later, when I went into the clubhouse, the first thing Lavagetto said to the press was, "Treat this kid okay."

I played for a lot of managers and picked up something from all of them, but Al Lopez's voice came back to me most of all. Whenever we played his team, I could talk to him after the game. From him I learned how to handle players. If a guy needed a boot, you booted him. If he needed a pat on the back, you gave it to him.

I was pitching Jim Kaat against Lopez's club one day and we had a 5–0 lead; suddenly they start hitting little nubbers around the infield, and before I know it, the score is tied, and I still have Kaat in the game. Afterward I said to Lopez, "What would you have done?"

He said, "Once in a while you get a game like that, and you got to get him out because the next guy you bring in may not be as good, but sometimes line drives may lead to a double play or an out. Some pitchers can be big winners because when they pitch, the line drives seem to be hit right at somebody, where a pitcher with more stuff gets beat by a lot of bleeders."

I only second-guessed myself once in my life, when I pitched Camilo Pascual in Game 3 of the 1965 World Series. We were up 2–0 over the Dodgers, and I had Jim Merritt, a good left-hander who could make the Dodgers' switch hitters bat right-handed and had a very good move to first base. The Dodgers had led both leagues with 172 stolen bases. I knew Pascual had a big high kick, and if they got on base, they would steal on him pretty easily. But Pascual had been my friend and done a lot of good pitching for me, and I felt I owed it to him to let him pitch in a World Series. With my heart I went with Pascual. As it turned out, Claude Osteen blanked us, 4–0. There were three stolen bases. I second-guessed myself, but I don't regret it. Pascual had done so much for me and for the Washington-Minnesota team.

After beating Don Drysdale and Sandy Koufax in the first two games, we could do nothing with them in Game 4, which Drysdale won, and Games 5 and 7, in which Koufax shut us out twice. Walt Alston wasn't sure who he was going to use in Game 7. Koufax had two days' rest and Drysdale three. Alston took those two guys out of a team meeting and told the others to decide who they wanted to pitch. They chose Koufax. He didn't have his best stuff that day, couldn't get his curve over, and Drysdale was up and down in the bullpen the first three or four innings. Then Koufax went just to his fastball and change-up, struck out ten, gave up three hits, and beat us, 2–0.

I was fired in June 1967. I don't know why; there was no particular incident. We were two games below .500 at the time. In 1965 we had gained 24 wins over 1964. We went from seventh to first. We did not have the fastest players, but we decided to run more. Billy Martin had them running from the start of spring training. Make the other team make mistakes. Our stolen base totals doubled. We won at least two games with guys on third feinting to steal home and drawing pitchers into throwing wild pitches. We had a lot of running situations. After winning in '65, there was no letdown. We worked harder the next spring. We had the same personnel, but we didn't get as many running situations. In '65 all year if we hit a pop fly foul, it landed a couple rows up in the stands. If they hit one, it stayed just in the field. The following year those breaks just didn't fall our way.

I had other managing offers, but in a way I was a little bit happy when I was fired. I had a tough time maintaining an even keel emotionally through a season because I was not a hard-shelled guy. I would think about things—like if a writer wrote something I didn't like—and carry them over too long a time, where other guys could put it behind them quicker. It bothered me when I lost, and when things were written about me that weren't true—or maybe were true. The writers who have to sound like experts and knock a guy wonder why the players don't want to talk to them. I couldn't tell writers what I thought of them; they had the last say anyhow. Now I wouldn't have to put up with that any more.

I had kept in touch with Mr. Yawkey, and he had a job for me any time. I went to work for him as a scout immediately after I was fired. I've been with them ever since.

As a scout, my best signing was Jim Rice. Mace Brown took me to watch Rice play a game in Anderson, South Carolina, where Rice was from. A lot of scouts were there, and Rice did not show up for the first few innings. The other scouts figured he didn't want to play bad enough to show up, so they left. One scout was with a club that drafted before the Red Sox. Brown and I stayed, and Rice showed up and played. After the game we asked Rice why he was late. He said he worked at a supermarket; his replacement did not show up on time, and he stayed until the guy showed up. Because Rice hadn't shown up on time, the team that drafted ahead of us did not take him. Another time a scout was back of the batting cage watching Rice hit, saw him miss on some curves, decided he couldn't hit a curve, and the scout left, but Mace Brown and I had seen him hit a fastball and figured he could learn to hit a curve. Houston also drafted before us, and their scout had orders to take Rice. But at the last minute Houston decided to take a pitcher instead, and that left Rice for us.

At Fenway both Rice and Wade Boggs went out early every day to practice, Rice in left field taking balls off the wall, Boggs taking at least fifty balls at third base before regular practice. I don't see much of that any more. I don't see guys working on their weaknesses, asking for curves or sliders in BP. They want the fastballs so they can hit them five hundred feet.

I was with the Orioles when they returned to the major leagues in 1954. It was very exciting, but I was here only half the year before being traded to Boston. Now I follow ten teams and try to see them eight or more times a year—at Fenway, Cleveland, and here in Baltimore. I like to come to Baltimore; the ballpark is good and the people are so nice.

30.

Wilmer "Vinegar Bend" Mizell
PITTSBURGH, JUNE 1990 PIRATES' REUNION

. . . .

Born in 1930 and raised in Leakesville, Mississippi, on a small farm adjacent to the Alabama border, Wilmer Mizell was a 6-foot-3½, 205-pound
left-handed pitcher with the Cardinals, Pirates, and Mets (1952–1962). The
tiny town had no post office; the family's mailing address was Route 1, Vin-
egar Bend, Alabama. Thus when he arrived as a rookie at Albany in the
Class D Georgia-Florida League, the club gave out his home town as Vin-
egar Bend, even though he never lived there. From then on the press seldom mentioned him without throwing in that nickname at least once. His
friends and family called him Wilmer, his teammates, "Mizell."

Elected to Congress from Winston-Salem, North Carolina, in 1968, he
served three terms, then held positions in the administrations of Presidents Ford, Reagan, and George H. W Bush. We talked in an empty meeting room at a hotel in Pittsburgh.

. . . .

MY DAD PASSED AWAY when I was almost two, and my mother
had very serious health problems after that, so my grandmother
Turner on my mother's side raised me in the log house my grandfather built when they were married. Had four big rooms and three
fireplaces. She cooked on a wood stove. Still lives there. We ran
cattle on open range, grew corn and vegetables for our own use.
No cash but we ate well. We lived in the southern timber belt. In
those days, to make a little money we worked in sawmills, sawed
and hauled logs, while we worked the farm.

I had a bunch of uncles and cousins, and we had great times. My
uncles had played some ball, and they encouraged us. We made
our own baseballs, sometimes using a rock for the center. When
my grandma went to the grocery store, they'd wrap the packages
with twine. We'd save that twine and wrap it around the center and
she'd sew some kind of cover on it. When we could get it, we'd use
this black tape and wrap the cover with that, and we were uptown.

We had one old Louisville Slugger that somebody had got hold of somewhere. It had got broke and we redid it.

I recall the older people talking about the St. Louis Gashouse Gang and of course Babe Ruth. But us boys didn't follow any major league teams. We didn't get a newspaper out in the country in those days.

Leakesville High School had no baseball team. Football and basketball, but not baseball. There was a county team for a while when I was a little boy, but Leakesville didn't have one. So the summer I was sixteen we decided we'd organize a little team out in the country. We had enough family members to put together the team. I recall that fall we played two games against another local team. The first one we got beat, 17–2. I had started in center field and had an uncle that started pitching. And before the game was over, I came in and started pitching. We played one other game that fall and got beat, 12–2.

The next year we were pretty well organized as a team. I was the pitcher, and my brother was the catcher. I had a first cousin at first base, first cousin at second base, first cousin at shortstop, and an uncle playing third. Three cousins in the outfield. Three Mizells and the rest Turners. We were just a pretty good bunch of country ball players. Our ball diamond was in the corner of a pasture without any fence around it, so if you hit a home run, you had to really hit one. We worked on the dirt to make it smooth, built our own pitcher's mound. Our pitching rubber was made out of a piece of white oak. We had homemade bases. Home plate was made out of a piece of white oak the size of a regular home plate. A fellow sliding in there had to be careful he didn't get any splinters. We had one ball that we called the game ball that was pretty good, but when it was fouled off down in the woods, we weren't against using one with tape on it. We didn't have uniforms or anything. I put on my blue jeans, or more often my overalls, and pitched barefoot. I was left-handed all the way, but all I had for a glove was an old right-hander's glove. The boys I was raised with all swung right-handed, so I did that too.

We were getting to be a pretty good group of knockers and sockers. We'd play any of those town teams, towns like Fruitdale and

Citronelle, Brusher Creek, Jonathan, McIntosh—we'd play anybody. Towns like Chatom [population over one thousand], of course, they didn't want to play us country boys. We'd go into those little towns and were winning our share. I wasn't thinking about baseball as a career. We weren't thinking more than a month ahead.

Our third year—1948—we actually ordered some bases from Sears Roebuck. And uniforms too. You can imagine how they fit. Didn't make any difference to us. I was wearing my shoes when I pitched. We were using an official ball. And we had a name. Called ourselves the Long Branch Rebels.

We played twenty-two games, won twenty, and tied two because we played doubleheaders and it got too dark to play. By now people were following our little team, knew where we were playing, and gave us enough money to buy balls and bats. We weren't paid anything. But, you know, that's when you had the most fun. It was great.

Most of the time we played Saturday afternoons, but sometimes you couldn't get a game until Sunday afternoon. My grandmother— she didn't like that too well. One Sunday morning the preacher in our little country church said, "You know, these young men are really fine young men, but if they got a game this afternoon, when this service ends, you better get out of the way." Oh me, oh my.

Along about the last of August one of us boys saw an article, in I guess the Mobile paper, that said the St. Louis Cardinals were holding a tryout camp down in Biloxi, Mississippi. Well, this was just a fun thing for us to do. Some of the others may have been dreaming about professional baseball, but I wasn't. We could go because it was the Labor Day weekend; school didn't start until after that, and we worked right up until school started.

So about six of us loaded up in an old car about 2:30 in the morning, heading for Biloxi. We get to the ball field, and they may have had a thousand boys at that camp. Those boys had come from as far as Texas and Arkansas, Tennessee, Florida, Alabama. I guess about half of them were pitchers. It was way out in the afternoon, about four o'clock, when they got to me to warm up. I was wearing my Long Branch uniform and had my shoes on. I was the last pitcher they brought in. My brother warmed me up. He had already been in the game. The little catcher who was catching when I come in, my first pitch I threw went right by his ear. So the scout in charge, Buddy Lewis, brought my brother in to catch for me. Then I threw nine pitches and struck out three men.

And that was the end of the camp. It was supposed to last three days, but there was a hurricane coming in off the coast. Man, it had started raining and blowing, and we were anxious to get out of there and looking for some high ground somewhere.

Now I was going to be a senior in high school. I was thinking about how I could go on to college with no money, but had the idea that at least some college would open the door for opportunities beyond what we had.

I played on the high school football team, and we had learned that Jones County Junior College was offering half-scholarships if you could make their football team. Some of us thought we'd go up there next fall when they had their tryouts and make that team and get that half-scholarship. We didn't know what that meant in money, but we figured we could make the rest somehow. That was my thinking at the time.

Back then baseball teams couldn't sign a boy until he or his high school class had graduated. On April 25, 1949, a cousin I was born and raised with and played ball with and I were to graduate that night. Buddy Lewis showed up at the house. My cousin and I were getting ready to take our bath for graduation down at the swim hole, which was about a mile back off an old dirt road, then down a little pass that went through the woods. Lewis drove up there on the creek bed where we'd been swimming. He wanted for us to go back to the house and for me to warm up. He wanted to see me throw. By the time we got back to the house, my brother had got home from work. So I warmed up. Buddy's comment was, "You're throwing harder now than you was last fall." I didn't disagree with him. One of the reasons I think we kept getting stronger was that my brother and I were living together and working together so much of the time; even when we were working in the fields, we'd come in, and after having dinner and putting the teams up to let 'em rest a while, he and I had a perfect area to pitch. It'd be hot. We had big old chinaberry trees in the yard, and he could be in the shade of one and I could be in the shade of the others and pitch across the front yard. By then he had a good catcher's mitt, and somebody had given me an old glove—a left-hander's glove.

So after I threw, Buddy and I were sitting in his car. He said, "I'd like for you to go to Albany, Georgia. Class D." All I knew was it was a professional league. He said, "I'll give you $175 a month." I didn't know what to say. So I didn't say anything. We just sit there for about five minutes. I'm thinking, all these things running through my mind. So he said, "When you get to Albany, I'll see that they give you $500."

Well, that woke me up, I'm telling you. Five hundred dollars. So after graduation my uncle signed for me. I don't know whether my grandmother would have signed for me or not. This all came up in just a few hours. I didn't even go back home from the graduation exercise. My grandmother said, "Now are you sure this is what you want to do?" And my uncle, same thing. I said, "You know, if I'm going to try it, I think I should go ahead and try it now." I was looking to do that summer what we'd normally do and try out for that JC football team. Four of my football mates made that team. Even right up to the last minute my uncle said, "Now are you sure you want to do this or wait a little bit?" I said, "I just feel like if I'm going to try it, I should try it now."

So Buddy took me and put me on the train from the graduation exercise. I rode that train all night and most of the day. Walter Shannon of the Cardinals met me at the station. I got off the train wearing my best blue jeans and carrying a very light little bag. He said, "Kid, where's your glove?"

I said, "I really don't have one."

"You don't have a glove?"

"No."

"Where's your shoes?"

"I got 'em on."

"Kid, we better stop at a sporting goods store."

We stopped at a store in the alley not far from the railroad station. He picked me out a Mort Cooper glove; you know, at that time that was one of the really famous pitcher's gloves. Well, I didn't really know who Mort Cooper was, but that was just about the prettiest thing I'd ever set my eyes on until I met my wife. Got me a pair of Riddell cleats made out of kangaroo hide and all the other paraphernalia a pitcher needed. Took me a while to learn how to wear all of it.

So we got to the ballpark and Bob Kline—big right-handed pitcher, weighed about three hundred pounds—had all the Albany pitchers out on the field, instructing them. Now, they told the story—I don't remember if this is true—they gave me a white uniform and a gray uniform, and I gave them the gray one back and said I'd keep the white one. I don't remember saying that, but, anyway, I got dressed and went out on the field. Kline was talking to them about the proper stance on the rubber and getting the sign and how to field the position, covering the first base side on a bunt with a man on first and the third base side with a man on second and holding runners on base—and all of this was brand new to me. So you can imagine I was really trying to look as inconspicuous as I could while I took all of this in. Nobody had ever carried me out to the mound and showed me all this.

Albany's season had already started, but that was the spring training base for all the Cardinals' lower minor league clubs, and some of them were still there. I remember a gentleman by the name of Harrison Wickel was in charge of that training camp. He came by and stopped at home plate with a fielder's glove and said to Bob Kline, "Let's see that new kid throw a few." I looked around for the new kid. Kline hadn't put me up on the pitcher's mound. I'm sure he could see I'm trying to take all this in, but when Wickel said that, Bob Kline just tossed me the baseball. I threw a few, four or five, pitches to him easy. Remember: I'd just been riding that train all night and most of the day. So he said, "Kid, is that all you've got?" And I thought, "Well, maybe they warm 'em up using fielder's gloves here." So I wound up and I cut that pitch loose just about that high. It hit that glove, stuck in that web, and went right up on the backstop, and he dropped his hand and left the ballpark. And old Bob Kline just chuckled.

Then he began to work with me, the first real instructions I had received. The manager, an old pitcher, Sheldon "Chief" Bender, had the patience to bring me along. It was almost six weeks after I joined the club that I pitched. Up in Americus, Georgia, one night, sixth inning, score was 15–0; we was getting beat. Chief looked down the bench at me and said, "All right Mizell, you can warm up." So this was it.

I grabbed that Mort Cooper glove and went down along the left-field foul line to warm up; with 2,500 people in that little ballpark you couldn't even see me warming up. But Chief gave me plenty of time to get ready, went out to the mound, took his pitcher out, waved me in. When I got to the mound, I knew something Chief didn't: I'd only thrown four pitches in that bullpen because the catcher was having to run that ball down after every pitch. So Chief gave me the ball and said, "Go get 'em, Mizell."

It was the first game I pitched with fences all around the field and lights.

Hal Smith was the catcher. He goes behind the plate and caught all my warmup pitches with a little effort. That first hitter up was feeling cocky, leading 15–0. So he dug in about knee deep, and Smitty gets down and gives me the sign: fastball. He and I know that's the only pitch I had. Needless to say, I was a little bit nervous. Nobody knew this but me: when I put my foot on the rubber, my foot would shake. It wasn't fear at all, just that nervous tension when the adrenaline flows, and so I'd take it off the rubber. When I cut that first pitch loose, I threw it right over everything. Smitty come running out to the mound, and he said, "Mi-Mi-Mi-Mizell, are you nervous?" And that hitter got way in the back of that batter's box. That next pitch was about a foot over and a foot behind his head.

This was my debut in professional baseball. They got hits. I hit some of 'em. I walked some of 'em. And I made it a point to forget the final score of that game a long time ago.

Later, when Hal Smith and I were both with the Cardinals, he told me, "You know, I was as nervous as you were that night until I realized I was the safest man in that whole ballpark." He said that's the only time he ever looked behind him and saw people lying behind their seats.

Chief brought me in in relief again, and I struck out seven of the nine I faced. Then he decided he'd start me in Moultrie, Georgia. I walked six men in a row before he took me out. Started me again, and I walked four before he took me out. I settled down and won eight in a row. We won the pennant.

That winter my brother and I sawed logs—six dollars a day. I had that $500—after taxes—in the bank. After a year at Winston-Salem in the Carolina League, I had a Houston contract but went to spring training with the Cards. They left me in Houston, where a former pitcher, Al Hollingsworth, was the manager. By then I'd picked up a curve but didn't throw it a lot. I had a good change-up but had no confidence in it. It was several years later before I really used it and picked up a slow curve as a change, not realizing what a great pitch that was. I was not all that wild off the plate, but my fastball had a tendency to stay up. Had to try to get that ball down.

In 1959 I was 10-3 around the All-Star break. Then one night I was pitching at home against Milwaukee; about the third inning or so came one of those sudden downpours, and they didn't get the mound covered in time. We had about a forty-five-minute delay. I had a runner on first and third. The first pitch I made, my foot slipped out from under me. I evidently tore those fibers loose from my rib cage all the way down to my hip. I went on and pitched about eight innings. The next day I felt like when they fold you up and squeeze the breath out of you. You can't breathe. I struggled the rest of that year. Then we went to Japan. I worked out that winter and went to spring training, and thanks to that injury, I really became more of a pitcher. I threw three different curve balls by then, a slow curve and straight change. I was pitching against Milwaukee in May, and it's the first time I felt really good and was really popping that ball and had good control. It had taken me that long. I struck out seven in seven innings. Then they took me out, and I know now why: 'cause they planned on trading me. [Two days later he was traded to Pittsburgh.]

I joined the Pirates at just the right time. Now I was pitching consistent ball. I won thirteen games for them. We had Bill Virdon in center field. We was laughing last night at the [Pirates' reunion] dinner they had when [the 1960 general manager] Joe Brown said, "Mizell made Virdon the star of the game sometimes." Yeah, I did more than one time. They'd hit those long fly balls in that big center field in Pittsburgh, and Bill ran them down. From right-center field all the way around to left field it was a big ballpark. This was an advantage for left-handed pitchers because those right-handed batters would try to pull the ball off you, and you could throw the off-speed stuff with Virdon and Clemente out there making unbelievable catches.

Danny Murtaugh was not only a great baseball man but a great manager of men, and 1960 was a great example of that. I thought about our team at the dinner when Joe Brown said that of all his experiences, his association with that team was his greatest. He emphasized the fact of being a team that won twenty-three games in their last time at bat. No superstars, just fellows who were really coming into their own, like Clemente. The nucleus had been brought up through the Pittsburgh organization, but the rest of that team had come from other organizations: Don Hoak, Smoky Burgess, Smith, Haddix, Virdon, Dick Schofield, Rocky Nelson, myself. You take all those different personalities coming in from all different organizations and see on a day to day basis how Danny Murtaugh was able to utilize all those players. That team just molded together like no other team that I played on. If we didn't play as a team, we didn't win.

After that I was pitching a lot with a sore arm. In the spring of '63 I knew my arm wasn't going to come around. I was just thirty-two, had anticipated pitching another five, six years. Now I had to think about what I was going to do. We went back to my wife's home town near Winston-Salem, and I joined the family-owned Pepsi-Cola bottling company, intending to settle down and make some roots. Then some friends of mine got me to run for county office—my wife's never forgiven them for it—and that led to Washington.

I became a Republican when General Eisenhower ran for president in 1952. In my youth around home everybody was a Democrat. They tell a story about the polls closing: they started counting votes and they came to a Republican vote, and they'd never seen one before. They didn't know what to do. Finally the old judge said, "Just lay it aside, boys, and keep on countin'." They kept on counting and came to another Republican vote. The judge says, "Throw 'em out, boys. That rascal voted twice."

31.

Rocky Nelson
PITTSBURGH, JUNE 16, 1990

Left-handed-hitting Rocky Nelson played in 620 games as a first baseman/ pinch hitter with five teams—Cardinals, Pirates, White Sox, Indians, and Dodgers—in nine years between 1949 and 1961. He had the good luck to wind up in two World Series (1952 and 1960) and the bad luck to just miss making it to two more (1949 and 1956). I sat down with him in a hotel lobby during a reunion of the 1960 Pirates.

IN MY ROOKIE YEAR with the Cardinals, 1949, we had a 1½ game lead over Brooklyn with five games to play against the sixth-place Pirates and last-place Cubs. The players' wives had flown to Chicago to go with us to open the World Series in New York. Nobody in the league liked the Dodgers. They all wanted us to beat them. In the first game in Pittsburgh, somebody slid in high on Pirates' second baseman Danny Murtaugh. That made him mad. He came over to our bench and said, "We wanted you guys to win the pennant, but you're going to have to work for it, 'cause now we're going to beat you."

We lost three in a row. In Chicago Bob Chipman, who couldn't break a pane of glass, beat us. We lost the pennant by one game. Our manager, Eddie Dyer, told us, "The old fellows lost those games for us." He named Stan Musial and Enos Slaughter specifically. They kept coming up with men on base and just did not drive in the runs. That World Series check would have almost equaled my full year's salary.

In 1951 we leased an apartment in St. Louis but never got a chance to unpack. After nine games, [Pittsburgh general manager] Branch Rickey traded for me. I had been signed originally by his brother, Frank, who lived in Portsmouth, Ohio, my home town. It was the craziest year I ever saw.

I sat on the bench for a week. They had Ralph Kiner playing first base. I never saw Ralph Kiner hit a cheap home run. He hit them over the farthest fence, even when they built a shorter one in front of it. Whoever wrote that Kiner wouldn't hit as many homers in today's ballparks never saw him.

Rickey calls me in. "Did you ever play the outfield?"

"I'll play anywhere you want me."

First game, I'm playing left field. I remember seeing Honus Wagner sitting in a rocking chair they put out for him in foul territory beyond third base. Don Newcombe is pitching. I got two or three hits. I was on base when the last out of the game was made. As I'm coming off, Kiner says, "You broke in pretty good." I said, "I didn't hit the ball well, just got a few bloop hits." He said, "Tomorrow they'll all look like line drives." I'll never forget that.

Next night, another right-hander pitching, I'm out there, game's ready to start, and here comes Pete Reiser. He says, "Rock, I don't know why, but I'm playing left field." I sat for two days then started playing again.

Bill Howerton and I were hitting about .345. One day in the paper it says George Metkovich and Jack Phillips are going to play regularly to help the hitting, and they bench me and Howerton. Every time somebody started to hit, they took him out. But never Kiner. It seemed like Rickey didn't want us to finish in the first division. [They finished seventh.] We go on a road trip and come back. At nine o'clock Monday morning I'm sitting on a bench outside of Mr. Rickey's office, and just as I get up to go in, here comes Howerton. I went in there, and the first thing—you had to know Mr. Rickey—he says, "You've been doing a great job for us; hitting about .340, aren't you?"

I said, "A little better than that."

He started talking about his ranch. After about fifteen minutes of that, the conversation went like this:

"Mr. Rickey, let's get down to brass tacks. I want to talk to you. I played in St. Louis last year, and we lost the pennant by one game. I come over here and I'm doing well when I'm playing, and all at once I'm sitting on the bench."

"Well, I have nothing to do with that."

"Who are you kidding? You've run the club everywhere you've been, and everybody knows it. It looks to me like the only man who can do well here this year is Kiner."

"What do you mean?"

"If somebody else starts going good, you bench him. Why don't you trade me or sell me?"

So he put me on waivers, and the White Sox claimed me.

[White Sox manager] Paul Richards told me if he can trade his first baseman, Eddie Robinson, I'll be his first baseman next year. He was trying to make a deal with the Yankees, but all he wanted in exchange was Mickey Mantle or Gil McDougald. So the deal fell through, and I went to Montreal in 1952.

I broke my ankle in the second game. They sent me to doctors in Brooklyn, and I wound up sitting in the Brooklyn dugout while I healed. I was activated in June and did some pinch-hitting and wound up in the World Series against the Yankees. That was the Series where Gil Hodges went 0 for 21. He'd had one of those years where he was doing everything wrong at bat and just couldn't break it. I don't blame [Dodgers manager] Chuck Dressen for going with him. He told me every day I was going to play first, but he left Hodges in there. I lacked six days of being there long enough to qualify automatically for a full share but got three-fourths.

I made myself into a pull hitter in Montreal in '53 and won the triple crown. The Indians drafted me. They had a first baseman who had driven in thirty runs for them. I told the manager, Al Lopez, I could get thirty RBIs batting right-handed. But he sent me back to Montreal. [The Indians won the pennant.] In 1956 the Dodgers brought me back up but traded me to the Cardinals before they went on to win the pennant.

[After two years in Toronto, Nelson was claimed in the rule 5 draft by Pittsburgh in December 1958.]

We were a bunch of misfits who jelled together and did the job in 1960. We never gave up and won a lot of games in late innings. Winning that World Series was my biggest thrill. It was a crazy Series. They scored all the runs, and we won four games.

After baseball I was in the insurance business, then became a painting contractor.

32.

Hal Newhouser
BLOOMFIELD HILLS, MICHIGAN, NOVEMBER 1984

. . . .

Hal Newhouser may be the only ballplayer who ever made it to a World Series before he graduated from high school. Although deemed "too young" by manager Del Baker to pitch in the 1940 Series, the nineteen-year-old Tigers left-hander was in the dugout after going to school in the morning of the Friday home game. Newhouser turned in one of the game's most spectacular three-year records: 80-27 in 1944–1946, earning—for a pitcher—a unique two consecutive MVP Awards (which would have been three, but he was edged out by Ted Williams in 1946). He pitched in two World Series and four All-Star Games. In fourteen complete seasons with Detroit (1940–1953) and one in Cleveland, he averaged 200 innings pitched.

I learned how he became a winning pitcher in a visit with the lifetime Detroit area resident at his home.

. . . .

I KNEW WHEN I was fifteen I was going to play in the big leagues. No doubt in my mind. My dad wanted me to learn a trade. He was a wood pattern maker. You have to be a very patient man to be a wood pattern maker, and I didn't have the patience for it. I went to Wilbur Wright Trade School and became a pretty good metal machinist. But I saw that machine work was risky. I had a car and took a lot of kids to the hospital when they made mistakes and injured their hands. My dad worked at Chrysler; they had their own school and they paid you to go there, so I went in as a drafting engineer. I worked in my trade for eleven years in the winter during and after the war.

Trade school went year round. In 1939 I pitched at Class D Alexandria in the Evangeline League and Beaumont in the Texas League. I was studying all that time and took my tests in September, when the Tigers recalled me. I fell behind when I went to spring training with the Tigers in 1940 and stayed with them into October, so my class graduated in June 1940 without me. I had gone back to school after Labor Day for three hours in the morning before going to the ballpark, including during the World Series. I graduated in January 1941.

Two changes turned the Tigers into contenders in 1940. In order to get Rudy York's bat into the lineup at first base, Hank Greenberg moved to left field. That gave us power at both positions. The Detroit infield was quiet. They got veteran shortstop Dick Bartell to liven it up, and he did. He was a rah-rah sort of guy, a pepper pot who kept everybody alive. He hustled and if anybody didn't, he'd holler, "Let's go!" Nobody on the club took offense to it. But it could get under your skin. Either you fought him or you did what he asked you to do.

Because I was a young boy, Bartell bothered me a little bit on the mound. I was sort of a hot-tempered young pitcher and I was wild, and he was quite a bit older than me. I guess they expected me to do more than what my age was, and Dick would be hollering, "Get the ball over the plate!" and of course that didn't settle with me. But I never held it against him. If I had been his age, I guess I would have taken it a lot easier than I did as a young kid. But he did a good job for us, kept the infield and bench alive.

With Birdie Tebbetts catching, we had two high-pitched pepper pots in the infield.

Dick got on Bobo Newsom too. A big guy, Bobo wore a size 52 coat. He probably showed up at spring training a little overweight and was a lackadaisical, fun-loving guy. He had fun on the mound but was a bear-down pitcher. Won 21 for us that year. Once when he was with the Philadelphia Athletics, he told the press, "If Hank Greenberg ever hits a home run off me, I'll shake hands with him at home plate." One day Greenberg hit one, and Bobo met him at home plate to shake hands. 'Course Greenberg wouldn't do it. That was Bobo.

Bob Feller was the fastest pitcher in the league. Dick was our leadoff man; Feller would strike him out, and he'd come back to the bench and holler, "You're fast but you won't last," in that high-pitched voice. Feller would strike him out three out of four times, and every time Dick would holler the same thing. It became a joke in the clubhouse.

We ended the 1940 season at Cleveland with a two-game lead over the Indians and three to play. When we arrived we knew that

Feller would pitch the first game on Friday. Our manager, Del Baker, called a meeting of all the players except the pitchers. We pitchers knew nothing about it. In the meeting Baker said, "We know Feller's going to pitch. We know we're not going to get many runs off him. We've got Newsom, Bridges, and Rowe. Should we give up one of our three top pitchers to pitch against him or use a youngster against him and in the last two games have all our three starters ready and Al Benton to back them up?"

The players chose Floyd Giebell, who had been called up from Buffalo, had good control, and wasn't familiar to the Indians. We pitchers were shocked. I thought I would get the start because I had pitched well against Cleveland. Baker said, "We'll put Newhouser in the bullpen, and he will start throwing as soon as Giebell goes out to the mound; if Giebell gets into trouble, we'll throw him and all the rest into the game."

I pitched the whole game in the bullpen. Every time the Indians got two men on, Baker would say, "One more and we'll bring in Newhouser." And Giebell would get out of the inning. Rudy York hit a home run with a man on in the fourth and we won, 2–0, and clinched the pennant. It was Ladies' Day, and the crowd in the bleachers showered the field with rotten vegetables, fruit, bottles, trash late in the game. The bullpen was right by the foul line against the wall. They dropped a basket full of stuff from the upper deck into the pen, and it hit Tebbetts on the back and shoulder; he went up and squared off against the guy he thought had thrown it and got sued for it and had to go to court.

The train station was about a mile's walk from the stadium over a viaduct above the tracks. After the Sunday game we sneaked out quick and walked along the tracks to the station to get out of town.

Floyd Giebell never got a World Series share. Nothing. Hank Greenberg led our meeting to vote the shares. He had the records of how many days each of us had been with the club that year and read off the names. When he got to Giebell, he said, "He'll be taken care of by Jack Zeller [the general manager] and Mr. Briggs [the owner]." So we went on. He told us later he never got anything. I'd have voted him a full share.

[In the seventh game of the World Series at Cincinnati, Bobo

Newsom, going for his third win, had a 1-0 lead in the bottom of the seventh. Frank McCormick led off with a double. Jimmy Ripple followed with a double to right field. Shortstop Dick Bartell and second baseman Charlie Gehringer went out for the relay. McCormick, a slow runner, was rounding third when right fielder Bruce Campbell threw to Bartell.]

I was in the bullpen, directly facing the play. I can see it now. McCormick was just rounding third. He sorta hesitated—I thought he was going to stop—then kept on going. The crowd was yelling, screaming. Dick had his back to the infield. I was hollering at him, "Home! Home!" We all were hollering, "Home!" Dick just held the ball. Later Dick said he didn't hear any of us for all the noise and thought that McCormick was already in the dugout by then. [Ripple then scored and the Reds won, 2–1.]

Some writers called Bartell the goat for holding the ball, but nobody on our club ever knocked him for it. If we had hit in the Series, that play wouldn't have meant anything.

The Tigers in 1941 got old over the winter, very old—Newsom, Rowe, Bridges—and us young fellows were to take over. The club fell apart. Bartell was released after five games. The same thing would happen to me after fifteen years with Detroit.

In 1945 we had to win the pennant on the last day and the World Series on the last day. In the first game the Cubs scored seven runs off me in three innings. Fortunately I started two more and won them, but how do you think I would've felt if I'd lost one more and we lost the Series?

We had three weird things happen to us in the World Series. In Chicago I'm pitching with men on first and second. A fly ball was hit between Doc Cramer in center field and right fielder Roy Cullenbine. Both of them cut over to right center. One says, "I got it," and the other says, "You got it." There's forty-some thousand people hollering. They stood there, and the ball dropped between them. Then each thought the other was going to pick it up. Fortunately we had a four-run cushion.

Another day a ball was hit between short and third. It hits a water sprinkler and bounces over Hank Greenberg's head in left, and the winning run scored. They gave Hank an error.

In another game we had a runner on second. There's a base hit. He rounds third, gets halfway home, and falls flat on his face.

After 1945 we floundered again, going nowhere. They hired Red Rolfe to manage. Red brought over Charlie Keller from the Yankees. Keller gave us 100 percent at bat and was a super person, a very refined, dignified, sociable man, and a lot of it rubbed off. They brought back Dick Bartell as a coach to shake up the younger players, and he did: hollered and screamed and kept them on their toes. They brought in Ted Lyons as pitching coach, like a father to the men. But something just didn't work.

Red could have been an excellent manager. The problem was he just couldn't get the college thinking out of his mind, and he had major league players playing for him. No shaving in the clubhouse before or after a game, even if you were going to dinner with your wife; nothing to eat between games of a doubleheader, but he'd have apples out for you; we called it Apple Day. That's college, and the players resented it. They folded. Red didn't like the way George Kell threw from third base—three-quarters; said he should throw overhand. Kell tried it and got a sore shoulder. Then Fred Hutchinson took over and we finished last for the first time in Tigers history.

I threw three different kinds of curves: overhand and straight down—what high school kids call a drop; a three-quarter curve that broke down and in to a right-handed batter; and a slow curve. At three-quarters I got more of a break than over the top. I didn't usually use the drop until I had two strikes on the hitter.

For my first three or four years I was struggling, trying to stay in the major leagues, until I grew up and found out how to pitch a little bit. When I went back to the three-quarter curve with one strike on the hitter, they just took it. It didn't mean anything. One day we had a four- or five-run lead. I got two strikes on a hitter, and I said, "Well, I'm not going to hang [a drop]. If I bounce it up there, so what?" I threw it and got it in a good spot, and he was so fooled by it that I used it for the next ten years, but only with two strikes—well, not always two strikes; you have to vary it.

Very few pitchers could throw an overhand drop. You need a long arm, long extension to come way up over the top, and that's what I had. The spin you gotta get is like a tire on the road, over and over. But if you hang it above the waist, there's no velocity; it's just turning—it's bye-bye. It's a dangerous pitch, especially if it might mean the ball game. It's a gamble, and I was a gambler on the mound. I'd gamble on curves or fastballs or changeups; when you shouldn't throw it, I threw it.

A change of pace is the most important thing for a pitcher to have and the hardest to cope with for a hitter. And it's the hardest thing to train a pitcher to throw. I've been in this business now since 1939. I go up to the University of Michigan now and then and talk to the pitchers. Everybody throws a fastball. Anybody can throw a slider. It's easier to teach than a curve. Some pick up a curve naturally, like I did. But the change-of-pace is the toughest because your body speed and arm speed have got to be perfect in order to fool the hitter. If your body speed is too slow and your arm speed is too fast—or the other way around—the hitter picks it up like nothing.

Bob Feller couldn't throw a change-of-pace. 'Course, why should he? Nolan Ryan, the same. But if you're a 92–93 pitcher—that's above the 88 average—and you throw a fastball by 'em and the batter has to get ready for that and all of a sudden the pitcher takes about three feet off that fastball, he's got you so far out in front, and then he plays a game with you. Once he's done that, the pitcher has a nice time. He has games that he can play with you, and that's what pitching is. To me it was a game. If the hitter got to you starting off, it became, "Okay, what do I do next?" Then it gets down to the late innings, and you're thinking, "How have I been working him?" And it all goes through your mind in a second—how I've been pitching him the last couple years and this year and today—and the catcher is doing the same thing—and you have to make a judgment: that rascal, he's looking for a breaking ball, you throw him a fastball, and he hits it out of the ballpark; he outfoxed you. So it's a game.

I'm eligible now to be considered by the Veterans Committee for the Hall of Fame. I don't know what they look for. It's so surprising as I sit here, waiting now for twenty-five years, to see fellows that are put in who probably should be in. If you look at their record and you look at mine, sometimes there's no comparison. There may be ten or fifteen who deserve to be in, but they can only pick one each year.

[Newhouser was elected to the Hall of Fame by the Veterans Committee in 1992.]

33.

Bill Nicholson
CHESTERTOWN, MARYLAND, MAY 1989

Voted by Cubs fans as their all-time favorite right fielder, left-handed batter Bill Nicholson was a two-time NL home run leader during his ten years with the Cubs, 1939–1948, followed by five years with the Phillies. Labeled "Swish" by Brooklyn fans who would holler that sound every time he stood at the plate waving his bat across the plate while awaiting a pitch, he was the third player in baseball history to be walked intentionally with the bases loaded.

On the way to his farmhouse out in the country, I passed a life-size statue of him near the small town's center.

I WAS ALWAYS A power hitter, even as a kid on the Chestertown team in an amateur league, the Chesapeake Bay League. Jimmie Foxx's father was an umpire. Jimmie was seven years older than I was; I never played with or against him until he joined the Cubs in 1942, on his way down fast, drinking too much.

Washington College [in Chestertown] had abandoned baseball for lacrosse the first two years I was there; then they brought it back. One day in 1936 a scout for the Philadelphia Athletics offered me $1,000 to sign with them. Nobody else had offered me anything, so I signed. A week later a Yankees scout offered me $5,000, but it was too late. I went to spring training in Mexico City with the A's in '37. The altitude didn't bother me; I was young, but they had to send a few of the older players back to the states. We played local Mexican teams, more Cubans than Mexicans. I wound up being traded to Chattanooga, and they sold me to the Cubs in August 1939.

The morning I got off the train in Chicago, I started my first game. In the fifth inning I hit my first home run.

My contract for 1940 was $5,000, $6,000 if I played regularly. I was in 135 games but had to battle to get that extra thousand. The most I ever made was $18,000 in 1943. After I led in home runs the second year in a row in 1944, the Cubs cut me $3,000. I got it back up to $18,000, but no raise.

Playing right field in Wrigley Field wasn't easy. It was the sun field—right was the sun field in six of the eight National League parks. It wasn't the fly balls so much as the line drives hit at you that stayed right in the sun's glare. You had to shield your face. I caught some after they hit me but before they hit the ground. But I had learned how to get a jump on the ball from the Chattanooga manager, [Hall of Fame outfielder] Kiki Cuyler. He taught me how to watch the batter's swing. I got to where I could tell even before he hit it where the ball was headed. A lot of years I had 16–18 assists because base runners didn't think I could get to a ball to catch it.

In the spring, when it was cold and wet and the wind blew in, home runs were scarce in Wrigley Field. When it got nice and the wind blew out, it was a good home run park.

I didn't mind getting thrown at by pitchers, except in Cubs Park, where you lost sight of so many balls coming out of the white shirts in the center-field bleachers. It was that way the whole time I played. The wild pitchers were the dangerous ones, not the ones you knew would be throwing at you.

One bright sunny day, lefty Johnny Vander Meer was pitching, wild as a jackrabbit, pitching out of those white shirts. We'd scored a couple runs on walks, and he loaded the bases again. I was hitting; he got me 3-2 and reared back and fired, and I've never seen that ball to this day. It just ticked the back of my head as it went by. We didn't have helmets. I was lucky. Coulda killed me.

Giants pitcher Ace Adams hit me up the side of the head. You can still feel the dent it left in my skull. But usually being thrown at didn't bother me. One day in St. Louis Lon Warneke, a former Cub, was pitching. Along about the fifth inning, the two hitters ahead of me each hit one on the roof of Sportsman's Park. I came up, and I knew I was going to get knocked down. Dusted me off. I got up, and he did it again. Next pitch he got over the plate, and I never hit one harder. When it went over the stands, it was just taking off.

In the 1945 World Series against Detroit we had some bad breaks and bad managing. Claude Passeau threw a one-hitter in Game 3 and started Game 6. He was leading when somebody hit a ball back up the middle. He reached with his bare hand, and it took the nail off a finger of his pitching hand. That was the end of him. The game went to twelve innings, and Hank Borowy pitched four of them. He had pitched five innings the day before. He was at best a seven-inning pitcher. When he started Game 7, we knew that was bad managing. [The Cubs lost, 9–3.]

I'd had a poor year, knew there was something wrong with me. Had a lazy bat. After the World Series they sent me to the hospital for a week of tests. The doctors never told me anything, but the nurse said they thought it was a kidney infection. I never thought any more about it, but in 1950, when I was diagnosed with diabetes, they sent for my records from 1945 and said, "You're lucky you're alive. You were showing sugar in 1945." I wasn't a drinker, but I'd have a few beers with the guys after a hot day in Chicago, and that's the worst thing I coulda done, I guess. It turned my career around. I didn't have those big years again.

I was traded to the Phillies after the 1948 season. In 1949 I was rooming with first baseman Eddie Waitkus when he got shot at the Edgewater Beach Hotel in Chicago. I went up to the room about 10 p.m., and there was a note on the dresser. I guess the bellhop had put it there. I picked it up and read it. It was for Eddie. A few minutes later he came in, and I gave it to him. It was from some woman he didn't know. He said, "I'll go up and see what she wants." We were on the fourth floor; "she" was on the twelfth. Later they found a list of ballplayers she was going to shoot. He was fourth on the list. I wasn't on it. Anyhow, he went up there and rapped on the door, and she said, "Come in." She was sitting in a chair opposite the door with a .22 rifle. She said, "I'm gonna shoot you." Eddie thought it was one of those old ballplayers' jokes, setting him up. He stood there, and she shot him right through the lung. That's the way it happened. I didn't hear any shots, but I heard the sirens. She said she was raised three blocks from him in Cambridge, Massachusetts, but she wasn't. She was from the Chicago area. Eddie played a few more years, but he never got his strength back. Died at fifty-three. They said he drank himself to death.

I bought this farm in 1952. Wasn't much of a farmer. I just wanted to live in the country, not in town.

34.

Mickey Owen
PITTSBURGH, JUNE 1990

. . . .

Arnold "Mickey" Owen is one of those star-crossed ballplayers remembered for one ignominious moment out of a long career. But there is more
to the story of his thirteen years with the Cardinals, Dodgers, Cubs, and
Red Sox, plus another 4½ in the Mexican League, beginning in 1937, than
that costly passed ball in the 1941 World Series. In his hotel room the morning after playing in an old-timers game, Owen, a knowledgeable student
of baseball history going back to 1840 and analyst of stats by decades, pre-
dicted the coming of ten-year, $100 million contracts for superstars more
than twenty-five years ago.

. . . .

I WAS BORN IN Nixa, Missouri, in 1916 but moved to Los Angeles with my mother and stepdad when I was seven. My stepdad,
a navy man, died young, and my mother sold insurance and real
estate, and we lived behind the office. I made money with a paper
route and as a professional marbles shark—won all the other kids'
marbles and lunch money until the mothers came to school to
complain and they stopped me. So I gave the kids back the marbles I had won from them. Next thing you know, they're out there
selling the marbles I had returned to them. A good agate went for
three dollars. So I won them back from all the ones who would
play with me.

I learned baseball at the Hoover Street playground. I was a shortstop, and the second baseman was Bobby Doerr. Later we got to
the Western regional finals of American Legion ball but got beat.
Doerr and two others from that team were signed, but nobody
wanted me as a shortstop. A Cardinals scout, John Angel, told me
they had orders to sign catchers. I could throw pretty good, but I
said, "I don't have a catcher's mitt." So he gave me one as a bonus,
and I became a catcher. Signed for $125 a month. This was 1935.

I went to spring training in Houston. There were thirty-five players there—three of them catchers. One had a sore arm, couldn't

throw across the room. One was 5-foot-8 and weighed about 245 pounds. So I got to do a lot of catching. They sent me to Springfield, close to my home town, in the Western Association. Eight games a week—every day and two on Sunday. I hit about .310.

The next year I went to Columbus in the American Association. They didn't have any catchers, so they started me and I hit pretty good. Up until then I had always been called "Arnie." The Columbus manager, Burt Shotton, pinned the name "Mickey" on me because I had big ears and I was fiery like Mickey Cochrane.

I made the Cardinals in 1937 but didn't play much. I remember catching Dizzy Dean. You know how a jockey can make a horse run fast or slow? Dean was the greatest at changing the pace at which he worked.

When they traded Dean the next year, they got a real smart pitcher in Curt Davis. A pitcher is the best for a catcher to learn from, and Davis taught me a lot. We were roommates. He could put the ball wherever he wanted to, jam you on the fists, had a great move to first base, good fielder.

Then all those great young pitchers came up from the Cards' farm system—and along with them came catcher Walker Cooper, and I knew I was dispensable. I had never lived up to what they expected. In December 1940 they traded me to Brooklyn.

The Dodgers had some mean pitchers—when they were on the mound. All you had to do was tell Whitlow Wyatt he was pitching today, and he'd turn mad. One day he's pitching and a fight broke out. A real brawl. I sat it out. I was too little. Wyatt says to me, "Those guys ought to put that much energy into getting me some runs."

Johnny Allen was a highly intelligent man with one of the worst tempers I ever saw. Raised in an orphanage, he had been abused, kicked around pretty good. He hated some players—Bill Werber, for example. Hated Werber with a passion. He'd throw four straight at him, aiming right for the chest. I said to him, "Why do you do that? You only make it tough on yourself." He said, "When I was in the orphanage, there was one person who gave me a rough time. He reminds me of him, and when I see him, I remember that so-and-so. I'm getting even with him."

Larry French was another highly intelligent man but not angry. He had a good fastball and screwball, but when he lost his fastball, his screwball was not as good. One thing about pitchers: they believe they still have the good fastball even when they no longer have it. They were creaming his. So we're sitting in the bullpen and he says, "I'm going to work on a new pitch." He came up with a one-finger knuckleball, but he wasn't sure he could control it. A couple days later he came in to pitch, and I gave him a sign for that knuckler. He says, "I'm not ready." I said, "Let's find out." I was not about to call for any fastballs. It worked. He was 15-4 before he went into the navy as a captain.

[In the 1940s pitchers who would come to be called closers came in as early as the fifth inning with the intention of finishing the game. Hugh Casey was the best of his time. In 1941 he combined eighteen starts (four complete games) and twenty-seven relief appearances, of which he finished twenty-one. He relieved three times in the five-game 1941 World Series. The Yankees led two games to one on Sunday, October 5, at Ebbets Field.]

In those days a lot of teams were good at reading catchers' signs. Hugh Casey absolutely didn't want anybody getting his signs. He'd throw at you if he thought you were getting them. And he would never throw a change-of-pace. He believed even a poor hitter could hit it. He had two good fastballs and two good curves. One fastball was across the seams, a riding fastball, and the other with the seams, and he'd give it a snap and let fire. His curves—he had a hard, quick curve, not a slider, that wouldn't break a lot, and he could throw it hard. Then he had that big curve that—shoom!—broke like that. He could throw either curve on the curve ball sign and either fastball on the fastball sign. I didn't know which curve he would throw; I just had to be ready for either one. And I didn't know which fastball he was going to throw. That way the other team couldn't pick it up either. All season long we used that system and never had any problems.

So he comes in to relieve [in the fifth inning, the Yankees leading, 3–2]. First pitch, he tried to roll off his big curve, and it didn't break, just hung outside. Ball 1. Next he tried the same curve; same result. Ball 2. From that time on I give him the curve sign, and he throws that tight one, and they couldn't touch it. So we go into the ninth inning [leading, 4–3], and hell, I've got a one-track mind anyway, so with two outs and nobody on and two strikes on Tommy Henrich, I give him the curve sign, expecting that tight one, and he throws that big one, and it broke—shoom!—like that. Henrich swings and misses, and I'm late getting my glove down, and it got by me. [Henrich reached first on the passed ball. The Yankees went on to score four runs and the next day won the Series.]

Funny thing about it: the Guinness Book of Records people sent three of us certificates because the three people who were the best at what they did absolutely failed miserably all at the same time. The reliever with the highest winning percentage lost the game; the "Old Reliable" hitter struck out; and the catcher in the middle of setting the National League record for consecutive chances without an error missed the ball.

I went into the service and then went to the Mexican League along with about twenty other major leaguers. I managed the Vera Cruz club in Mexico City. Some fans carried guns down there for protection. Only once did I run for my life.

Babe Ruth came down for an exhibition game. Ruth was an old man, and that high altitude got him. I was catching one of the best Mexican pitchers, Ramon Brigande, an overhand fastball pitcher with a hard-to-follow delivery. Babe was up there, and he couldn't hit one out of the park. That pitcher was zinging it in, and Babe just fouled 'em off. The manager of Ruth's team came out and said to the pitcher, "Why don't you let the batting practice pitcher come out and pitch to Babe?" Brigande said, "No." They got into an argument, and the pitcher shoved the manager in front of all those people; our club owner came out and told the pitcher to sit down, and they put in the batting practice pitcher He was laying them in there, and Babe hit one into the bleachers, and the people went wild. We thought it was all over.

We had a dressing room under the stands, and there were three players in there: myself, the pitcher Brigande, and Danny Gardella. This fourteen-year-old clubhouse boy comes in; he's the brother of the manager who got shoved, and he's got a pistol and says, "Brigande," and Brigande makes a rude gesture to him. We're in the corner of the room. There's a wall about six feet up and a three-foot space between it and the stands for cooling. We heard some people talking to the clubhouse boy in Spanish through the door, trying to stop him from killing Brigande. We went over that wall.

When the Vera Cruz owner fired me, I went home. I guess I was a lousy manager. I sued him for what he owed me and won, but then he took it to their federal court and I lost there. They said I'd waited too long, by three or four days or something.

I came back to Brooklyn in 1949, and a week later they sold me to the Cubs.

I was disappointed that I wasn't a better ballplayer than I was. I don't believe I was as good as I could have been. Nobody's fault but my own.

My mother saw me play once, in an old-timers game in San Diego. At those games I always got a dozen balls and had them signed to give to friends. I put her in the stands and asked the people around her to watch her. She was pretty old, and they said they'd take care of her. After I got the balls signed, I took them up to her to hold onto them. When I came up to bat, Satchel Paige was pitching. I hit one against the fence with the bases loaded, almost went out of the park. My mother was saying, "That's my son," and hugging everybody. She was so happy, she started passing out the signed balls. When I got back to her, she didn't have a single ball left in the box. Six of the people around her gave them back to me.

Back in Missouri I was elected sheriff in the third largest county in the state, served fifteen years, had seventy-five deputies. My son and I plan to go into the memorabilia business, authenticating things, representing players who want to sell stuff.

I sincerely believe that when you have a great player, he will be so valuable you won't want to lose him. I predict that within the decade of the 1990s there will be players who will get $100 million contracts for ten years because the owners don't want to lose that name. They'll have the players insured against breaking down. Worldwide TV marketing is where the money will be. That's not too much when you look at how many people they are selling that Budweiser beer to.

35.

Mel Parnell
New Orleans, January 29, 1993

. . . .

Mel Parnell was the rarest of pitchers—a left-hander who loved to pitch in Fenway Park. While right-handed sluggers taking aim at the Green Monster in left field intimidated most lefties in the American League, to Parnell the Monster was his friend—so good a friend, he used it to compile a 71-30 lifetime record in 117 starts with sixty complete games at Fenway, while becoming the winningest southpaw in Red Sox history, 123-75 over eleven years beginning in 1946.

A lifetime resident of New Orleans, Parnell provided a seminar on the art of pitching at his home (later destroyed by Hurricane Katrina).

. . . .

I WAS A FIRST baseman and outfielder in high school and enjoyed that more than pitching. At first base I was right in the middle of the game at all times. Hitting was fun too. Even in the majors, I took as much extra batting practice as I could because I felt that if I could hit, that would keep me in a lot of close games late in the game and maybe pick up a win. Most pitchers can't hit because they aren't good athletes; all they can do is throw the ball. I played every sport.

I was a lowball pitcher, kept everything down. That was my key to success. My high school coach gave me the nickname "Dusty" because of it. I was a skinny six-footer. The higher I could release the ball from, the more it sloped toward the plate. I thought by pitching straight up overhand and keeping the ball low, the ball was going out of the batter's line of vision. The hitter sees only the top part of the ball, and he'll hit more ground balls than in the air. Casey Stengel once accused me of throwing underground.

We had a power hitter who was drawing a lot of attention from scouts. Red Sox scout Eddie Montague was at the game to look him over. I pitched that day and struck out seventeen. The Cardinals and Tigers were interested in me. New Orleans was a Cardinal farm team. I had some friends who had signed with them, and they warned me that the Cards' "chain gang" had so many players, they were numbers, not names. So when [Cardinals general manager] Branch Rickey came out to the house and talked to my dad, I told him I didn't want to sign with them. I was told how Irish Boston was, and I figured I'd be better off there, being Irish myself. Right after graduation in June 1941 I signed a minor league contract for $150 a month.

I broke in at Centreville, Maryland, in the Class D Eastern Shore League. It was a friendly town. Everybody knew everybody. We stayed at a boarding house. A local hardware man ran the club. We had a horse to cut the grass. No road trips. We rode the bus home at night after every away game, had a ball holding amateur contests where everybody got up and took a turn doing something, maybe stopped and raided a watermelon patch on the way. We were all young. No family responsibilities. Those minor league days were the most fun I ever had in baseball. Once you get up to the major leagues, it becomes more businesslike.

In '42 I was with Canton, Ohio, in the Mid-Atlantic League. I filled in in the outfield on opening day, two for four, drove in all our runs. I wanted to stay in the outfield, but the word came down from Boston: put the little skinny kid back on the mound. I was a little disgruntled over that. The orders were to pitch me once a week. So I pitched every Sunday.

The war interrupted my advance to the major leagues [three years in the army air corps], but I played on base teams. Sometimes we had all pros on a team, playing other service teams and some pro teams. Once we played a Memphis service team against [Phillies pitcher] Hugh Mulcahy. He told me if I could get my release from Boston, he could get me $75,000 to sign. That was big money then. So I wrote to the Red Sox requesting my release and [Boston manager] Joe Cronin wrote me back: forget about it.

At Scranton in '46 we ran away with the Eastern League pennant. I set the league record with a 1.30 ERA.

I started '47 with the Red Sox. In spring training there were six of us fighting for two openings on the pitching staff. Two of them were veterans. Rookies were assigned high-numbered uniforms, but I got 17. I thought that was a good omen. Harry Dorish and I won the two spots. Other players resented us for costing their old friends their jobs. They looked down on us for the first year.

Boston people told me my style was identical to [Hall of Famer] Herb Pennock's. The same smooth delivery. He was the Boston general manager then. I talked to him a lot, but I never saw him pitch.

We opened at home against Washington. The manager, Joe Cronin, comes up to me and says, "Kid, you're starting in Washington." That was three days away. It was a shock to me. I didn't expect to be used that early. I got beat, 3–1.

After you pitched, Cronin would let you know when you'd start again. I liked that. You could set yourself up for that day. If you know when you're going to start, you take it easy the day before, don't run as much. You start thinking about the opposition.

In midseason I was sent down to Louisville. In my fourth game there I was pitching, and a big, strong, muscular guy who looked like Samson hit a line drive back at me. I threw my bare hand up at it, and it broke my ring finger.

Joe McCarthy replaced Cronin in 1948. A manager affects the outcome of maybe five games a year. He has to be the good humor guy, know whose toes to step on, who to pat on the back. He was good at that. A lot of guys were afraid of McCarthy, but I thought he was great. If I owned a team then, I would have hired him without a doubt. He didn't take any bull from anybody. He didn't play up to the press. They would ask him who's pitching tomorrow, and he'd name the whole pitching staff and say, "Pick one. I'll pitch him for you." You knew how you stood with him. If you committed a wrong, he'd take you into his office and chew you out, and you could hear your back end hit the floor. He never showed you up in front of anybody. You respected the man. Cronin never showed you up either, but he never gave you the chewing out that maybe you deserved.

McCarthy didn't like pipe smokers, thought they were too contented, I guess. We got Billy Hitchcock, a pipe smoker, from St. Louis. He joined us in St. Louis. We were in the hotel lobby, and I told him, "The old man doesn't like pipe smokers. Watch out for him." McCarthy walks out of the elevator and heads for us, and Hitchcock grabs his pipe and puts it in his pocket. You could see the smoke coming out of it. McCarthy didn't say anything then, but I bet he did say something later on.

Under McCarthy I'd pitch sometimes with two days of rest. If I was a surprise starter, it didn't bother me. I already knew the hitters. In one series against the Yankees I pitched the first game. Dizzy Trout was supposed to pitch the fourth, but he was frying some chicken and the grease splashed on him and burned him, so I pitched that game too.

I pitched a little differently from most left-handers. I had a good slider, and I kept the ball in tight on right-handed batters, especially at Fenway. The hitter couldn't detect it until the very last minute, and it was too late for him to make an adjustment. I was just talking to Ted Williams about it two days ago. Williams said it many times: the slider was the hardest pitch for him to hit. It looked like a fastball coming to the hitter, and all of a sudden it would dart in on him. If they hit it, it was on the handle. In one game against the Yankees I broke eight bats. But so many pitchers don't throw the *good* slider. They throw a nickel curve, snapping their wrist on it like a curve ball, and get hurt by it. On a lot of occasions I'd throw the curve ball off the plate just to let the hitter see it. I wouldn't want him to hit the curve. Then I'd come back inside with the slider. A good slider is as good a pitch as you can throw. It was my bread and butter, and nobody would change that. If you grip the ball too tight, it won't move. I held it so loose, if I just brushed my hand on my pants leg, the ball would fall out.

I loved the power hitter who wanted to hit the ball out of the park. I could make him overcommit himself, and he's working for me. That happened a lot in Fenway Park—hitters looking at that left-field wall and trying to hit it. I'd throw my slider inside, and these guys are swinging as hard as they can; when the ball moves in on their fists, I've taken the bat out of their hands. The guy going to the opposite field would have better luck. That Green Monster is supposed to be a detriment to pitchers, but the biggest detriment to pitchers at Fenway is the lack of foul territory. Every foul ball that goes into the seats gives the hitter another shot at you. In most parks it's an out. The high fly ball that just kept carrying and went out is the one that got you in Fenway.

When I pitched, I checked with my catcher after the first inning to find out what each of my pitches was doing, so when I got in a jam, I'd know what pitches to go to.

We had a meeting before the first game of every series, and everybody had a chance to comment on how to pitch to them. Pitchers and catchers did most of the talking. Ted Williams was a good observer of opponents. My book on Joe DiMaggio was to keep it in tight on him; don't let him swing with his arms extended. I had good luck with him and Mantle. But Luke Appling, Harvey Kuenn, Lou Boudreau—free swingers, not power hitters—gave me trouble.

We finished the '48 season tied with Cleveland. The one-game playoff was at Boston. I was in bed at nine the night before, all set to pitch the biggest game of the year. McCarthy always put a new ball under your cap in your locker if you were starting that day. When I got to the clubhouse, the ball was under my cap. I'm sitting there and after a while I start getting dressed. He comes out of his office and comes up behind me, puts his hand on my shoulder, and says, "Kid, I've changed my mind. I'm going with the right-hander. The elements are against a left-hander today." He had seen the wind blowing out to left field and figured it wasn't a left-hander's day. Then he said to the clubhouse boy, Don Fitzpatrick, "Run outside and get Galehouse."

I was disappointed not being able to pitch that game, but it was his decision. Galehouse had pitched well against Cleveland on the last road trip. He comes in and McCarthy tells him he's pitching, and it's a complete shock to Galehouse. I got dressed and went out on the field, and all the guys are asking me, "What are you doing out here?"

"I'm not pitching."

"You gotta be kidding."

"I'm not kidding. Galehouse is the pitcher today."

Cleveland manager Lou Boudreau thought McCarthy was playing tricks on him, trying to make him get a left-hand-hitting lineup in there against Galehouse while I was warming up under the stands. He sent outfielder Allie Clark to look under the stands to see if I was there throwing. [Boudreau hit two home runs in Cleveland's 8–4 win.]

In '49 we got beat out by the Yankees by one game at the end. They had a little bit better club than we had. They had the big guy who could come out of the bullpen—Joe Page. We didn't have that. We could have. Chicago was trying to get rid of Max Surkont, and he could have been our Joe Page in the bullpen. But [general manager] Joe Cronin didn't make the deal. Why he didn't, I don't know. Maybe they wanted somebody he wouldn't give up.

Our pitching staff wasn't deep. Kinder won twenty-three and I won twenty-five [Parnell worked 295 innings, led the league with twenty-seven complete games, with a 2.78 ERA.] But the rest of the staff could not match us.

By the stats you'd think I was wild [134 walks], but I wasn't. In Fenway you pitch around some hitters, and that gives you more walks.

Joe DiMaggio missed the first half of the season with a heel injury. But he came back and destroyed us in a three-game series at Fenway the end of June. I pitched the third game. I vowed he was not going to hit one off me if I had to walk him four times. New York led, 3–2, in the top of the seventh. He's up with two on and two out, and I'm thinking on the mound, "If this guy's going to beat me now, he'll have to beat my best pitch." That day it was my fastball. My first pitch, he hits a pop fly outside first base. Billy Goodman is under it, and it hits the heel of his glove and drops to the ground. I groaned inside. But you have to keep your composure, can't let it get you. You know you make mistakes of your own. Now I'm thinking, "Should I throw him something else?" He was late on my fastball. So I threw him another one. He hits a little topper that spins around near home plate foul. Two strikes. I threw a breaking ball off the plate and then came back with my fastball. A pitcher can tell by the sound if it's gone. He hit it into the light tower in left field, and I can hear the steel of that light tower ringing for five minutes after. I'll never forget that one.

That year my arm hurt all the time. I'd be in the whirlpool before I went out and started throwing. A lot of games I pitched using Capsilum, a red salve that's as hot as can be. It will burn the daylights out of you. Not too many people can use it. It would create heat in my shoulder. And if you didn't get it all off and got into the shower, it got twice as hot. I talked Ellis Kinder into trying it. He came in screaming, it hurt so bad. And I had elbow trouble that led to an operation. Sometimes the trainer gave me a shot of cortisone in the elbow. A lot of guys would be sore after pitching, and they'd go out and throw the next day. I couldn't until the second day. The elbow trouble was from tearing a muscle from the bone. My shoulder problem was probably rotator cuff, which we didn't know about then.

We took pride in finishing what we started. That's gone. One day in 1951 I was pitching. It was one of those days when I felt real good, but I was getting hit pretty hard in the first inning. The manager, Steve O'Neill, sent a coach out to take me out. I told him, "Get the hell out of here. I started this thing, and I'm going to finish it." He goes back to the dugout and tells O'Neill. Next thing I know, I see him coming back out to the mound. He says, "If you don't get out of here, it's going to cost you $500." I said, "For $500 you can have the ball." I threw it up in the air and left.

I tried to talk Lou Boudreau out of taking me out of a game one time. I was leading, 3–0. I told him afterward, "Don't ever do that to me again. If I'm pitching a shutout, there must be something working for me." He said I was getting tired. I said, "I'll tell you when I'm getting tired. Don't tell me."

Boudreau was the only manager I ever had who tried to call the pitches. When I pitched, I told him, "Forget about it. I'll throw what I want to throw, not what you want me to throw. I get a different view of the game when I'm on the mound than you do in that dugout." He can't detect movement by the hitter in the batter's box. I could and my catcher could. He can't tell when I have a ball in my hand if it's suitable for a breaking pitch or a fastball. A new ball is a little slicker with not much friction, and a ball could slide out of the fingers real quick, and that ball sometimes would react differently, almost like a knuckle ball. Balls are all the same size, but sometimes one ball would feel a little bigger in your hand than another. Sometimes you get a ball with high raised stitching on it. That gives you a chance to get a good grip to throw a breaking pitch and get the rotation on it. That's as important as the hitter and the count and the situation. The catcher calls the game, but the pitcher can shake him off. It's his game. You shake him off if you have a ball in your hand that feels different and something in mind that you want to do with it. Pitchers have a sixth sense of what they are able to do with that particular pitch that nobody else knows or feels. Boudreau called pitches with some guys but not me. It's my game to win or lose. I got that settled right quick

Sammy White was to me a great catcher. We had a lot of confidence in him. A good catcher is one who can handle a low pitch, has a good arm, can understand you as well as you understand him. He'd say, "Just throw it. If I can't catch it, I'll block it." A fellow tells you that, you have a lot of confidence in him.

I thought it was ridiculous to throw at a hitter after the guy ahead of him had hit a home run. That guy didn't do it. I never had any pressure to throw at anybody. But some other pitchers did. In spring training one year we had a young pitcher, Russ Kemmerer. We were playing the Phillies in Montgomery, Alabama, and Karl Drews was pitching for the Phillies. He hit one of our players, and Lou Boudreau told Kemmerer, "Next time Drews comes to the plate, you hit him." The Phils had big numbers on their uniforms, and Drews was number 22. Kemmerer hit him right between those twos. Down went Drews. Granny Hamner was the first one out of their dugout. Steve O'Neill was their manager. Our catcher, Sammy White, hollered to O'Neill, "Steve, you better get back in the dugout. You're too old. But let Hamner keep coming." With that, Hamner's steps kept getting shorter and shorter.

I think it's a falsehood about the Red Sox being so well paid and contented that they did not have the drive to win in '47–'48–'49. Mr. Yawkey was such a great man, you wanted to give a hundred percent for him. It wasn't a country club ball club. We battled all we could and just got beat. The press wanted to find other reasons. So they always went back to the notion that we were treated too good.

Most travel was by train then, but we would always fly back from a road trip. Yawkey wanted us to get back and have more time with our families. Jackie Jensen and Del Wilber feared flying. They took the train when they could. But they were aboard on one of the worst flights we ever had. We took off from Washington, and everything was fine. Then we got tangled up in a cluster of thunderstorms around Philadelphia. A hole broke open in the top of the plane, and we dropped about fifteen hundred feet. Some guys were about to go berserk and panic out. Hy Hurwitz, the writer, had a little mezuzah, and he was rubbing it. One of the guys told him to put it away; he couldn't trade it for a parachute. A coach got flipped out of his seat and busted a rib. I was sitting by the stewardess in the rear, and the pilot kept buzzing her. She told me she wasn't about to try to walk through that airplane. We figured school was out. The pilot told us afterward he had never experienced anything like it. He was soaking wet, perspiration rolling off him.

The wives were waiting at the airport, and all they were told was the flight was delayed. They knew nothing else. We were a mess when we landed in Boston. When I got home, my wife made me a cup of coffee. I took one swallow, and it wouldn't go down. My heart was up there in the way.

On the trains there were some regular card games, but we talked a lot of baseball: how to pitch to hitters, strategies, opinions of other players. They don't do that now. Rookies started out in the upper berths until they got promoted to a lower. I was lucky; at least I started out in the middle of the car, not over the wheels.

Who kept us loose? Maury McDermott. Al Zarilla. And of course Jim Piersall. You never knew what he was going to do. I was pitching in Chicago one day, and I heard a roar from right field. I stepped off the mound and looked around, and all I could see was the back of his uniform. He's leading a locomotive cheer with the fans, spelling out P-I-E-R-S-A-L-L. If I had continued pitching and a ball was hit to right field, he wouldn't have seen it, and there's no way he could make a play. To get a big hand from the fans, he'd time himself to get to a fly ball just in time to catch it. Sometimes he didn't get there in time.

McDermott was my roommate on the road. In 1954 he was with Washington. One day he's pitching against me. We were going to go out to dinner that night. I'm batting lefty, and he threw a pitch that looked like it would be a strike. I started my swing, and all of a sudden it tailed off into me. I threw my left arm up in front of my face, and the ball hit the ulna bone and broke it. Maury was tearful when he came to see me afterward. I didn't start again for three months.

Ray Scarborough was our loudest bench jockey. We'd ask Lou Boudreau to run him to the bullpen to get him out of the dugout. He got Bill McGowan suspended once, needling him from the dugout. McGowan got tired of hearing it and comes over to the dugout and gives Ray some choice words and throws his ball-and-strike indicator at him. It went under the bench. Ray is down looking for it. When he gets it, McGowan says, "Give me my ball-and-strike indicator." Ray says, "Like hell. See [league president] Will Harridge. He'll give it to you."

McGowan says, "I better not be behind the plate when you're pitching."

Ray says, "Don't worry. I won't be pitching that day. I'll have a sore arm."

Will Harridge suspended McGowan.

Ted Williams was and is a good guy. He got a bad press because they wanted to dig into his personal life and his past. Ted didn't want to talk about that kind of stuff. They'd keep probing until he told them where to go, and it built up a hate relationship. He worked hard on his hitting. I give him credit for some of my success. I'd throw batting practice to him under game conditions, not tell him what was coming. If I could figure him out, the rest of the guys would be easy. In left field he didn't look impressive covering ground, but he played that wall as good as anybody could. I thought he was a better left fielder than Yaz [Carl Yastrzemski].

One time Ted was called out on strikes at Fenway, and in the dugout he and Cronin got into a discussion about home plate. Williams said, "I wouldn't have been called out if home plate was in line, but it isn't." All of us pitchers sitting on the bench are laughing out loud. Home plate looked fine to us. The next morning he and Cronin are out there with the grounds crew taking measurements and checking the alignment from the mound to home plate, and darned if home plate isn't out of line.

I was a good hitter. I liked to hit against fastballers like Allie Reynolds. On slow stuff I'd lunge too much. I hit one home run, in Chicago, over the bullpen in right-center. I can still see that pitch coming toward me, a hard fastball right down the middle, belt high. I took my time around the bases, and when I got back to the dugout, the guys gave me the silent treatment, which was the practice when a pitcher hit one. I gave them a big blast, and they broke out laughing.

I can also still visualize some pitches I threw. I remember the best curve ball I ever threw. It was in Yankee Stadium. Tommy Henrich, a left-handed batter, was up. The pitch was low, knee high, just over the outside of the plate, right where I wanted it. Somehow Henrich got the bat around to pull that ball into the upper deck. I couldn't believe it. Cal Hubbard, the home plate umpire, came halfway out to the mound to give me a new ball. He says, "Kid, you keep throwing like that, you'll win a lot of ball games." I said, "Yeah, that's fine. But how did I make out with that one?"

The day I threw a no-hitter, I could put the sinker any place I wanted. I mixed it with my slider for an in and out pitch. During the game it was very quiet on the bench. Jackie Jensen came over to me in the seventh and said, "You're going for a no-hitter. Don't let them hit it to right field. I don't want to be the guy to mess it up." I said, "Jackie, forget it. If it happens, it happens. I want the win; that's all I'm looking for." The other guys got a little uptight, not me.

Last guy up was Walt Dropo, an ex-teammate. He hit a ground ball to the first base side of the mound. I fielded it and continued to first to make the play unassisted. First baseman Mickey Vernon said, "What's the matter, you don't have any confidence in me?" I said, "I might have thrown the thing away." It's the only no-hitter where the pitcher made the last putout unassisted.

I don't believe it when a pitcher says he didn't know he was going for a no-hitter. Every time you look at the scoreboard you see all those zeroes. From the seventh inning on, the fans let you know it, making noise on every out, and you hear all that.

[Mel's wife, Velma, joined us, and I asked her about her life as a baseball wife.]

Velma: I loved the life of a baseball wife in Boston. Our children did too. They got to meet and know other people from outside the south.

Three of them were born in the north. When school was out, they couldn't wait to see their friends, who were waiting for them. We never took them out of school early. Some baseball kids were in four schools in one year. Our children are all in the medical field today.

All the packing and driving and getting settled and driving back in September was up to me. I'd drive up with my mother, three kids, and a dog. Two-lane highways, no motel chains, took four days. Once I was stopped for speeding somewhere in Maryland, and the cop said, "What's with you wives? I just stopped [third baseman] Hank Majeski's wife for speeding."

My mother babysat, and I went to a lot of games. We always sat behind the catcher. One night it was sold out, so we had to sit behind first base. Mel started and wasn't doing too well, and this drunk behind us said, "The trouble with Parnell is too much wine, women, and song." My face turned red as a beet. I turned around and said something to him, I don't remember what. He said, "Boy, thirty-five thousand people in the ballpark, and I had to sit behind his wife."

People want others to think they know players better than they do and spread this kind of stuff. Somebody said something like that to Ellis Kinder's wife, and she was going to get up and hit him. They had Vern Stephens and me starting a riot in a bar in Springfield, Massachusetts. We had never been there. A lot of that goes around.

Bench jockeys didn't bother me—most of them. Al Simmons, then the Cleveland third base coach, could break my concentration, yelling stuff like, "You have no right beating us." One day I called time and walked over and told him, "If you open your mouth one more time, I'm going to drill you right in that coach's box." He shut up after that. Yankees pitcher Tommy Byrne bothered me, trying to impress on you that he was stealing pitches. I told him, "Go ahead, keep calling them," and I'd whistle a fastball under the hitter's chin.

If I could choose one umpire to work behind the plate when I'm pitching, it would be Bill Summers or Bill McGowan, who was hard to get along with but a great umpire. They were real bear-down guys, took control of the game, even though they missed some.

We could say more than players can today, and the fans liked it. The ump would let you sound off, and then he'd say, "Okay, I've had enough. Any more out of you and you're gone." Or they'd just walk away. Today it's ridiculous. The umps yell back and go after the players. That's bad. The fans loved to see a little rhubarb. They've taken one of the most colorful scenes out of the game.

McGowan ran me once at the end of a game. Nellie Fox walked on a pitch right down the middle and ran to first base laughing. He was sacrificed to second and wound up scoring the winning run. I gave McGowan some choice words and he ran me, but the game was over. "You'll get a letter from the league office," he said, and I did.

Who would I want for a defensive lineup behind me when I was pitching? Third base George Kell, shortstop Phil Rizzuto, second Bobby Doerr, first Mickey Vernon. Sammy White or Jim Hegan catching. I'd take Dom DiMaggio over his brother Joe in center field, put Joe in left, and Piersall in right when he wasn't clowning

If I had one game to win today, I would choose Roger Clemens. He's the bulldog type, strictly business out there, and that's the way you gotta be. You have to be a bully out there.

When a muscle tore from my elbow and the doctor told me I'd need an operation and then two more, I said one's enough, and I was finished. The Red Sox talked me into doing some managing in the minors, and I didn't like it. Putting up with the kids and their problems, you had to be mother, father, doctor, lawyer. There was always something: parents knocking on your door, complaining about something between their daughter and a player, police knocking on your door about shooting street lights out or something. I decided, man, I don't need this. I scouted for a year, did some broadcasting in Chicago and Boston, but got tired of the travel and came home, started a pest control company, sold it, and retired.

36.

Claude Passeau

. . . .

Claude Passeau may be the only pitcher who ever won a World Series game and didn't like baseball until he was in his thirties—and then only because it paid better and was easier than farming. Despite that, he was an old-fashioned workhorse of a pitcher; in twelve full seasons with the Pirates, Phillies, and Cubs (1936–1947), he averaged over fifteen complete games and 227 innings pitched, with a high of 292 in 1937.

Passeau is also the game's greatest nemesis for minor league researchers; he played under so many different names, even he could not remember them all. (Not to mention that his "real" name kept changing with the whims of family members, including himself.)

Camellias and azaleas were in bloom, yellow finches were at the feeders, redbirds and quail flew by as he and his wife invited me in. She then excused herself: "I've heard these stories before."

. . . .

MY PEOPLE CAME FROM Alsace-Lorraine, France. They came to Escatawba, Mississippi, across the river, to a community called Passeauques. That was too long, so they cut it to Passeau. People couldn't understand that, so my grandmother said, "I'll settle that," and spelled it Passo. In my second or third year in college, I changed it back to Passeau. No legalities to it.

My father was a sawyer in a sawmill. I was born in 1909 in Waynesboro, Mississippi. In those days they moved the sawmills around to the trees, not the other way around. Every little town had a baseball team.

In high school we only had twelve boys, and I was number 12. When somebody was out, I played third base, outfield. Never did get around to pitching until my senior year. I pitched a few games, and we won the southern division state high school championship and got beat in the state championship. But I wasn't interested in playing baseball. All I wanted to do was hunt turkeys, geese, and quail, and fish.

When I was fourteen, I was going fishing with my brother one day, driving along this bumpy country road. He had put his .38 pistol on the seat under him with his coat over it. He said to me, "Take that gun out from under me," and I did, and it went off, right through my left hand.

I tried to get in the navy when I was sixteen. I told them I was eighteen. They wouldn't take me; said I couldn't even shave.

I went to Millsaps College—about nine hundred students—at no cost and a little [money] on the side, and during my freshman year I played football and basketball. It was all in the same dressing room; when I turned in my football uniform, I got my basketball uniform. I didn't go out for baseball. I wanted to be a football coach.

I didn't want to work. I thought school teaching would be ideal. After my freshman year some of my studies were just eating me up. I was always so tired. I played football and basketball, ran the 440, and threw the javelin on the track team for a month or so and finally just quit track.

It was understood that if you weren't playing some athletics, you would be sweeping out the dorm or waiting on tables in the cafeteria, and one day the coach said to me, "Why aren't you out for baseball?" I told him, "Coach, I don't play baseball." He said, "Yes, you do. I saw you play in the state championships." I had played center field in one game. So I went out for baseball. I was just like all hard-headed youngsters. I didn't want to, didn't like it. So I just went out in the outfield and dogged it. I wouldn't even take batting practice. Finally the coach got disgusted with me and had me pitch batting practice. I acted like I didn't know how to stand on the mound or anything, just to get out of playing. I didn't want to be there, so I started throwing hard, and the hitters didn't like that. We had two starting pitchers and were losing games, and he would put me in as a relief pitcher.

After my freshman year I couldn't find a job, so I went up to the Delta and played semipro ball, which students weren't supposed to do. A Detroit scout, Eddie Goosetree, kept after me to sign, and I kept telling him, "I just don't like baseball. Only reason I'm playing here is I can't get a job doing anything else." He said, "Well, my job is to sign you, even if you don't report." But $350 a month was a good contract in those days. I signed under the name "Passo."

This was all illegal. I played under the name "Jones" for a few months—all Class C and D—played for two or three paydays, quit, and went to another team under a different name. I played from Montreal to Mexico City. I believe I played under the name "Newman" in the Western League. In the Carolina League a boy walked up to me one day and said, "What's your name?" I told him whoever I was then. He said, "I coulda sworn I played against you last year and your name was something else." I was playing under so many different names in 1929-'30-'31, sometimes I really had difficulty remembering who I was.

I believe it was my first year in the major leagues that I got a letter from the president of the minor leagues: "Will you please make up your mind what name you're going to play under? All our records are messed up."

I was still the property of the Detroit club when I graduated in 1932. They sent me to Decatur in the Three-I League. After thirty-two days the league broke up. Then they sent me to Moline. The next year at Beaumont in the Texas League they tried to change the way I threw. The changes threw off my control.

Now I was just pitching. But I never learned how to throw a curve ball. Never. Best I could do was what I called a spinner. Broke about four inches. All I ever used was an overhand fastball—made it drop or sail a little bit—some change-up. Location. That was it. The ball came off my middle finger. End of a game, it was raw. For years hitters complained that I was throwing a spitter. Commissioner Landis even called me to his office one time to talk about the complaints and warn me that if I was doing it, I would be suspended. But I wasn't using it, and nobody ever found any evidence that I was.

In 1935 I went to spring training with Milwaukee, and they released me. Des Moines offered me $250 a month. I wanted $300. I said, "I'll stay a month, and if I'm not worth $300, release me." I stayed and got the $300. I was 20-11. That's where I became friends with a young radio broadcaster—Ronald Reagan.

Now I'm twenty-six years old and decided that was my last year. Eating hamburgers and riding buses was not for me.

Then Pittsburgh bought me. The Pirates had an older team, and I'm a rookie. The clubhouse boy led me to a locker in a corner. One player came over to me and held out his hand and said, "I'm Paul Waner." I rose up about that high. After that, whenever a young fellow joined our club, I made it a point to go over and introduce myself to him. After I got into one game, they made me the throw-in in a deal with the Phillies. The owner, Gerry Nugent, was a fine fellow, but he had no money. I made $3,000 my first big league year; the next year, $4,500. In two years I pitched in ninety-nine games. With the Phillies I asked for number 13. I tried chewing tobacco; damn near killed me when I swallowed it in a game.

Because of my being shot in the left hand, some fingers were drawn up, and I had to put my glove on slowly, one finger at a time. So I had them make me a smaller glove. I practiced my fielding extra because of it. And I would rub the ball in my glove rather than in my hands. One day Bill Terry came out to umpire Bill Klem and complained about it. I said, "Mr. Klem, I've got a crippled hand; if I take the ball out of the glove and rub it, I'm slow enough as it is. We'll never get through the game." I showed him my crippled hand. That was the end of that.

The Phillies traded me to the Cubs in May 1939. I reported to them in Brooklyn. And they started me. Gabby Hartnett was the manager. In the meetings he'd tell the pitcher how to pitch to each man. I'd faced Brooklyn before and knew the hitters and they knew me. They knew I didn't have a curve and I couldn't throw my little spinner outside. So Hartnett is telling me to throw curves down and away to left-handed batters. He gets down five or six left-handed batters that way, and finally I said, "Skipper, I just can't pitch that way." I struck out a bunch and we won the game, and afterward Hartnett says to me, "When I tell you how to pitch to hitters, don't pay any attention to me."

I had a good year, 20-11 with a 2.50 ERA. I went up to see the owner, Mr. Wrigley, and we talked about sailboats and airplanes. Finally he said, "I know you didn't come up here to talk about that." I said, "Mr. Wrigley, I'd like to sign my contract before I go home. I don't want to go home in doubt. I won twenty games." I'm thinking maybe I'll get a $500 raise. We always had beer in the clubhouse. I'd drink one or two after a game, but that was the extent of my drinking. I said, "You never have to worry about me being ready to pitch." I got through telling him about my pluses, and he said, "You forgot about one thing. You lost eleven."

I pitched everybody inside and didn't give up many home runs. When I was pitching, I didn't talk to anybody, and nobody talked to me on the bench. My catcher on the Cubs, Clyde McCullough, said when I was out there, I was the meanest SOB he ever saw. I didn't care if I hit a batter or not, and they all knew it. Nobody ever came at me out on the mound 'cause they knew if they did, the next game they would get it worse. Leo Durocher was always on me. Once he was set to bunt, and I threw the ball right at him. The ball hit the bat and then him. One day I wound up and threw it right into the dugout where he was. To hold a man on first, I just stood there and held the ball till he relaxed, and he'd lost a step that way. When I was being relieved, I never left the mound until the reliever arrived. I wanted to hand him the ball myself. Nobody else did that.

I never took the game home. Win or lose 1–0 was all the same. When I left the ballpark, I was in a different world.

[In the 1941 All-Star Game, Passeau threw the pitch that Ted Williams hit for the game-winning home run in the bottom of the ninth. **NM:** Can you still see that pitch?]

I see it every time somebody asks me about it. I had pitched two hard games on Thursday and Sunday before going to Detroit on Tuesday, not expecting to play at all. Reds manager Bill McKechnie is the All-Star manager. He says to me, "Passeau, you'll pitch the seventh and eighth." I was dead tired. But I went out and pitched the seventh and eighth. [The NL led, 5–4.] Then I headed for the clubhouse. McKechnie says to me, "Don't go in. Go ahead and pitch the ninth."

I went out there and grit my teeth. [With two on and two out] Williams hit a fly ball that dropped into the overhang of the upper deck. I just stuck my glove in my pocket and walked off the field.

In 1943 we had Eddie Stanky, a little gamecock second baseman, and Lou Novikoff, the mad Russian. Stanky didn't get along with anybody. We left him alone. Opening day Rip Sewell was pitching; he couldn't crack a window. Stanky's leading off. Second pitch, Rip hit him on top of the head. Stanky fell over. Hack, batting second, and the umpire looked at him and didn't help him in any way. Our trainer didn't even come off the bench to see if he was all right. Stanky's on the ground two or three minutes. That's what we thought of him. I just didn't like his ways. I guess in his way he was a nice fellow. It just wasn't my way.

One of Stanky's boys in Mobile wound up marrying my niece.

One day I'm pitching and Novikoff's playing left field. A fly ball was hit to him; he's charging back toward the fence and turns, and the ball lands way in front of him. When the inning was over, I said to him, "Lou, there's a little girl in the stands can play left field better than you." I finally got to like the game a little for the simple reason that when I was at home, I worked like a slave from five thirty or six in the morning to eleven at night. I had some land, and we didn't have machines to clean up underbrush. I wanted to farm some of it, and we did the cleanup by hand, and that was hard. So when I went to spring training, I was going on vacation. That's the only reason I liked baseball. But I gave it my best.

In 1945 I had bone chips in my elbow. Little pieces of cartilage would chip off. I never had an operation.

[The Cubs lost the 1945 seven-game World Series to Detroit. Passeau won Game 3, 3–0. Rudy York's second-inning single was the Tigers' only hit.] I didn't know I had a one-hitter, just knew we had the lead. [The Cubs had acquired right-hander Hank Borowy from the Yankees in midseason.] Borowy was a frail fellow. Good curve ball. Could go five innings and that's all. He pitched in Games 5 and 6, and we were surprised when [Cubs manager] Charlie Grimm started him in Game 7.

In February 1947 I had a back operation. They trimmed a few discs. I thought I was through. I had some therapy, and in August I was pitching. I was making about $18,000. Then the Cubs released me.

I missed the game a little but not the traveling. I missed the paydays mostly.

I managed in the low minors for the Cubs at Centralia and Visalia, had two last-place teams, then quit. I couldn't put up with halfhearted boys who wouldn't work.

Later my poker pals put me up to running for sheriff here. I was elected twice, 1967–1975. Domestic disturbances mostly. Half the time I didn't even carry a gun.

37.

George Pipgras

George Pipgras was a right-handed pitcher for the 1923–1933 Yankees, leading the league with 24 wins and 301 innings pitched in 1928. Pipgras was 3-0 in three World Series. After he broke his arm in 1934, he became an American League umpire for nine years. He reminisced while sitting in a wingback chair in his home in Inverness.

DESPITE THE PRESENCE OF so many Hall of Famers—Ruth and Gehrig and Lazzeri and Combs and Dickey and Hoyt and Pennock—and Bob Meusel belongs there too—there were no rivalries. I never saw any kind of friction in the clubhouse.

Babe Ruth's heart was as big as he was. But us young players risked a thousand dollar fine if we went out partying with him. He was considered hazardous to our health.

With all that power in the lineup, we pitchers didn't feel any pressure. We paced ourselves and pitched a lot of complete games. We'd get ahead and let up, still putting something on the ball but letting them hit it.

When I was sold to the Red Sox in 1933 and had to pitch to Ruth, I copied the way Ted Lyons used to pitch to him: get behind in the count, then throw a strike or two past him. One day I faced him with the bases loaded. The count went full, then I gave him a big motion and threw a slow curve. He was way out in front, figuring fastball. He could be fooled that way.

Miller Huggins was a very nervous manager but a good guy. I was sitting alongside him on the bench one day, and he put a pitcher, Joe Bush, in to pinch-hit. Bush hit it out of the park, but Hug never saw it. He had his head down. He says to me, "What did he do, George? What did he do?" I said, "He just hit one out of the ballpark."

Huggins was also very demanding. In 1928 I had 22 wins by September, but after I lost one, he called me into his office. "I'm not going to tell you how good you are," he said. "I'm going to tell you how lousy you are." Then he explained the mistake I had made on the pitch that cost me the game. "You think it over," he said, and the meeting was over. I left there thinking, "I've won 22 so far; what else do you have to do around here?"

Hug was a little guy, 5-foot-6½, and weighed 140 pounds. He never came out on the field to change pitchers but sent out a coach. I rarely saw him argue a call or get thrown out of a game. Once, in 1922, he was coaching first base when the leadoff man, Whitey Witt, beat out a bunt. But the umpire, Bill Guthrie, a burly 240-pound Irishman from Chicago, called Witt out. Witt lit into him and was thrown out of the game. When Huggins got into it, Guthrie jerked a thumb in his direction and said to Witt, "And take da batboy wid ya."

Guthrie was fired soon after that, but they brought him back in 1928. In the meantime, Bill ran a flower shop in Chicago. One day somebody came in and asked for some bachelor buttons, and Bill says, "Dis is not a tailor shop; dis is a flower shop."

I never argued with an umpire. Herb Pennock once told me, "Remember, you make more mistakes than they do." The first year I became an umpire, the players didn't say much to me. The second year, they started in a little. It's the third year where you make or break yourself. That's when they found out I wouldn't take anything from a player. One day in a Browns–White Sox game in 1940 I cleared both benches—seventeen players.

I was behind the plate one night in Cleveland. Bob Feller and Elden Auker were the pitchers. Suddenly the air was full of Canadian butterflies that came in off the lake. It was like snow falling on the field. When you walked, you heard them crunching under your feet. I told both pitchers and catchers I didn't want to hear any squawks out of them that night, and I didn't.

One day in Philly I was working first base and there came a play where I called the runner safe, but under the photo in the paper the next day it said he was out. The caption said, "Pipgras misses another one." I took the picture to league president Will Harridge and said, "How would you call this?" He said, "Out." I said, "I called him safe." He said, "Show me how." I showed him and told him that the best evidence that I was right was that nobody on the field squawked at my call.

I called a balk on one of Connie Mack's pitchers one day. The pitcher stood back of the rubber and made a motion like he was going to pitch, then turned and threw and caught the runner fifteen feet off the bag. After the game Mack and one of his coaches came into the umps' dressing room, and Mack said he didn't think that was a balk, and I showed him where it was in the rule book. The coach pulls out a dog-eared book and says he can't find it in his book, and I said, "What year you got?" It was about fifteen years old. They turned and walked out.

Umpires aren't infallible. Pants Rowland was the worst umpire I ever saw. He had no minor league experience. One day he said to his partner, Bill Dinneen, "I had a good day today. I didn't miss one." And Bill said to him, "You missed a hundred."

I have two world championship rings and a wristwatch. I also had a pocket watch from the 1923 world champions, but it was stolen. It was a Gruen with a gold chain and a little gold baseball for a fob. In the spring of 1926 I had to change trains in Memphis, and while I was waiting outside the station, two stickup men robbed me. I started to chase them, but one guy turned around, and I was looking down the barrel of a pistol that looked as big as a cannon. That was the last I saw of them or the watch.

[The watch turned up in the shop of a Virginia memorabilia dealer three years after Pipgras died in 1987.]

38.

Johnny Roseboro
PITTSBURGH, JUNE 10, 1990

• •

Born in Ashland, Ohio, in 1933, Johnny Roseboro was a catcher for the Dodgers in Brooklyn and Los Angeles (1957–1970), then two years with the Twins and one with the Washington Senators. He played in four World Series and three All-Star Games. At the time I visited him in his hotel room while he was in Pittsburgh for an old-timers game, he was a roving minor league catching instructor for the Dodgers.

When I called him to request an interview, he was at first reluctant but finally agreed. At the appointed time I knocked on his door with some apprehension. The door opened. A stocky, six-foot man with an unwelcoming expression said, "How long will this take?" "As much time as you will give me," I said.

Ninety minutes later I had learned about the art and science of catching, what it was like to catch Don Drysdale and Sandy Koufax, and the frustration of a black man trying to break into baseball management in the 1970s and '80s.

• •

I WAS SIGNED IN 1952 as a catcher by Dodgers scout Cliff Alexander, who happened to be Walter Alston's brother-in-law. They sent me to Sheboygan in the Class D Wisconsin State League. I chipped a knuckle in my first game, and after that I played outfield and some first base. I really preferred the outfield. I could hit and run and threw well. My first manager was Joe Hauser. He taught me a lot about hitting to all fields and bunting. He showed us how to take infield practice and made it fun. We put on a show. I still prefer to see infield taken that way today. He would hit shots and tell us, "If you can't catch it in practice, you can't catch it in a game."

I went to C ball, then the army for two years in Germany, then A ball for a month, mostly as an outfielder. I wasn't a very good catcher, so they sent me down to Class B Cedar Rapids to learn catching.

[**NM:** What was the hardest thing to learn as a catcher?]

I ask the same thing of the kids I teach now, and I wonder why they don't tell me what I consider the most difficult thing of all, and that is why you put the finger down that you do, what you want to accomplish when you call a pitch. Mostly catchers try to fool hitters. They say, "I got a curve ball over; let me try a fastball," or "I got a fastball over; he's looking for a curve; let me put another fastball." After my first year it got to be a chess match back there. If I wanted a ground ball to the right side of the infield, then my infield would play that way, we'd pitch that way, and most of the time we'd get what we wanted, unless we missed the spot.

You are not trying to outfox the hitter. Satchel Paige and Sal Maglie both taught me a basic philosophy of catching which I've carried over for years: the object of pitching is to take away the hitter's power and make him hit the ball where you want him to hit it. Strikeouts come after you have worked to a certain point. Take away the hitter's power and you can beat him.

I was at Montreal in June 1957 when the Dodgers called me up to replace Gil Hodges, who was sick or hurt at the time, so I played my first three major league games at first base.

I didn't have many big offensive days in my career. The biggest was a three-run home run off Whitey Ford in Game 1 of the 1963 World Series that gave Sandy Koufax a 5-2 win.

The move from Ebbets Field to the Los Angeles Coliseum was a dread for us left-handed hitters. The short porch was in left field, with a screen. From left-center to right was a pretty good drive in a taxicab. But the good thing about the Coliseum was that it taught us how to pitch. We had to pitch away from the hitters' power and get them to hit to the long part of the park. That did us well when we got to Dodgers Stadium. We had learned how to keep the ball from the middle away most of the time.

[**NM:** Do you go with a pitcher's strength even if it's the hitter's strength too?]

If the pitcher is a fastball pitcher and the hitter a fastball hitter and the pitcher doesn't know where the pitch is going, he's in trouble. When you talk about Don Drysdale and Sandy Koufax, and the hitter's strength is fastball, there are very few hitters that can handle a fastball on the outside part of the plate. Even a guy throwing 70 can throw a ball on the outside corner—the black—that'll get most hitters out. Drysdale and Koufax, who are throwing 90-plus on the black part of the plate and using the fastball to move batters back off the plate when we get ahead in the count—I defy somebody to get a hit. It's just not possible. Occasionally a Harmon Killebrew might hit one on the black out of the park in right field, but those guys are few and far between.

I told Ted Williams once, "If you were hitting against the Dodgers and hit .400, you would do it to left field and off your ass, 'cause we would knock you down or make you hit the ball to left field, or, better yet, not even pitch to you, 'cause the guy coming up behind you can't be as good as you are. We'd put you on first base and let you clog up the base paths."

Koufax's fastball tailed just a hair on the outside part of the plate. He didn't throw any fastballs from the middle in unless he was moving batters back off the plate or striking them out. He wouldn't knock you down, but he would come up under your chin. When you throw 94 miles an hour and you throw one up and in, God can't hit it.

Koufax had a great curve, better than Drysdale's. If we work our system right, by the time you get to two strikes, you don't know whether it's going to be a fastball in or a fastball away or a big curve ball, so we're sitting in the driver's seat with three pitches we can throw. I could put down any finger and get the best pitch from the best pitcher in either league.

I've read a lot of people getting credit for it, but nobody really knows why or how Koufax suddenly gained control. One day he was shipped out to Montreal 'cause he was so wild, and the next thing you know, he's striking out everybody.

With an 0-2 count on a right-handed batter, Drysdale would come sidearm inside with a 96 m.p.h., and when the hitter saw me move my glove inside, his intestinal fortitude will not let him look outside. So many a time Drysdale would then just throw that ball on the outside corner—strike three. Better than messing with a waste pitch where the count becomes 1-2 and you come back and miss with another pitch, and suddenly it's 2-2. Now the hitter's in the driver's seat 'cause you got to throw a strike or you are in deeper.

I didn't talk behind the plate to distract the batter, but I might say something to fool him. After I gave a sign for an outside fastball, I might move inside and say something so the batter hears my voice close to him and is looking for an inside pitch. But the pitchers knew that no matter what I did, the outside target would be there by the time they got to their release point. Or I'd move away from the batter so he's looking outside after I've signed for an inside pitch.

In a possible double steal situation, I'd go out to the mound and discuss with the infielders the four or five options we had on how to play it. If Koufax was pitching, he'd say, "I don't care about the base runners. I have a better chance of getting the batter out than making one of those plays." Drysdale would try to pick somebody off.

I loved the slider. It's hard for a left-handed batter to hit it breaking in on his knees. For a right-handed batter it gives you two curves. It's easier to control than a curve, and if you miss, it's usually on the outside of the plate. A curve is more dangerous if you screw up in the strike zone or it hangs.

I tell kids you need two breaking balls. You need the good yellow hammer that breaks down, but you can't throw that curve when you're behind 'cause the hitter is not going to swing at it. Behind in the count, a good three-quarter curve ball is ideal 'cause he's sitting on fastball or slider. On 0-2 you might want to go yellow hammer 'cause he has to go at anything close. It's a mental game.

The pitcher is the most important man on the ball club. The catcher's job is to make him perform at his best, and you don't get that out of a pitcher by throwing the ball back at him 90 miles an hour and breaking his hand whenever he misses a pitch or calling him a stupid son of a gun and all that. You coddle a pitcher, very much so. It's a rapport like brother and sister, man and wife, and when you're cooking, when you put down a sign, his mind will be on the same track that yours is. Say you have a right-handed batter up with men on first and third and one out. We want to get a double play, and I'm thinking fastball away to get the ground ball to second or short. I put it down, and he's thinking the same thing. After a while with pitchers you get that kind of feeling where both of you are thinking alike. That's what I call cooking.

I teach more philosophy than mechanics. Catching is knowing how to take away the hitter's power; knowing the pitcher; knowing the hitter's personality, stance, likes with a bat—all these things determine what he's trying to do when he gets to the plate. If you make a game of looking at a guy's stance, his bat, his ego, his personality, pretty soon you've got a profile of 450 guys. When he comes to the plate, automatically you've got it in your head and know what he is capable of doing.

What makes me wince at today's catching? Catching with one hand behind their back and with a first baseman's glove. They're off balance, with the top of their bodies leaning forward, and that takes the ball out of the strike zone. They're not in position to throw; they have to come up straight.

Roy Campanella taught me years ago the face of the glove is like a ping pong paddle, and you use that to stop the ball. When the ball is low, the book says catch it fingers down. With fingers up there's a lot more passed balls.

I used to think that LA manager Walt Alston was too sedate, too laid back. He put men in position to make decisions, then sat back and rode the boat. He'd ask you, "What do you think we should do?" He'd leave a lot of decisions up to us.

Then I was traded to Minnesota. Billy Martin was volatile and unpredictable. He had the Durocher fire to win, but he wasn't very good at handling players. Angry a lot, jumped on your case a lot, got on pitchers.

My last year was with Washington. Ted Williams was a one-dimensional manager. Strictly interested in hitting. He let coaches deal with the rest. He didn't know much about other aspects of the game but knew more about hitting than anybody. First time I talked to him, he told me, "I want you to start taking a swing at that fastball like you do in BP. Any time you get the pitcher in a hole and you study him, you look for the heat, and if you get it, I want you to jump off the ground swinging at it."

But on defense he raised holy hell if we got behind in the count and had to throw a fastball and the batter got a hit. When that happened, the pitcher and I would go back and tell Ted it was a slider. Then he wouldn't get as angry.

A lot of guys go up to bat with nothing on their minds, not looking for anything. You need an idea of what you are going to do at bat. Ted taught discipline. Hank Aaron went to the plate one time looking for a changeup off Johnny Podres. Made out three times looking for the change-up he never got. Fourth time up he got it with three on and hit a home run. Ted taught you how to think at bat. I was thirty-seven, and he taught me more about hitting than any man I've ever seen. And all it was was anticipation and discipline. Look for what you want to hit until you get two strikes. If you don't get it, don't swing at it. That can be taught to anybody.

He was the nicest man I ever met. I loved him.

In 1972 I was the bullpen coach for the Angels. The next year I was the first base coach. Then we had a very funny situation. The third base coach was a little hesitant in giving signs and made some bad judgment calls. So one day they told me they wanted to move him to first base coach.

I said, "That's fine. What about me?"

"We want to move you back to the bullpen."

That was going backward. I said, "Wait, wait. If he cannot do his job at third base and you want to move him to first, why don't I go to third?"

"Well, we want to bring someone else in for that."

I got very pissed off, very vocal. They sent me back to the bullpen. Same old story: you can coach first base, but you can't coach third base or manage.

Dick Williams came in as manager in midseason. One day near the end of the season he told me he was going to take someone else on the road trip and I could stay back home. I said, "You gotta be out of your mind." I packed my bags, left the clubhouse, didn't say I quit, nothing. I just left.

I started a public relations business with my wife. That's still my fallback position. I went back to that not because I liked it. I did that for ten years, wrote a book in 1978 about my observations as a young man coming into baseball from Ohio and all the carousing and drinking and problems that athletes have. When Al Campanis made his public relations mistake on TV a few years ago [Campanis said that "blacks may not have the necessities to be . . . a manager"], I thought the doors were going to swing open a little more than they had been in the past, and I wanted to get back in immediately to see if I could go up the ladder. I'm still trying, but it's been a few years now, and if it goes to four or five, I'll get out. I'm not going to stay in this little minor league position the Dodgers gave me in baseball.

I was out of baseball over ten years. That's a long time to be frustrated. There's an instinct you have as a catcher: when a guy is going to steal, when they're going to hit and run—all the little things that can happen. You learn to anticipate, and when you anticipate correctly 90 percent of the time, you know you're cooking. So I immediately started analyzing baseball again, and I found out you don't lose it. It's there, and as you get older, you sort of fine tune it. I hadn't lost it at all.

Some managers are just plain dumb, think they know everything about baseball. They may know how to play the infield or outfield, but I'll be damned if they know how to pitch or catch. They don't know it; they've never done it. And only Campanella and God know it better than I do.

[**NM:** Given the importance of pitchers, is it surprising that the least represented among managers are pitchers?]

I don't know about that. I believe the least represented people among managers are black catchers.

[**NM:** Do you want to manage?]

Like I need air. As a catcher you are almost managing anyway. If certain other people can do it with high school educations or no education, then the only reason you are not doing it is the color of your skin. I would not manage in the minor leagues. I am as capable as any manager out there. Many managers came right from the field and managed. I don't need minor league experience. That's not ego; that's fact. Offering me a minor league managing job is like—what's the word—a pacifier. I was asked about it. I don't want to be a minor league manager for five years. I'm too old for that. I have more experience and success at what I did than 90 percent of the managers in the major leagues, and they go out and hire these guys that continually lose year after year, and they keep putting them on the clock. That irritates me because they're losers.

I have no expectations. We don't know if baseball is ready for minority managers in certain cities. Wherever you do have a minority manager, somebody's going to be racially pissed off. You just go day by day and put a ribbon on how long you're gonna play this game. I'm away from home a lot. I love baseball, but I'm not gonna spend my waning years traveling around trying to teach kids making $4–5 million a year how to play ball, and they get sent up without anybody asking if they can do the job until they find out they can't.

A lot of people in baseball now are business majors, corporate people not into the talent side of it. You call the Dodgers office now, you get a computer. You don't talk to people any more.

I gotta get ready for the game tonight.

39.

Hal W. Smith
COLUMBUS, TEXAS, NOVEMBER 5, 2008

. . . .

If you want to know how fleeting fame can be, just ask Hal W. Smith. For fifteen minutes on the afternoon of October 13, 1960, the catcher who played for five teams during a ten-year major league career (1955–1964) was destined for a legendary status that eludes most lifetime .267, fifty-eight-home-run hitters. He told his story at his home near Houston.

. . . .

I WAS BORN ON December 7, 1930, in West Frankford, Illinois, and grew up on a twenty-acre farm where we raised what we needed to eat. My father was a coal miner. I grew up listening to Cardinals games on the radio. When the mines closed during the Depression, we moved to Detroit.

I had thirty-six football scholarships when I graduated, but I wanted to play baseball. Scouts told me if I went to college for four years, I'd never make the major leagues. I had to learn the game in the minors. That's what they told us in those days. So two days after graduation in 1949 the Yankees had me and my father on a train to New York. There were about sixteen other boys there. We took BP and worked out. I was a pitcher and infielder. At the end of the day the general manager, Lee MacPhail, had us up to his office and said they wanted to sign me as a catcher. They gave me $5,000 and a contract for $225 a month and sent me to Ventura.

I was assigned to room with a pitcher, Dick Aubertin, who turned out to be a 6-foot-4 Indian who packed a Colt .45 and a big German luger—both loaded. The other players warned me when he got to drinking, you never knew what he might do. Frank Lucchesi, who later managed the Phils and Rangers, was the center fielder, scared to death of Aubertin. One afternoon we're playing cards in a room on the seventh floor, and there's a knock on the door. A pitcher, Tom Morgan, went out the door for a minute and came back and says to Lucchesi, "Aubertin is out there drunk as a skunk, swearing he's gonna kill you." I said, "He's my roomie.

I'll talk to him." I went out, and there he is, holding his gun. He said to me, "I haven't had a drink. I'm just going to scare that Lucchesi." He had a big firecracker and a lit cigarette.

I went back in and told Lucchesi, "You better get out of here." The door flies open, and Aubertin's pointing a gun at 'Chesi. Tom Morgan gets between them, and there's a boom! Morgan goes down like he's been shot, and 'Chesi's white as a sheet, trying to get out the window. How he kept from dying of a heart attack I'll never know.

They sent me to Idaho Falls to finish the season. Charlie Metro, the manager, drives our school bus into Billings, Montana, in the middle of the day, and I see all these people walking around with six-guns in holsters, just like in the movies. One night we're going over those curvy mountain roads and got stuck in a snow bank. Metro says, "Boys, we're going to spend the night here." What an adventure for an eighteen-year-old from the Midwest.

I never played for the Yankees. After six years in the minor leagues I was part of a seventeen-man trade between the Yankees and Baltimore on November 17, 1954. Then I went to Kansas City for three and a half years. One spring the manager, Lou Boudreau, said to us, "Let's look good losing this year. Let's do things right, like hitting the cutoff man." While I was there, they were always trading their good players away. Roger Maris was a lot of fun before they sent him to New York. He would have us all over to his house after a day game. He didn't change; he just couldn't handle what went on in New York.

In December 1959 the Pirates traded for me as a backup catcher to Smoky Burgess. Danny Murtaugh was a good manager. He had a veteran team that knew how to play the game, and he let us do our own thing. He knew nothing about pitching and left the pitchers and catchers to have their own meeting. In a bunt situation with men on first and second, we designed our own strategy on who would field the bunt, who would cover third. One day after we made a double play in that situation, he said, "I'm going to start getting here earlier so I don't miss anything."

We won the 1960 pennant by seven games and were surprised when Casey Stengel didn't start Whitey Ford in the first game of the World Series. We won it, 6–4. Our bullpen was thin after Clem Labine and Elroy Face. We knew if they got to our starters early, we were finished. So when the Yankees shellacked us in the second, third, and sixth games, we just shook it off. That's easier to do than when you lose a one-run game.

In Game 7 we were behind, 5–4, when Burgess was lifted for a pinch runner in the bottom of the seventh. We didn't score, and I went behind the plate in the eighth. Face didn't have much that day. The Yankees added two more runs to make it 7–4. In the last of the eighth we made it 7–5 and had two men on with two out when Clemente hit a bouncer to second. First baseman Bill Skowron was off first base, but their pitcher, Jim Coates, didn't cover first. If he had, they'd have won the Series. Clemente was safe; the score was now 7–6, and I'm up with two men on base. I was a little tense until I stepped into the batter's box. I was talking to myself: "Okay, Hal, all you want to do is get good wood on the ball, drive it hard, and get at least one run in and tie this game." I just concentrated on getting a base hit. As soon as I hit it, I knew I'd hit it out of the park. It always felt good to hit a home run in a game, but that's all I felt. When I got to second base and looked up, there were people on top of the dugouts going crazy, screaming and yelling. I thought they were going to come out of the stands onto the field. Then it hit me what I'd done, and then I was excited. I said, 'Wow." When I got to home plate, Clemente was there to grab me. Other teammates came out of the dugout, but they were calm. There was no big celebration, high-fives and hugging and all that stuff. We led, 9–7, but the game wasn't over.

The writers up in the press box would be tearing up the stories they were writing and starting over. They told me later that the typesetters at the Pittsburgh newspapers had headlines set in big letters: "Smith Home Run Wins World Series for Bucs." Bob Prince, the Pirates' broadcaster, went to the clubhouse to set up for the postgame interviews believing my home run had won it.

Bob Friend started the top of the ninth. Bobby Richardson singled. Dale Long singled. McDougald ran for Long. Haddix came in to pitch to Maris, who fouled out. Mantle singled, making it 9–8. Berra hit a ground ball to first. Rocky Nelson stepped on the bag, then fell asleep. Mantle ducked back to first without a play. McDougald takes off from third. I'm standing at home plate ready to make an easy play on McDougald and there's no throw. McDougald scores, and it's 9–9.

That's what gave Bill Mazeroski the opportunity to become the hero. [Maz hit the Series-ending home run in the bottom of the ninth.] Bob Prince didn't know how the game had ended. When we came into the clubhouse, he was looking for me to interview as the hero of the game until somebody told him that Maz had hit the game-winner, so he interviewed Maz instead. But the general manager, Joe Brown, told me I was his hero; my home run was the most exciting hit he'd ever seen.

We were all happy to have won, but I couldn't resist asking Rocky Nelson why he hadn't thrown the ball to me for the play at the plate. He said, "I couldn't find you."

I said, "Well, I was standing right there at that home plate."

There's somebody else who was affected by my home run, a catcher for the Cardinals at that time named Hal R. Smith. We were often taken for each other by fans. He got a lot of compliments for hitting that home run.

40

Billy Sullivan Jr.

SARASOTA, FLORIDA, SEPTEMBER 1990

. . . .

A 6-foot-1, 170-pound left-handed pull hitter with a .289 career batting average, Billy played every position but shortstop, center field, and pitcher with seven teams—White Sox, Reds, Indians, Browns, Tigers, Dodgers, and Pirates—in 12 seasons between 1931 and 1947, with three years in the navy. About half his games were as a catcher.

His father, Billy Sullivan Sr., had been a catcher with the Boston Beaneaters (1899–1900) and the White Sox (1901–1912), managing the club in 1909. Junior caught Bobo Newsom's three starts in the 1940 World Series, becoming with his father (1906) the first father-son duo to see World Series action.

I visited him in the den of his home in Sarasota, the two-story Spanish-style former winter residence of Barnum & Bailey circus magnate John Ringling North.

. . . .

I WAS BORN IN Chicago in 1910. I have the vaguest memory of when I was about four, walking through the White Sox clubhouse with my dad. All I remember is the smell of the liniment. Sometime around World War I some fast-talking real estate salesman must have come through the White Sox clubhouse selling all these ballplayers on buying land in Oregon. Dad bought twenty acres of apple and walnut orchards outside Newberg, about twenty-five miles from Portland; called it the Home Plate Orchard. Another player bought the adjoining ninety-eight acres; called it the White Sox Orchard. We moved there in 1916.

I was encouraged by my dad to play ball but get my education first. He told me what to say if anyone wanted to sign me: "I want $25,000 to sign, a two-year contract at $1,000 a month, and no reduction if farmed out." One day the general manager of the Cubs called me, and I recited what I wanted, and I heard a click. Goodbye. The Yankees' standard approach was, "We'll give you $1,000 more than anybody else." I was a first baseman. I said, "You got a guy on first base who's going to be there another ten years. What am I going to do?" And they wouldn't go along with my continuing school and missing spring training and the first two or three weeks of the season.

The closeness with my dad worked for me with the White Sox. They gave me the $1,000 a month for two years, but only $10,000 to sign. Then they said, "We don't want to give you this money and then you don't show up. We'll give you $3,300 each of the first two years and $3,400 the third year." Later that would come back to bite me. They had no objection to my reporting late until I was done with school. I never went to spring training for five years.

I went to Notre Dame, where I played first base two years and graduated with a BA in 1931, then went to law school for two years and passed the bar exam but never intended to practice law.

In June 1931 I got on a train to join the White Sox in Washington. Overnight trains always arrived early the next morning. I got to the Wardman Park Hotel, a scared kid, sat in the lobby a couple hours, saw some tanned young men going by, got a cab to the ballpark by myself. The manager, Donie Bush, says, "Go to the clubhouse and have them give you a locker." Now they're going to have a pregame meeting. I'm way off in a corner sitting on top of two uniform trunks, knowing I'm not going to play, overwhelmed but enjoying it all. Bush is telling them how to pitch to the batters and how the fielders should play them. Then he reads off the lineup— so-and-so, so-and-so, and then he says, "Billy Sullivan, right field."

I nearly fell off the two trunks. I'd never played outfield in my life. And I'm batting fifth.

Alvin "General" Crowder was pitching for Washington. After I struck out, I came back and said, "Boy, he's fast." The veterans all said, "Fast? No, he's one of the slower ones."

We were down about eight runs after the bottom of the eighth. In those days you left your glove out on the field. I tossed my glove back of where the second baseman plays. Joe Cronin, the Washington shortstop, is standing on second base. He says to me, "Hey, kid," tosses me my glove and says, "If you get eight runs, you can bring it back out."

I got my first hit in the ninth inning, a line drive to center field. We go to New York and I'm rushing to get the New York papers to read about my hit. It said, "Billy Sullivan got a scratch hit in the ninth inning." Those New York writers could be a sarcastic bunch.

I walk into Yankee Stadium, and that big ballpark was awe-inspiring. Here are these names that are just magic to me: Ruth, Gehrig, Dickey. So here I am, again out in right field. There were so many home runs going over my head I got a sore neck.

After two games in right field, I'm in the lineup at third base. I had never played there before either.

Eddie Collins always emphasized the importance of the little things in baseball. Now that I'm playing third, I paid attention to whether base runners touched the bag when they came around. A lot of times they didn't. One day the Yankees had runners on first and second with two outs. Ruth lined a bullet off the right-field fence. Two runs score. Ruth comes into third on his spindly legs. I went to the mound and told the pitcher to give me the ball. I went back to third and stepped on the bag and the ump says, "The runner missed the bag. He's out." Force out. No hit. The two runs don't count. Boy, was Ruth hot.

In 1930 on my way to Notre Dame I had worked out with the White Sox, and Luke Appling was trying out at the same time. Now we were roommates. Luke was always moaning low. If he felt okay, there was something wrong. Then he'd go out and foul off twenty balls till he got one he liked, get four hits.

Train travel made for team cohesiveness, a fellowship that's gone with air travel. Now that has to develop in the clubhouse, and I don't think there should be any writers or anybody else in the clubhouse after a game. Do their interviews outside the clubhouse.

The food on the trains in those days was magnificent, the best chefs. Many trips were overnight; we boarded around six, had a great steak dinner. Breakfast was a big deal with the players; you didn't eat lunch. Night ball threw that schedule all off.

There was a camaraderie among ballplayers, not just team-mates. Some players went out of their way to be kind to me. One day before a game with the Athletics I was taking some infield practice at first base, still using my glove from Notre Dame, when Jimmie Foxx walks by. He stops and says, "Hey, kid, let me see that glove." I gave it to him and he says, "We don't use a glove like that up here. It's too little." I said, "That's all I could get in South Bend." Next day he hands me a glove and says, "Here." It was broken in, better than brand new.

I thought I was pretty sharp about manners and etiquette and such, but I learned a lesson early in the game about life and tipping. In the Depression a quarter was a lot of money. One day on the train I saw Ted Lyons tip a porter a dollar. I said, "You gave him a dollar tip?" He said, "The difference between a quarter and a dollar is only seventy-five cents. At the end of the year maybe it amounts to 15–20 dollars. It helps that fellow a lot, and think what it does to your image."

Lyons was a wonderful guy. Everybody loved him, even though he was a fierce competitor. And strong? He lifted Jimmie Foxx into an upper berth on a train one day.

A couple years later I caught my first game at Yankee Stadium. Lou Gehrig is at bat, hits a high pop-up back of home plate. I take off my mask, running back toward the screen. That ball is so high it looks like an aspirin tablet, and then I start backing up and backing up, clear back to home plate, and the ball comes down and tips off the end of my glove, five feet fair, and Gehrig's on second base.

The Yankees' dugout was on the third base side. A runway ran from it to both clubhouses. Players from both sides would sit along that runway, talking, smoking, before a game. The next day Yankees' catcher Bill Dickey is sitting there, and I sat down next to him. He said, "Sully, you had a little problem out there yesterday, didn't you?"

"Yeah."

"The ball goes in the direction in which it spins. You have to learn that in a closed-in ballpark, especially this one, the wind blows in, hits the stands, and has to come back out."

Here's a star, talking to a novice catcher. That's camaraderie.

The White Sox had two outfielders who were good hit, no field: Bob "Fats" Fothergill and Smead Jolley. Fothergill's initials were RRF. He said, "That's Runs Responsible For." I got into a slump, went four days without a hit. We're behind eight or nine runs. I work up a 3-0 count. Naturally you're supposed to take a strike. Not me. I swung and hit a line drive single. Got hell from Donie

Bush. "You're not supposed to do that." I said, "I saw Fothergill do it." He says, "You're not Fothergill."

Smead Jolley's locker is next to mine. Bush's locker is next to mine on the other side, then the coach, Mike Kelly. Seems like I'm getting yelled at every day by Bush. "You lost that game today." In my face with those bushy eyebrows. One day I'm taking my shoes off, and he lit into me and about got me crying. When he finished with me, he started in on Smead, and that big moose is bending down like me and smiling and winking at me—didn't bother him.

One time Smead hit a long single and tried to make it into a double and got caught midway, and Bush lit into him. "What were you thinking?"

Smead said, "You know, Donie, I was thinking the same thing myself. I got halfway and I said to myself, 'Smead, what are you doing out here?'"

In September Lefty Grove was going for his sixteenth win in a row. First inning, I hit a home run. He's following me around the bases cussing me out. That was the only run we scored.

I never caught the spitball, but I played behind Red Faber, one of the spitball pitchers who had been grandfathered in when the pitch was banned in 1920. One day in Yankee Stadium I was playing third base, and the ball was hit to me. I gripped it where this glob of slippery elm was and threw that ball into the camera balcony that hung from the second deck. Faber was a very smart pitcher. Once when Babe Ruth was up, Faber moved me to play in front of the shortstop, challenging Ruth to hit to left field. Then he pitched him in on the fists, and Ruth was so anxious he just hit a little blooper right to me.

I'd been playing at Notre Dame in '30 and '31 and didn't need any spring training. But in '32 I was in law school and couldn't play, so I joined the team with no spring training. I'd come in on weekends, pinch-hit, and go back to school until mid-June. I still led the team in batting at .316.

In September Ed Walsh Jr. was called up by the White Sox. Because his dad and mine had been battery mates, they asked me to catch. I agreed but left after five innings when he did.

My original two-year contract was up, and I got a new one for the same money. No raise. I was screaming, but they knew I had to sign to get the last installment of my bonus. On top of that, they wanted me to be a catcher. I'd caught in a few games but mostly played first. Here I'd led in batting, I'm not getting a raise, and they want me to change positions. I held out and finally got them to add to the contract that I would not be required to catch.

Lew Fonseca is the manager. He figured he could play first base. He said, "I know what's in your contract. You'll sit your ass on this bench until you catch." I didn't play much, hit only .192.

While I was at Notre Dame, I fell in love with a student from St. Mary's, the girls' school across the road. On October 9, 1932, I proposed to her at a hamburger stand. She said yes, but she was only sixteen. I said she was too young, but if she still felt the same way next October 9, we'd get married. Now October 9, 1933, comes around, and we're in the City Series with the Cubs. Only way I could get married on October 9 is if we won or lost four out of five. We lost the first game, and now we had to win four straight. And we did. The next morning we got married. Went to Hawaii and Australia for our honeymoon.

Then I had to report to Pasadena for spring training. No wives were allowed, and we had no home. Hadn't given it a thought. I stayed in an apartment in Pasadena, but the club insisted: no wives. I took it up with Commissioner Landis, said we have no home and my wife can't be barred from living with me in my apartment. He agreed, and I got a reputation for being a clubhouse lawyer. I also got a ticket to Milwaukee.

The Milwaukee manager was the best I ever played for: Al Sothoron. Never made it to the majors as a manager. He knew that young players needed different treatment. One day after a game he sat down next to me. "Billy, you have a great background. Your father was a great ballplayer; he really knew the game, and he taught you. You know too much baseball to make a play like you did today." Is that ever psychological or what? I'd have torn the place down for him. I hit .343 and batted in over a hundred runs hitting second. But I made only $2,000 for the year. I was ready to quit baseball and do something else.

That winter the White Sox shuffled me on paper to Indianapolis, then St. Paul, and finally sold me to Cincinnati. I didn't do any catching for them. They had Ernie Lombardi, the only one I ever saw catch a pitch barehanded. I roomed with him once; when he snored, you could hear it everywhere. I didn't get along with the manager, Chuck Dressen; not his type. Cocky little guy. One-fifth manager and four-fifths big-time gambler.

A veteran catcher, Steve O'Neill, had seen me catch once in Chicago and told me if he could ever work with me, he thought I'd be a fine catcher. He was now the manager at Cleveland. At the end of the season I asked the Reds' general manager, Larry MacPhail, for permission to talk to O'Neill. He said okay, but if they wanted me, they'd have to pay at least what the Reds had paid for me. They started bickering and got within $5,000 of each other. I said, "I'll put up the other $5,000." Finally they split the difference, and I offered to pay the $2,500. I may be the only player willing to contribute to his own purchase price. I was hitting over .400 in the middle of June, and the Indians said to forget about what I owed them. I wound up hitting .351.

At Cleveland I became a catcher. My dad had been a talker behind the plate. He caught the great spitballer, Ed Walsh. A spitter has to be thrown low to be effective. One day Larry Lajoie was at bat. Dad called for a fastball, but as Walsh wound up, Dad yelled, "Get it low, Ed." Lajoie figured spitter and let the fastball go by for a strike.

Dad was mild-mannered but had his tricks. When Ty Cobb was at bat, if Dad walked out to the pitcher, Cobb would follow him. One day Dad went out and Cobb followed, and Dad said to the pitcher loud enough for Cobb to hear, "When I give you this sign, you throw right at his head."

We had been taught to holler and make noise on the bench to distract the other team. I became a talker behind the plate to distract the batter just as the pitcher was ready to throw.

In the fall of 1937 Bob Feller went barnstorming through the northwest. His catcher was Rollie Hemsley of the St. Louis Browns. Feller liked pitching to him and came back and persuaded the Indians to trade me for him. Now I'm with the Browns. One day Feller is pitching against us, really had his stuff. We had no hits until about the sixth or seventh. I was a good drag bunter, and he knew it. I faked a drag bunt, and he came off the mound toward first, but I pushed it toward shortstop, and he couldn't field it. Only hit we got. I still hear from Feller about that.

Gabby Street, an old catcher, was the Browns' manager. Gabby had a friend, another old catcher, Joe Sugden. They both had fingers all twisted and gnarled from foul tips. The joke was, when they shook hands, it took a locksmith two hours to get them apart.

The Browns traded me to Detroit in 1940. Our road trips could sometimes last for three weeks at a time. At the end of one trip we stopped at Cleveland for a series before returning to Detroit. I decided I'd fly to Detroit and see my wife for one night and fly back the next morning. When I got my next paycheck, there was a hundred dollar fine taken out. I wondered how they knew I'd gone to Detroit for one night. I asked about it and they said, "That's for not sliding at home plate in St. Louis." What had happened was I'm heading for home plate; the next hitter is the one who signals whether you need to slide or not, and he's not giving me any kind of sign. I didn't slide. The catcher had the ball. Only fine I ever got.

At the end of the season we went into Cleveland needing to win one of three to beat them for the pennant. When the manager, Del Baker, held a meeting to ask our opinion on who we should pitch against Feller in the first game, I voted for Hal Newhouser. But Floyd Giebell was chosen by Baker. I was catching, and I noticed a white towel sometimes appearing in one of the open squares in the big scoreboard. They were reading my signs. So we changed the signs every inning and threw them off. Giebell pitched a fine game and won, 2–0.

In 1942 I was holding out at Detroit and got traded to Brooklyn. The Dodgers had a good team. Won 104 games. Had an 8-game lead in August, lost eight in a row to the Cardinals, and lost the pennant by 2 games.

We had played a game at the Jacksonville naval base, and all those sailors were hollering at us, "Why aren't you fighting? Got flat feet?" I felt very uncomfortable. The Dodgers sent me a contract, but I told them I didn't feel right about playing ball. They said I'd be suspended unless I asked for voluntary retirement. So

I did. I went to join the navy, figuring they could use a lawyer, but they said they needed construction contractors more, so I became a government contractor. They were building an air base in Venice, just south of Sarasota. I bid on it and got the contract and wound up building about thirty bases; then I went into the navy and got out in 1946 and went back to the construction and building supply business in Sarasota.

Hank Greenberg was now with the Pittsburgh Pirates. He called me from Miami in the spring of '47. He said, "The players' pension plan is going in and you have to be on a major league roster on April 1, 1947, to qualify, or all your past years are wiped out. They want you here."

So that's how I wound up in Pittsburgh. Hank Greenberg is the smartest baseball man that ever lived, in my opinion. He and I had dinner together about every night that season. He studied every aspect of the game. There is more to being a star than hitting a ball. How you dress, how you act—he was a star. He took Ralph Kiner under his wing. Kiner had ability, but Hank made him into a star.

41.

Bobby Thomson

WATCHUNG, NEW JERSEY, OCTOBER 28, 1992

Bob ("Call me Bob; I'm too old to be called Bobby") Thomson is best remembered for hitting the most dramatic home run in baseball history—his 1951
"shot heard round the world" that turned an imminent Brooklyn Dodgers'
pennant-winning playoff game into a New York Giants miraculous come-
back victory. The third baseman/outfielder's fifteen-year career (1946–
1960) included four years with the Milwaukee Braves and two with the Cubs.

Forty-one years after he was struck by the lightning bolt of fame, I sat
in the living room of his comfortable suburban home and learned the story
of his life leading up to that moment and after it.

I WAS BORN IN Glasgow, Scotland, in 1923, the youngest of six
children. My eldest sister, Jean, was eleven. We lived in an area
my mother called Toon Heath. As a girl my mother worked in a
bakery. She was a plain cook but a wonderful baker—what they
called "sweets."

We were quite poor. Before I was born, my father decided he
was going to move the family to America. When you stop to consider the substance of those people back then, making those decisions just to pick up and go to a new country made me admire and
respect my dad very much. I lost him at an early age, forty-seven.
Back then you had to apply to come over here, and there was a
long waiting list. He had a number, and wouldn't you know, my
mother was expecting me when his number came up. So he had
to make a decision whether to wait until after I was born and get
back on the end of the line. He decided to get started and took off
by himself, a decision I wonder if I could make today.

He was a cabinetmaker and had a tough time over here, sometimes out of work. He had to make enough money to live on, save
for our passage, and send money home to support us. There were
a couple times he wavered and thought he may not make it. But
he survived, and we made it. I was two and a half when we made

the voyage. I had never seen him until we arrived. We looked like typical Scottish kids of the time. I had a woolen scarf around my neck and a cap.

We lived on Staten Island in New York. My dad had taken to baseball and became a Dodgers fan. The rationale was that we had a tough time when we came over here and the Dodgers were called the Bums. They were always losing, and I wonder if he related to that. The Giants and Yankees were much more successful at that time. When I was seven or eight, we'd walk a couple miles on Sundays just to see a sandlot game on Staten Island. My dad took me to a couple games at Ebbets Field when I was about eleven or twelve. His favorite player was Dolph Camilli, a strong man playing first base for Brooklyn. My dad was not a demonstrative person, didn't have much to say. One day Camilli hit a home run, and my dad jumped up and put his arms in the air—I'll never forget that— and it was a wonderful thing. I was always proud of him. Later I had the opportunity to meet Dolph Camilli at an old-timers' game in California; I really got a kick out of telling him that he was my dad's favorite player.

I had an older brother who played ball and got me started playing. My brother rooted for the Yankees. I don't know what got me started as a Giants fan. In high school I was an infielder and worked out a few times with the Giants at the Polo Grounds, but apparently they weren't interested in me. I worked out more at Ebbets Field with the Dodgers, even played with a team called the Dodger Rookies. Now I'm getting out of high school and realize I'm going to sign a contract. The Dodgers told me, "Please talk to us before you sign. We'll better anything the Giants offer you." But I never had any intention to sign with any team other than the Giants. There was mutual hatred between Giants and Dodgers fans. I was a loyal Giants fan and was never going to sign with Brooklyn.

The Giants sent me to Bristol, Virginia. I was just out of high school, a scared little kid, wet behind the ears. I remember there was a fan in the stands, a big, fat, leather-lunged woman—scared the heck out of me. They had a good team, a good third baseman. I just sat, didn't play much. Bill Terry was in the Giants' front office. He wanted me to be playing, so I was shipped to Rocky Mount,

North Carolina, and got into about twenty-five games. I lived in a rooming house with four guys in one huge room. The clubhouse was very tight, had two showers. The old bus we rode had the worst-looking tires I'd ever seen. There were no windows in the last two rows of seats. One trip was 150 miles, and on that bus it seemed like a thousand miles. We stuffed our uniforms and gear and stuff into our uniform pants legs and pulled the belt tight and carried them on the bus. After a hot, sweaty game, we'd stuff those wet uniforms in the back of the bus. As a rookie, that's where I ended up. It got kind of chilly at night coming home. I used to lie on top of those sweaty old uniforms to help me keep warm.

I was such an immature youngster; it was just a way of life. Why do you become a ballplayer? You love to play baseball. You don't make an overnight decision; it just comes on you gradually, and it's just something that's there, like following a star in the sky. What else would I have done if I couldn't play baseball? I had nothing else in my mind but being a ballplayer.

I was drafted into the army air force in late 1942 and never left the U.S. I began training as a radio operator and that was killing me, so I applied for air cadets and wound up in bombardier school. In advanced training I got an ear infection that put me in the hospital for a month and was pushed back one class. My original class went overseas. We were ready to ship out when they dropped the A-bomb and our orders were canceled.

I always had my glove with me. We'd play catch occasionally, and they'd throw grounders at me. One night our barracks caught fire and we all ended up out in the street, and there I stood with whatever I was wearing and my baseball glove on my hand.

In 1946 the Giants sent all their returning servicemen to their AAA Jersey City spring training camp in Jacksonville. There were hundreds of us there. I expected to go back to Bristol, and I didn't look forward to going back and listening to that fat lady with the leather lungs. We had races and I won them all, and the Giants decided my speed was wasted in the infield and they put me in center field. I was still very inexperienced. But I made the Jersey City team.

The Giants thought I'd be a third baseman when they called

me up near the end of the '46 season. They were playing the Cardinals, who were fighting the Dodgers for the pennant. The manager, Mel Ott, told me it wouldn't be fair to play a rookie against them. "Just sit and watch Whitey Kurowski play third base," he said.

I remember Ernie Lombardi sitting on the bench with his pancake catcher's mitt under his arm, his shoes untied. Ott would walk down to him to pinch-hit. He'd nonchalantly tie his shoes, walk to the bat rack, take a bat, maybe take one swing, and go up to hit. Most guys would have to loosen up, take some practice swings. Not old Schnozz.

In 1947 Giants pitcher Hal Schumacher had retired and gone to work for Adirondack Bats. In the spring he came into the locker room with a bunch of bats, and we used them. Walker Cooper put some little nails in his bats, and they didn't catch him for a while. We set a home run record with 221. We got rings with "221" on them. They talk about cheap home runs down the short foul lines in the Polo Grounds; I hit a few of those. But as a left-center hitter, I lost a lot of 400-foot fly balls in the Polo Grounds that would have been home runs in most parks. In the first playoff game in 1951 at Ebbets Field, the home run I hit off Ralph Branca was left-center, right over the 375-foot sign. That would have been a pop fly in the Polo Grounds. In '47 we lacked pitching but finished fourth, up from last the year before.

I got into a slump in '48, and everybody and his uncle is telling you how to hit. Two I listened to were Mel Ott and Hank Greenberg. Slumps start in your head. It's like trying to make a three-foot putt in golf. Your mind has a lot to do with how you approach things. I changed batting stances. Feet wide apart, bat held back—copying Joe DiMaggio, they said. But I didn't know from Joe DiMaggio. I just had my hands entirely different from the year before, and I don't know how these things come about.

It was a shock when Leo Durocher came over to manage the Giants in 1948. Mel Ott was a real gentleman, and Leo was a fiery noisemaker. He was aggressive, smart, could be obnoxious. But who's perfect? In his first meeting he said, "Boys, let's just forget everything that's gone on in the past. What counts now"—he rubbed his hand across his uniform shirt—"is Giants. We all go down the road together or we go different ways and don't win." We got used to him in a hurry.

Like the Giants' fans, I used those words: "We hate the Dodgers." But we didn't know them as people; we knew them as players. I always thought of Branca, with those big baggy pants, as a pitcher. He didn't like us, and we didn't like him. They were the enemy, and that's the way it was. In Ebbets Field the locker rooms were right next to each other and we had a common runway, so you had to pass guys on the other team between the dugout and locker room. I never talked to them except to say hello to Gil Hodges because he was such a respected guy.

The walls between the locker rooms were thin. When they beat us, we could hear them banging on the walls, singing, "Roll out the barrel, we got the Giants on the run."

[The Dodgers had a thirteen-game lead on the morning of August 12. They were 26-22 and the Giants 37-7 the rest of the way, finishing in a tie.]

Leo would tell us, "Don't get them mad. When the time comes, kick their teeth in." One day at Ebbets Field they had two on, two out, first base open. Leo plays the percentages—intentional walk. Bases loaded. Carl Furillo is up. Hits the first pitch for a grand slam. Ebbets Field is so small you can talk between the dugouts. Carl goes in and hollers, "Hey, Leo, how did you like that?" That got us mad.

I remember once facing Don Newcombe with Monte Irvin on third, losing 1-0 about the sixth inning, and Newcombe getting two strikes on me. Now I'm fighting for my life, and I'd never felt that way before; I had to get that run in. The next pitch is right under my chin, and I swung at it and hit it right over the Dodger dugout. I couldn't leave that guy on third. The next pitch was probably outside a couple inches. I just got my bat on it and hit a long fly ball. I remember really like fighting for my life that one time at bat.

The last week of the season the Dodgers were in Boston, which was loaded with former Giants—Buddy Kerr, Sid Gordon, Walker Cooper, Willard Marshall. The Braves were going nowhere. In the next to last game of the series, the Dodgers led, 13-3, in the eighth inning, and Jackie Robinson stole home. He's on the bench, laughing, making all kinds of gestures. That got the Braves mad. Walker Cooper coulda wrung his neck. The next day the Braves were out to show them, tried a little harder, wound up winning three of the four games.

The week before the season ended we couldn't afford to lose a game. We finished with two games in Boston. I was playing third base. The last game, when Willard Marshall came up with the tying run on second, my heart was in my mouth. I hadn't felt that way the week before. With the pressure you get more determined to do whatever you can do. Fortunately Willard hit a fly ball to left.

There was always a lot of press ballyhoo and big crowds whenever the Dodgers were at the Polo Grounds for a weekend series. Leo would tell us, "Let's just play our ball game. But"—there was always a "but"—"as soon as one of their pitchers comes too close to one of our hitters' chin, I want two for one." Typical Durocher.

[After the Giants and Dodgers split the first two playoff games in 1951, the deciding game was played at the Polo Grounds. The Dodgers, behind Don Newcombe, had a 4–1 lead after 8½ innings.]

When we came in for the bottom of the ninth, I was totally dejected, threw my glove down on the floor. I thought we were just good enough to come this far, but not good enough to take that last step. I knew I was the fifth hitter. I didn't expect to get a chance to bat. Newcombe had walked right through us in the eighth.

[With one out and two on, Whitey Lockman doubled in a run. It was now 4–2 with men on second and third. Don Mueller hurt his ankle sliding into third, holding up the game. Thomson was the next batter.]

It was a once in a lifetime situation. Don was a good guy, good ballplayer; he's lying there really hurting. You could rationalize that Don hurting his leg stopped the game, broke the tension, got my mind off the game. I think that coulda been a factor. They carried him off the field, and now all of a sudden I'm thinking I gotta get back to bat; there's a ball game going on here. I didn't pay attention to the crowd. I didn't even know they had changed pitchers. So now here I head toward home plate, and I remember Leo putting his arm around my neck, saying, "If you ever hit one, hit one now." I thought, "You're out of your mind." I didn't even look at him, certainly didn't answer him.

And then fundamentals seem to take over. I try to rationalize this. The only thing I can do to make sense. You're supposed to be a professional. You can go up there in a tough spot, be a little afraid of it. But over your career you face situations where you maybe feel a little tighter than others. I just started talking to myself: "Wait and watch. Get up and give yourself a chance to hit, you SOB." I'm swearing at myself all the way. It seemed like a long walk from third base to home plate. "Wait and watch. Give yourself a chance to hit. Do a good job, you SOB. Wait and watch." The idea being, don't get overanxious. Keep your weight back. Give yourself a chance. That's all you can do, and let the good lord do the rest.

It wasn't until I got to home plate that I realized they had changed pitchers and put in Branca. So now I get in the batter's box. I took the first pitch right through the middle of the plate. I remember Larry Jansen saying later, "Jesus Christ, we wanted to kill you when you took the first one right down the middle."

It wasn't a matter of being nervous, just total concentration. It's a daze or whatever term you want to use, but you're just totally concentrating. Nothing's going on around you except this thing in front of you. I'd never been in a situation like that where it was that critical. I wasn't fighting for my life, but I was totally concentrating, waiting and watching. And now I'm in my crouch, and he winds up, and I remember just getting a glimpse of it—I use that term, "getting a glimpse of it." Maybe I didn't see it all the way to the bat. It's coming high inside. If it's inside, your hands better get out in front of it. It was a bad ball, but obviously it wasn't that bad.

For days afterward, wherever I went, people would tell me where they were at that moment. I still get letters from people telling me where they were.

I was still living with my mother on Staten Island. I wasn't one for the night life. After the game I went home.

After what we'd been through, playing the Yankees in the World Series was like playing a sandlot game. I never felt more relaxed in my life. I couldn't believe how hard Allie Reynolds threw. Monte

Irvin was on second base with two outs, and I hit a single so hard to left field, Irvin couldn't even score.

[Thomson was traded by the Giants in 1954 before they went to the World Series, and by the Braves in '57 before they wound up in the Series. He retired from baseball in July 1960.]

I walked away from baseball and didn't miss it. I began a new, more normal life. I learned the meaning of work, became aware of the value of time and money. Baseball was play. Now I experienced a working life, rode trains and subways, setting out each day with a goal to accomplish, things I never felt playing baseball. As a ballplayer, you are self-centered: how am I doing? How am I hitting? It's always "I, I, I." It was satisfying to become aware of others around you and their needs. I worked in sales for paper and carton manufacturers until I retired.

I remember Mel Ott telling me after a game, "Bobby, stay with it as long as you can. You never know what's going to happen after baseball." I didn't feel that way. I feel I've grown a little bit.

42.

Bob Turley

. . . .

A big right-handed high fastball pitcher for the St. Louis Browns, Baltimore Orioles, Yankees, Los Angeles Angels, and Red Sox (1953–1963), Bob Turley pitched in five World Series with the Yankees. His best year was 1958: 21-7, Major League Cy Young Award, World Series MVP—working in four games with a 2-1 record.

Turley was living in a thirteen thousand square foot mansion at the south tip of Marco Island in southwest Florida when I visited him. A column of stately royal palms lined the driveway. A wall-sized plate glass window looked out on the Gulf of Mexico. A small yacht was moored at a dock. His Cy Young Award plaque was mounted on the wall of a huge open area in the house.

. . . .

I WAS BORN IN a small town, Troy, Illinois, about twenty miles outside St. Louis, and grew up in East St. Louis. My high school coach, a bird dog for the Browns, arranged a tryout for me at Sportsman's Park. A Browns scout, Jack Fournier, recommended they sign me. But they had to wait until I was no longer in school. The night I graduated in 1948, I signed for $1,200–$600 bonus and the rest salary. They sent me to Belleville in the Illinois State League, close enough so I lived at home. I was used to pitching four or five games a week—never had a sore arm. But for about two weeks I pitched nothing but batting practice. One day the Browns called and asked why I wasn't pitching. They wanted me to start that night. I had just thrown BP for thirty minutes and was running in the outfield when they told me I was pitching that night. So I pitched against West Frankford, beat them, 3-1, struck out ten or eleven. The next day they fired the manager. I finished 9-3.

In 1949 I went to spring training in Pine Bluff, Arkansas. The Browns had twenty-six farm teams at that time, and all of them except the AA and AAA teams trained at this old army base, must have been about five hundred of us of all ages. I was eighteen, and there were some guys in their thirties. We slept in the barracks. During the summer they grew corn in the field there. In the spring they plowed. They lined us up, and we walked across the field picking up corn stalks and rocks. Then they used machines to smooth it out and put down four baseball fields. We did our running alongside the air strip.

They were paying me the same $200 a month I'd made in '48, and sent me to Aberdeen, South Dakota, in the Class C Northern League. Long bus trips. We played a July 4 doubleheader at home, about 104 degrees; got on the bus, drove all night and the next day to Duluth, Minnesota; got off the bus—and there were snow flurries. I was 23-5, never taken out of a game starting or relieving, and won two playoff games.

After the season we played an exhibition game against a local semipro team. In the first five innings I struck out everybody. One inning we had nobody behind me on the field except the first baseman.

I trained with the Browns in Burbank in 1950. They sent me to San Antonio. I pitched two games, lost, 1-0 and 2-1, and they sent me down to Class A Wichita in the Western League. Never figured that one out. That's where I ran into Don Larsen. He was twenty; I was nineteen. Joe Schultz was the manager. He had more to do with my career than anybody because he was an old catcher, so I learned from him how to play the game from the pitcher's point of view.

The next year I was 21-7 at San Antonio and was called up by the Browns, pitched one game, and got beat by the White Sox. I was about to be drafted into the army, so I went back to Texas and enlisted. I knew the general there, and he wanted me to pitch on his base team. All I did was play baseball for two years and got back to the Browns for the last month or so in 1952.

The '53 Browns were a lot of older guys near the end of their career. Marty Marion was the manager. I remember sitting next to him when a sportswriter asked him, "How come you don't play anymore?" He said, "I ain't going out there and embarrass myself with these bums."

One of the catchers was Clint Courtney, who fired the ball back to the pitcher. I think if he threw it back easy, it would be erratic, all over the place. When Duane Pillette was pitching and nobody was on base, he would step aside and let Courtney's throw go out to center field. I knew a lot of catchers who, if there were men on base, couldn't throw the ball back to the pitcher. It's a mental thing, just like a pitcher's control.

Satchel Paige was there. He was always chewing gum, and he'd warm up by taking the gum wrapper and laying it down and throwing over it. He had a rocker in the bullpen, and he'd fall asleep out there during the game.

Harry Brecheen was the pitching coach. Once, when I was eleven years old, I was on a kids' team that was on the field before a Cardinals game. The manager gave me a baseball to get signed. The only player I wanted was Brecheen. He wouldn't sign it. Maybe he was pitching that day. Now he was my roommate. He signed a ball for me. Brecheen and Whitey Ford cheated by throwing from in front of the rubber. But us hard throwers couldn't do that. Power comes from the legs, and we needed to shove against the rubber for power.

I made $6,000. Even with the [54-100] Browns, players were paid for helping win games, not just the stars. Like hitting behind the runner, stuff that they don't keep stats on, or a reliever who comes in and stops a rally. How many times do you see a man on second base and the batter hits in front of him, not behind him? Things like that make a difference in winning. Hit it on the ground to the right side, move him over, and another ground ball can score a run. The attitude was, "Gotta get the run in." It's the .240–.250 hitter who's asked to sacrifice for the good of the team. The front office has to recognize that and pay them accordingly.

The move to Baltimore in 1954 was exciting. In St. Louis we had maybe eight hundred people at a game. But we found out very quickly we were the same team, just in different uniforms. Jimmy Dykes was the manager. Dykes loved the press, being the center of attention. He did more talking to the press than to the players. You'd find out more about yourself from the papers than from the manager.

There were all kinds of prizes you could win, trips and things. First home run would win a diamond ring, for example. We had a meeting and somebody suggested putting all the prizes together, turn them into cash, and divide it because some guys had more chance of winning something than others. One player said, "If I win something and you think I'm going to divide it with you guys, you're crazy." He hit the home run to win the ring. Joe Coleman, Cal Abrams, and I were the finalists for MVP voted by the fans. I won a Cadillac and a trip to Japan. We couldn't split up the Cadillac, but we took the cash for the trip and divided it, about $1,000 each.

Tim Cohane from *Look* magazine wanted to see how hard I threw. The Orioles agreed to it, but it had to be after I pitched. So one day I went to Aberdeen Proving Grounds. They put a machine on home plate for me to throw through. I threw 98-point-something, and that's where the nickname "Bullet Bob" came from. Now they time it halfway to the plate. On that basis a lot of guys I knew could top 100.

I stayed in Baltimore that winter. One night I was watching Steve Allen on the *Tonight Show* on TV, and all of a sudden my picture flashed on the screen: "Bob Turley traded to the New York Yankees." I was so excited it was unbelievable. [Turley, Don Larsen, and five other Orioles were traded to New York for ten players.] The phone was ringing. Fans said they were sorry to see me go. I was kind to them, but in Baltimore they had averaged maybe one or two runs a game. In New York they averaged maybe six runs a game.

My first spring training with the Yankees, I walk in and there's a couple drinks in my locker. Mickey Mantle walked over and said, "I'm so glad you're here, another guy I can't hit."

Casey Stengel didn't have meetings to go over the hitters. Going over how to pitch to hitters didn't help much anyhow. The manager or pitching coach would say, "Don't throw a high fastball to this guy" or "Throw curves to that one low and away." I lived on my high fastball. What was I supposed to do? If I could control a curve low and away, I'd be winning forty games a year. The outfielders wanted to know how you were pitching to a hitter. The infield would relay the signs to the outfield.

Before a World Series game Stengel might talk about hitters, but it would be like, "Now this guy is a low ball hitter . . . likes it low and away," and then he'd wander and talk about how some old-timer like Heinie Manush couldn't hit an outside pitch—something like that.

Toward the end of the '56 season we're getting ready to play the Dodgers in the World Series. And the pitching coach, Jim Turner, suggested to Don Larsen that he try pitching without a windup because teams were stealing his pitches. Then Turner says to me, "I want you to do the same thing but for a different reason. Your windup is no good to you, and you always lack control." The day after Larsen's perfect game in the '56 Series, I pitched the best game of my major league career [a four-hit, eleven-strikeout, eight-walk, ten-inning 1–0 loss] in that bandbox Ebbets Field, but nobody remembers my game. Enos Slaughter lost three balls in left field. In the tenth with two on and two out, Jackie Robinson hit it real hard to left. All Slaughter had to do was stand there. He came charging in; the ball went over his head.

Larsen went back to the over-the-head windup. I stayed with the no windup, got criticized, booed, written up: "You're going to ruin your arm." But it became very easy for me; I didn't have to get in a rocking position. With better control I didn't have to try to strike everybody out. I could try to get them to hit my pitch.

Here's an example: With Minnesota outfielder Bob Allison, my routine was first pitch, curve ball in the dirt. Second pitch, up around the neck. I'm 2–0. The next pitch would be a high slider, and he'd hit the softest fly ball. I threw him two pitches, got behind, and in that situation hitters are really going to jack up on the ball. Then the high slider. I could follow that pattern because now I could control my pitches. Never once did he realize how I was pitching. I was able to switch the ball in my hands. I could switch to a sinker and get a double play ball. It made me able to do what pitchers should do. Before that my high fastball produced fly balls, not double play grounders. Now they all do it.

I'm pitching in Washington one day, fifth inning leading 3–0, two out. Need one more out to be eligible for the win—and wins is what we got paid on. A left-handed batter hit a ball over the shortstop's head. Only man on base. I look over and here's Stengel coming out of the dugout, waving his hand for a pitcher to come in from the bullpen. I thought, "What the hell is going on here?"

He came out to the mound, didn't talk to me. I don't swear a lot. I called him every dirty name I could think of, following him around the mound; he kept walking away from me. I went in the clubhouse. I was so mad I tore my uniform off and was trying to flush it down the toilet. For about a month Stengel avoided me. One day we're on a train; I'm in my roomette reading a book, and he stopped by and said, "Now that you've quieted down, I'm going to tell you why I took you out of that game. You weren't striking anybody out."

I said, "Casey, get out of here." I had been pitching a hell of a game. What can you say?

[In Game 2 of the 1958 World Series against Milwaukee, the Braves scored seven runs in the first inning off Turley. He came back to shut them out in Game 5. **NM:** How do you explain that?]

In that second game my stuff was good, but maybe the ball wasn't moving, maybe I was throwing the same speed. I don't know. Any pitcher will tell you out of four games you pitch, you'll have exceptional stuff in one. Your object is to win two out of three you're pitching. I had many times when I'd go out there and just have extraordinary stuff and times when I felt so good it was unbelievable.

Yogi Berra was a great all-around player. Smart, not excitable. Learned how to get rid of the ball and throw guys out. Elston Howard was more into the emotional side of it with a pitcher. He'd come out and talk to you, encourage you. Both great catchers.

Ralph Houk was a players' manager. He kept everybody excited, happy, talked to you, made you feel like you were part of the team, like *you* were doing it, not him. Appreciated what you were doing.

I had the ability to call some pitchers' pitches. Great hitters can pick up the spin on the ball right out of the pitcher's hand and adjust. Not many hitters can do that. Mickey Mantle and Gil McDougald especially wanted the tips. Mickey said, "You're right 85–90 percent of the time." I'd go into the TV room to look at pitchers' motions to see what I could pick up. I might tell Mickey, "Watch his foot. When he's going to throw a screwball, he moves his foot to the other end of the rubber."

Billy Pierce always wore a long, heavy sweatshirt. When he

went into his glove to throw a fastball, his sleeve would go down to his wrist. For a curve he would go deeper into his glove, and his sleeve would be off his wrist. So I told Mickey that.

All pitchers try to work on their stuff and be consistent in what they do. Early Wynn, with somebody on base, if he was going to throw a knuckleball, he'd do something in his stretch; a fastball, he'd come up even with his chin; a curve, he'd be up around his forehead. Or I'd tell them, "Watch the glove. It spreads more when he's gripping a curve than a fastball." I picked up on things like that. When you throw a curve, you shorten your stride. Pitchers would alter their windup a little from fastball to curve. With no windup, it's more difficult to pick up those things.

When I was on the DL, they'd buy me a seat in the stands, and I'd call pitches from there. Whistle to them to give them the signs.

I could read our pitchers too. I called Whitey Ford's signs all the time. He called his own games, giving the signs to Yogi. If he bent over and shook his head, it was a fastball. If he stood up, it was the reverse of that. I asked him once, "How long you been calling your own games?" He looked at me. "What do you mean?" When I was traded, they changed their signs.

The hardest thing is to get pitchers to realize what they are doing. They get into a routine and don't realize it.

I never had a bad arm, but it was sore during the 1960 Series. I didn't pitch much in '61; we had a good pitching staff. At the end of the '61 Series I had it operated on to remove the bone chips. In '62 we had another good staff, and I didn't get to pitch much. The older you get, the more you have to pitch, especially for me to maintain my control. Your muscles don't come back as fast. You have to do more throwing, more working out. Your work habits are more than those of all the young guys put together. Like Ryan. Like Clemens. We didn't know anything about icing your arm after pitching a game. We used hot water in the shower. We never used the whirlpool. We had one trainer, not six or seven. I could still throw pretty hard, but I was just not into it.

Some of the Yankees had an active night life. Mickey was one of them. But he was like Babe Ruth: when they put that uniform on, that overcame anything they did the night before. I've seen some guys miss a game because of the night life, but not Mickey. He loved to play and win. In 1961 Mickey hurt his shoulder and hit few home runs in September. But he still wanted to play, even though he could barely swing a bat. He never complained, never moaned. He liked to kid around, always laughing. He loved to warm up with rookies—he could throw a knuckleball, and he'd throw that thing to them and laugh when it tied them up.

Roger Maris was the opposite: a good guy but not outgoing, a family man. It's true that the guys were rooting more for Mickey to break Ruth's record than Maris. But Roger was probably the best right fielder the Yankees ever had. Hank Bauer played against the fence and came racing in and made diving catches. Roger played way in and could go back on a ball. Very fast.

Then I was traded to the Los Angeles Angels. The only game I can remember not walking anybody was with the Angels. And I pitched a one-hitter against Chicago. We called manager Bill Rigney "Mr. Hook." Every time he took me out of a game, everybody on base scored off whoever came in. One day about the fifth inning he came out to the mound. Bases loaded. I said, "Look, if you check it out, every time you bring somebody in, everybody scores. I can't do any worse than that. Pitching is very simple with nobody on base. I'm good with men on base if you'll just let me get 'em out." All this is on the mound. He looked at me, said, "Okay," went back, and I struck out the next three guys.

Umpires have different strike zones. They are human beings and they take a lot and they hear it. Ed Runge was a pitcher's umpire. But if you showed him up, forget it. I pitched 24 shutouts and I bet half of them were with Runge behind the plate. Hitters knew it too. With Runge they wouldn't take pitches. He'd call them out on pitches that were outside. The Yankees would use me when he was behind the plate. I don't think I ever lost a game with him umpiring.

Ed Hurley for some reason didn't like me. I don't care what I did, he couldn't call a strike. One day in Chicago I was throwing the ball right down the middle of the plate. He's calling, "Ball. . . . Ball, . . . Ball." They had to take me out. Guys in the dugout were yelling at him. He thought it was me. One day he came out to the mound and said, "Don't worry. I'm not going to throw you out of the game. I'm going to let you pitch yourself out of the game." I wrote a letter to the league president; nothing came of it.

[Turley was the Yankees' player rep in 1958.]

I remember when J. Norman Lewis was our union head and we proposed to the owners that they allocate 20 percent of all their baseball income to players' salaries. I've never seen grown men act like we just killed them. I remember Buzzy Bavasi saying, "You mean to tell me we came in last, and just because we drew four million and made a lot of money, we gotta pay you guys 20 percent of it?" Tom Yawkey's on the other side and he says, "Here's my books. I'm already paying that now." Today they'd be the happiest people in the world if they'd signed that contract.

I was at Mickey Mantle's funeral. When the services were over, the comedian Billy Crystal came rushing over and shook my hand. He said, "I've been waiting a long time to talk to you. When I was a little boy, my mother used to take me to the Yankee games. I'd try to get autographs and never could. One day you came out and were walking across the grass, and my mother asked you if you'd sign. You said you'd be happy to. Then my mother asked if she could take a picture with me, and you said you'd be happy to." I sat him on my knee for the picture. He said, "That's my favorite picture. It sits on my desk." Made me feel good.

43.

Broadway Charlie Wagner
READING, PENNSYLVANIA, DECEMBER 9, 1991

Charlie Wagner was the definitive baseball lifer: seventy-two years (minus three years in the navy), all of it in the Boston Red Sox organization—as a pitcher, coach, assistant farm director, scout, and (his favorite role) roving minor league pitching instructor.

A lifelong resident of Reading, Wagner spent the last evening of his life at the Reading ballpark, where he died at ninety-three, shortly after the last out. Almost to the end his attitude was, "There still isn't a day that I don't want to put on that uniform."

I spent a wide-ranging afternoon with him, his keen memory and strong opinions, at his two-story brick home in Reading.

ALL MY LIFE I have enjoyed dressing well. In the old days, the 1920s and '30s, wearing a coat and tie was mandatory for major league ballplayers on the road and the higher minor leagues too. I always believed that if you represent a big organization, you should look the part. You're somebody. I still believe it should be that way in the big leagues. I get annoyed at today's players, the way they dress.

I was with Minneapolis in 1937. I had two suits, brown and gray. I mixed them every day, never wore either full suit. We had a shortstop, Fresco Thompson, who started calling me "Two-toned." He asked me, "Don't you have anything at all that matches?" Later he changed the "Two-toned" to "Broadway."

In those days we were very friendly with the sportswriters. When I got to Boston, John Drohan of the *Herald* and I became good friends. He called me "Broadway" in the paper, and it spread and stuck.

That dress code didn't apply down in the bus leagues, but even in Class B I wore a jacket. Not on the three- or four-hundred-mile bus trips, but when we got off the bus, I was wearing a jacket. Most of the players wore dark shirts, what they called "thousand-mile shirts." They got on my case about wearing a jacket.

My father was a meat and milk inspector for the city of Reading for twenty years. There were no athletes in the family until I played four sports—baseball, basketball, soccer, and track—in junior high. In those days if you scored ten points in a basketball game, it was a big deal. We won championships in all those sports. This part of Pennsylvania was strictly Athletics country. My father was not a fan, but somebody would drive us to Shibe Park to see all those great pitchers in the 1920s. When I started pitching in junior high, my father came to the games.

The Red Sox had a farm club in Reading in the International League. I was a batboy, a gofer—go for cigarettes, go for hot dogs. I watched those big guys, then went home and aped them, throwing a ball against a wall. We all did that; we wanted to be like Babe Ruth or somebody.

I quit high school before graduating. In those days your parents were more interested in your getting a job and earning some money. I worked at a knitting mill for a few years. Meanwhile I was pitching semipro ball: Anthracite League, Lancaster League, Industrial League. A former International League outfielder named Doc Silva was now the editor of our local newspaper. He and I played on the same teams. I pitched three times a week, got five dollars, sometimes eight dollars, a game.

The Reading manager, Nemo Liebold, let me pitch batting practice. He asked me if I wanted to go away to play ball. I was interested, but he wanted me to go to Mahanoy City in western Pennsylvania. I said no, that's too far away for me.

So Doc Silva called the Scranton manager, Jake Pytlak, and asked him if he needed a pitcher. Pytlak said, "Send him up. I'll look at him." This is 1934. I'm twenty-one. Scared to death. I signed for $100 a month. I was pitching batting practice, and a mean little shortstop was up. I hit him in the back, and he flung the bat at me and cussed me out. I lasted two weeks, never got in a game, and came home.

Liebold persuaded me to sign a 1935 contract with the other Red Sox farm club, Charlotte, in the Class B Piedmont League. Frank O'Rourke was the manager. First thing he told me was, "Never give your right age." I was born in 1912. He said, "Tell 'em you were born in 1916." I demurred, but he insisted. All the old pros told me the same thing. So I did. The reason was that in those days of limited farm systems the minor league clubs owned most of the players and hoped to sell them. Scouts would come to see the minor leaguers, and the first thing they'd ask is, "How old are you?" And I told them the lie. I was twenty-two and said I was eighteen. I didn't want to, but that was the way it was.

Later on I would kid Ted Williams, my roommate. He'd say, "How old are you?" I'd say, "A year older than you." Years later we're at spring training, and I'm in the front office. I'm fifty years old, and I signed up for the baseball pension. They put my age in some bulletin, and Ted read it and said, "You lying so-and-so. . . ."

Herb Pennock was the general manager at Charlotte, a wonderful man. I signed for $100 a month. He said, "If you stay all year, I'll give you a $100 bonus." Charlotte had a bad club with a shortstop who couldn't catch the ball or throw, definite handicaps for a shortstop. There wasn't much coaching; we learned more from the former major leaguers on their way down. Pennock wanted me to go to a younger club in Danville, Virginia. I was homesick and told him, "Give me my release, and I'll go home and forget about this." Frank O'Rourke said, "I ought to kick you in the butt." That woke me up. I started to pitch better and wound up 7-16. And got my bonus.

The Red Sox switched their farm to Rocky Mount, and that's where I went in 1936. George "Specs" Toporcer, later our farm director, was the manager. He knew more baseball than you could ever think about. It was a joy to play for him. He gave you confidence. I won twenty games. We learned from him how to live the right way. Four of us roomed in a house and ate our meals out, the usual junk food. Three of us were in a restaurant in Norfolk that was next to a rundown hotel where prostitutes and sailors hung out. We ordered some stuff and French fries. Toporcer saw us, came in, ran us out of there, and paid the bill. Outside on the sidewalk he told us, "You gotta eat right, not in a dirty joint like this." The next day he held a meeting about how to eat the right food, and it was the start of my no more junk food. He taught us about baseball and living right.

The ballparks were okay in the Piedmont League, but the lights weren't too good. Vander Meer was in that league, and hitting against him under those arcs was no picnic.

I never worked in the winter. Even at $100 a month, you could save money. I was single until 1942, then away three years in the navy. But I'd have to borrow $100 from my dad to go to spring training.

The end of the season, Toporcer said, "We're going to send you to Minneapolis next year"—AA at that time. Now I'm really twenty-five. Later I came to believe that 95 percent of pitchers come into their own at twenty-five.

The Minneapolis club owner, Mike Kelly, sent me a 1937 contract for $225 a month. I sent it back. Next one I got was for $250. I said to Doc Silva, "Twenty wins deserve a bump up." He said, "You got $125 last year."

"Yeah, but I jumped up to AA." Doc wrote a letter, and they went up to $325, but I didn't sign. I called the farm director, and he said, "Sign and go, and I'll work it out." I wound up at $500.

In those days they paid you in cash. No checks. They put an envelope on your chair at your locker, and when you took it out and counted it, anybody could see how much you were getting. Some of the veterans were making less than I did and were shocked when they saw me counting mine.

We trained in New Braunfels, Texas. I thought I was on that train forever. If I ever got lost, I'd never get back to Reading. Nobody met me. I got to the hotel and didn't know what to do. Fresco Thompson came over to me. "You must be a ballplayer," he said.

"Yes. Do I sign something?" "You register, then come over to me. You better go in and see Mr. Bush [the manager] and Mr. Kelly."

"I'll see them tomorrow."

"They're in the bar. I'll take you in."

And he did. Kelly, a big guy, says to me, "You're the little cracker-ass writing all those letters to me?"

I mumbled all over the joint, saying nothing. He said, "Well, nice to see you."

I won 20 for Minneapolis that year and made it to Boston in '38.

As a rookie in the major leagues you had to work your way in to be accepted. They wanted to see what kind of fellow you were. You were really alone and had to make it on your own. That's an adjustment. So we're in Sarasota in spring training, and it's all new to me and when Jimmie Foxx says, "You want to go to dinner with me?" I said, "That'd be nice." We're at a bar and it's about 6:30 and I don't drink; then it gets to be after eight, and we still haven't eaten yet. I'm tired of eating pretzels and that other junk. I said, "Well, it's about time to eat, right? I'm hungry as a bear."

He's half in the sauce. "Yeah," he says. It gets to be 11:30, and I'm scared to death I'm not going to get in by midnight curfew. I said, "Jimmie, I gotta get back." He says, "Aw, don't worry about it." I said, "I gotta go." I made it back quarter to twelve. I'm thinking, "What am I doing out so late?" I'm in bed nine thirty, ten o'clock.

I did this a couple times with Jimmie. I'm in the outfield one day, and I feel a little bump on my butt. It's the manager, Joe Cronin, with a fungo bat. He says, "Hey, that Foxx is a big guy, isn't he? Look at him hit up there. You think you can keep up with that guy?"

"I guess I could, Joe."

"I don't know," he says. "I recommend you don't try to keep up with him."

I wasn't quite sure what he meant. That evening John Drohan and I took a walk. I said, "Joe patted me on the ass today and said something about keeping up with Jimmie Foxx. I thought Foxx was just being nice to a rookie and all."

"Well," he said, "don't let him pat you again."

Whatever you had done had nothing to do with making the team now. You have to prove yourself. Lefty Gomez tells a story about when he first got to the major leagues. He was in the bullpen. Big crowd. Herb Pennock was pitching. Gomez is saying, "I hope they don't have to use me. I don't want to pitch." Something happened to Pennock on the mound, and they quick called in Gomez. He said, "I hope I fall down and hurt something on the way in." He gets to the mound, and they told him, "Pennock broke the webbing on his glove. Give us your glove and go back to the bullpen." Lefty said, "Thank you very much."

One day Gomez was pitching and Rogers Hornsby was the batter. Hornsby stood way back in the box. Gomez just stood there on the mound. Finally Bill Dickey yelled at him to throw the ball. Gomez said, "That guy is still in the on-deck circle."

I pitched well in a few games but lost. My worst day was June 10. White Sox pitcher Monty Stratton hit a grand slam off me in the second inning in Boston. Giving up a grand slam is a horrible feeling. You're standing out there, and nobody is looking at you but your manager, and he's looking all over you and coming out to get you. That long walk off the field is a tough walk. When you get to the dugout, there's nothing to say. They know how you're feeling. I said to myself, "I'm going downtown and eat, and I hope I get ptomaine poisoning, and then I'm gonna sit through two lousy movies."

So I get on the subway, and I'm sitting next to a fellow who was at the game. I figure nobody's going to bother me. He says, "Were you at the game today?" I said, "Yeah." He says, "Did you see Wagner pitch? What in the hell are they doing with him around?" He's ripping me good, moaning about what a bad day it was. Took the starch right out of me. Didn't recognize me. He says, "Do you get out to the ballpark often?" I said, "I try to get out there every day. My stop is coming up." He said his name was Harry Klump or whatever it was. I said, "I'm Charlie Wagner. I'll see you."

I wasn't pitching enough to stay alive and had an awful time. I didn't want to sit around and watch other guys pitch. I was going to lose all I had. So I asked Cronin, "Why don't you send me to Minneapolis?" And he did.

And that's where I began a lifelong friendship with Ted Williams. We roomed together as long as I was an active player. We were a compatible, early-to-bed pair. Didn't drink. The carousers—Foxx and Cramer, and a few others—called us the "milk shake boys." We didn't care.

One year Ted had the flu, and Cronin suggested I room with Foxx for a while. Jimmie had a room by himself. I didn't see Foxx all week except at the ballpark. He'd say, "Hey, roomie, how we doing?" I'd say, "Oh the room is beautiful."

But when Foxx hit a home run, it had a distinctive ping sound. You didn't have to be looking to know who hit it.

In those days they'd give you a steamer trunk in spring training, and you used that all season. Ted had a lot of outdoor-type clothing in his. He has two pair of shoes, and I have about fifteen; I'm stretching my stuff out, and he says, "Where am I going to go with my stuff?"

He never wore a tie, but he wore a jacket and looked neat. Well, he wore a tie once, for me. They had a banquet in Reading for my fiftieth year in baseball. Ted was a speaker, and he borrowed a tie from me and put it on just for me. Then he stood up and said, "The minute this thing is over, I'm giving this tie back to Charlie."

Ted would stand in front of a mirror with a bat, studying his stance and his swing. They had these four-poster beds in the room in one hotel. He's practicing his swing, and I'm lying on the bed watching him. He swings a little too hard and hits one of those bedposts, and the whole thing collapses with me on it.

We had no long-term contracts. A hungry player has that motivation to do well and get paid well for it. Ted had that. He'd say, "I'm going to hit and they're going to pay me the gees." He called money "the gees." He never wanted to be embarrassed.

When Ted made up his mind to do something, he'd do it. You'd hear him say, "You know what he's gonna do to me today? He's gonna come in here. Well, I'll clean his clock." I'm pitching in Chicago one day and it's tied in extra innings, and he said to me, "Do you think you can hold them if I hit one out of here?" I said, "Yeah, you get 'em, and I'll do it." He said, "You got it. I have an early dinner date. You better hold 'em." So he hit it out of the park in the eleventh inning and we won. That's how he could determine himself. He believed in himself.

Mr. Yawkey invited me to Fenway Park for Ted's last game. Before the game Ted said, "I'm gonna hit one out of here today." And he did.

One day in Sarasota Donie Bush, who had been with Detroit for twenty-two years and was my manager in Minneapolis, and Eddie Collins, our general manager, were watching Ted hit, and they agreed they had never seen a better hitter. They tried to think of who would come the closest and finally settled on Shoeless Joe Jackson. They said they never saw Jackson hit a ball that wasn't hard hit with a pop to it.

So it's 1939 in Sarasota, and I'm set to go north with the Sox. We're sitting in the lobby waiting for the bus to go to the train station, and I see Donie Bush's Cadillac in back of the hotel. I wondered what he was doing there. I knew that he and Tom Yawkey and Frank McKinney had bought the Louisville club that winter. Johnny Orlando came over to me and said, "Mr. Cronin wants to see you." I went over. Cronin says, "Charlie, I don't know how to say this. I'm scared to death to tell you." I said, "I don't know what else I can do to prove myself to you." He said, "That isn't the point. Mr. Yawkey wants to know if you'll go down and pitch the opening day in Louisville. They want a good start to draw people. Mr. Yawkey is asking for it." I said, "Holy geez. If that's the way it is, I'll do it." I was so mad I said to Donie Bush, "If I ever see you again, I'm going to punch you out."

So I went to Louisville, and Mr. Yawkey came down for opening day. As I'm warming up, I said to him, "You're the only guy I'd ever do this for." He took care of me almost the rest of my life. A nice, beautiful man. He paid his players well at a time when most club owners were tight with money. When Johnny Murphy was our farm director, he told me that once he had a great year with the Yankees and they cut him $1,500. He goes to see Ed Barrow. "What's this? I lose $1,500 after a good year?" "We won the World Series," Barrow says. "The Series money was $6,000." Murphy says, "That doesn't have anything to do with my career." Barrow said he'd give him the same as last year. No raise. The players were dead in the water. They couldn't go anyplace. It's also true that a lot of clubs made no money. I don't buy that "country club" reputation the Sox had. It's true we often finished second to the Yankees in those years. But what the Yankees had that we didn't was a great defense, and defense is the last word in winning.

Anyhow, I was in Louisville until July. Pee Wee Reese was the only good player we had.

Lefty Grove was a spoiled brat, temperamental sort of guy. Not a bad guy; a nice guy. At Fenway in those days the bullpen was on the field. You could see pitchers warming up. One day I'm in the pen with Moe Berg. Grove is pitching. I wanted to throw a little. Berg says, "You don't get up in the pen when Grove is pitching." I said,

"Come on, Moe. I want to loosen up." He said, "Don't do it." I got up anyhow and was warming up while the Sox were at bat. But I'm not quite finished when Grove goes back out to the mound. He stopped the game and watched me until I sat down. Moe says, "I told you."

In 1940 I had my tonsils taken out just before spring training and was sick as a dog. I spent most of the year back in Louisville. Cronin didn't use me much, but in the fall he told me, "You'll get the ball in '41." I did and had good years [12-8 and 14-11]. Could have been great years. Lost a lot of close games. Pitched one day, rested the next, threw batting practice, rested, and started again. Did a lot of running in between starts. All we had in the training room was a heat lamp and some oil. No ice. Some of the trainers were fight trainers. If you had a stiff arm, you pitched it out. We warmed up at 50 percent, not 80 percent. Built up our legs with a lot of running, not our muscles.

My fun day was after I pitched. I could sit on the bench and watch the pros play. They played hard. I never felt like I was going to work. A lot of players today don't enjoy it enough. They think they're working hard and playing all out, but they're not. Today players with multi-year contracts sometimes get back on their heels and don't even realize it. There's a nonchalance about them.

We used the brushback but not to flatten a guy. Except for some like Grove. If you bunted on him, he'd go after you. Barney McCosky, a rookie with Detroit, bunted on him one day. Grove told him, "Don't you ever do that to me again." He flattened McCosky four times, walked him. Nobody said a word. Doerr batted behind Foxx. After Foxx hit a home run, Doerr would get knocked down. We'd retaliate, usually against a guy who was bothering us. Or throw at the pitcher, and if you didn't get close to him, it'd cost you fifty bucks with some managers. Those things happened. But we all brushed back hitters. A guy like Dave Winfield would have been knocked down a thousand times a year because of the way he swings and the way he looks at you. Every time you go inside to him, he goes out of his mind.

Luke Appling could hit at midnight with no lights. Right-handed batter, always punching the ball to right. I used to move him back a little, and he'd stand there and yell, "Not me, Charlie, not me."

Complained every day: "I don't know if I can play today. My legs are killing me." And he'd kill you out there.

Paul Waner was high every day of his life. He told me that Pat Malone of the Cubs would ring your bell every day. He'd tell Malone, "Go easy today. I had a terrible night. Don't ding me today." And he'd get four hits.

The hitters accepted it. It was a legitimate part of the game.

Of the Red Sox in those years, Bobby Doerr was the finest man you could ever meet. Doc Cramer—a jubilant guy, walked all winter to stay in shape, chopped at the ball to get his hits. Dom DiMaggio: quiet charm. At a banquet in 1941 honoring Ted Williams and Joe DiMaggio, somebody said to Dom, "I just said hello to Joe," and Dom said, "Gee, I better say hello to him while he's in a talkative mood."

On the train trips we did a lot of talking. The guys knew if you were in a slump or a rut; they'd come over and sit and talk to you, and it was a helpful thing. You feel lonely when you're not doing well. They'd help build you up. That's what was great about trains. Today the players don't really know one another.

I enlisted in the navy in July 1942. New Guinea, Australia, the Philippines. I never felt good in the Philippines and came home in '46 with dysentery that plagued me all year. In July Mr. Yawkey asked me to work in the office. I was thirty-four. I thought about it and finally said yes. I didn't want to be a manager. That's how guys get fired. I scouted and was assistant farm director. I pitched batting practice to our kids till I was sixty. I felt great, never felt old in baseball. It annoys me when I see former players who get fat and out of shape. Later I did more scouting.

I was the pitching coach for Eddie Kasko in 1970. When I was in a close game, I used to try to talk Cronin out of taking me out. A manager can tell if you want to be there or you don't. So one day Kasko sent me out to take out Ray Culp. We were ahead, but he was in a tough spot. He says, "I'm not coming out, Charlie, no way."

"Kasko sent me out to get you."

He said, "I don't give a damn. I don't want to come out." Well, he said more than that. I said, "I'm going to get fired if I don't get you out, but I'm gonna leave you here. If I get fired, it's your fault."

I came back to the bench and said, "Eddie, he didn't want to come out and he meant it. I bet you he's gonna get out of this inning, and if he doesn't, I'm gonna die."

He got out of it, and we won the game. If he hadn't, Kasko would have fired me.

Pitchers today go six innings and start looking in to the bench. That to me is a give-up. Drives me crazy.

Another thing that drove me crazy was that sometimes it seemed the coaches were the only ones who were mad when we lost. Gene Mauch once lost a doubleheader; he comes in and the players are digging into this big food spread, eating like pigs, and he just turned that table full of food right over. Some of it landed on a guy's suit in his locker, and Mauch said, "I don't care. Go buy a new suit," and he lit into them, used words you never heard of. That's how I feel sometimes. I want the players to think about it after they lose a game.

I enjoy working with young pitchers. Herb Pennock taught me to give kids this assignment: throw three straight strikes. You'd be amazed how hard it is for them. If they miss on one of the three, they have to start over. When they do, I tell them, "Okay, now throw a fourth and you're done." Pitchers don't do that today.

In the first few years in the minor leagues, a young pitcher has to get the ball over the plate, then figure out if a guy is a low-ball or high-ball hitter, and that solves your problem.

When I see college pitchers get to an 0-2 count, I hear coaches yell, "Waste one." That's the dumbest thing. I hate that expression. An 0-2 pitch is a purpose pitch. Find a spot for it and hit it. It should have a purpose: close enough to swing at but out of his power spot.

The most delightful time I ever had was sitting with Branch Rickey in Danville, Virginia, where we had a team and his team was playing ours. It was my first year as assistant farm director. Rickey always had a secretary alongside him taking notes. He'd say things like, "That kid never went after that ball properly." Another thing he said that I never forgot was, "Whenever you see a fellow who's been a great pull hitter all his life and he starts to hit to the opposite field—even though he may lead the league in hitting, that's the greatest time to trade him. I can get maybe three young pitchers for that guy." I still watch for that every day. It happened to Mike Schmidt.

The Yankees were good at making trades. One year they spent two weeks looking at Johnny Mize, who had been with the Cardinals for years. He could still hit, could always hit, even in his casket. They traded for him as a pinch-hitter and won with him. Same with Enos Slaughter. They asked Phil Rizzuto, who was in his thirteenth year with them, what he thought of Slaughter. He said, "Grab him." So they did. Now they had to remove somebody from the roster to make room for him. Who did they cut? Rizzuto. He's still mad at Casey Stengel about that. They won with Slaughter too.

I got close to Joe McCarthy when he managed the Red Sox. Joe was a teacher. If a guy went up to pinch-hit and took a called third strike, he'd tell him, "Pinch-hit means hit; you go up there to hit. It's okay if you strike out swinging the bat, but swing the bat."

One day in spring training Billy Goodman struck out and came back to the bench grumbling at himself. McCarthy called him over and said, "You got mad too late. The time to get mad is when you go up to bat. Coming back is too late."

McCarthy knew how to handle men and get the best out of them. When he quit he said, "I'm just too old for these boys now." He always made sure that you were learning something when he talked to you. One day I was sitting in his office with him and he said, "Goodman's in a little slump right now. I think I'll bring him in and talk to him."

I said, "I'll get out of here."

"No, stay here."

He asked Johnny Orlando to get Billy, who was putting on his socks. We could see him through the window into the clubhouse. Joe said, "Let's see what reaction he has."

We could see Billy saying, "Me? Me?" It wasn't fear. He just didn't want to go into McCarthy's office. He's thinking he might get squealed out a little bit. He comes in and McCarthy says, "You know, Billy, the other day when you made a play at second base? I thought it was a terrific play. You remember it?"

"Yeah. I remember it."

"It was a terrific play I just wanted to say what a great reaction you had. That play saved the ball game for us. I haven't been able to talk to you about it. I didn't want to forget it. That's all I wanted to say."

After Billy left, McCarthy says, "Now let's watch his reaction."

Billy goes back to his locker. You could see the smile on his face, the elation. McCarthy had just given him a bump. That's what McCarthy was good at.

Joe didn't want anybody talking anything but baseball in the clubhouse. If players were talking about fishing or golf and Joe came in, they'd switch to baseball talk. Like Cronin, McCarthy wasn't a bed checker.

I think the secret of managing today is handling pitchers. There's nothing I'm going to do as a manager that's going to fool another manager. You win with knowing who can do what, not with strategy. You've got to know your pitching staff's personalities, what they're feeling. Some pitchers pitch better when they are one run behind than one ahead. Lefty Grove was a great one-run-ahead pitcher. Had perfect mechanics. He and Ted Lyons and Mel Harder—you could wrap up the bats. They were the greatest finishers. They had that determination that you were not going to beat them.

In the majors a lot of pitchers are getting beaten on what they think is their best pitch, and that drives me crazy. I see it every day in the big leagues. Big leaguers live on fastball hitting. Nobody hits curve balls. If you have a great curve, work on getting it over the plate. Grove and Feller and Gomez were the only ones I knew who could throw fastballs and nothing else. Feller had a great curve also.

I've seen so many guys who couldn't drive in a man from third base if they had six bats up there. They drive in 125 runs, and they do it in 12–1 games. The guy who drives in 50 runs but they are tying or go-ahead runs—that's the winning player.

You can never say if a kid will be a big leaguer. Nobody can know that. Some kids you think are gonna make it, but they stay in the minor leagues. Some can't adjust to constant pressure. If a scout signs somebody and he makes it to AAA, I'd say that was a successful scouting job.

44.

Monte Weaver

ORLANDO, FLORIDA, DECEMBER 29, 1991

Right-handed pitcher Montie ("I dropped the 'i' when I started playing ball") Weaver earned a master's degree in mathematics from the University of Virginia while pitching for the Washington Senators (1931–1938) and Red Sox (1939). He may be the only player who ever received a percentage of his sale price in the form of a free appendix operation.

Weaver's home, where we talked, overlooked a yard of orange, grapefruit, and kumquat trees.

I WAS BORN IN 1906 and grew up in Helton, North Carolina, a tiny town in the northwest corner of the state. My father was a blacksmith and farmer. Major league baseball was too remote for us to follow. No radio or newspaper coverage. I knew nothing about any of the players or teams. The town was too small for a town team or any high school sports. We had a county team, but it was mostly pickup games. I played some as a barefoot catcher and played any position I could. I never gave pro ball a thought.

I enrolled in Emory & Henry University, $450 a year including room and board. After two years I paid my way pitching for teams in the Kentucky coal fields, made $10 a day for sixty-six days.

I was working on a master's degree in mathematics at the University of Virginia and teaching when Dr. L. S. Booker, a surgeon who owned the Durham club in the Class C Piedmont League, offered me a $500 bonus, $275 a month, and 25 percent of any sale price in 1928.

Our manager was George "Possum" Whitted, who had been on the 1914 Miracle Braves. He was also the first baseman, bill payer, and groundskeeper. We had a skin infield, and every morning he attached a scraper to the back of his Ford roadster and scraped the infield. The ballpark was next to a tobacco warehouse. The smell was so strong it almost made me sick. I tried chewing once, but that was enough.

One day I was pitching, and the batter hit a line drive that split my chin wide open. I went down, and Whitted came running over. My chin was bleeding profusely, and all he said to me was, "Don't get blood on your uniform." The laundry bill was the first thing on his mind. There was a doctor in the stands, and he dragged me out to his car and put some metal clips on the cut until I could get to a hospital. I was back pitching three days later, stitches and all.

After my first year I was sold to Baltimore, but I was teaching in the offseason and did not want to mess that up. Besides, I was still not sure about playing pro ball, so I returned to Durham. I pitched nineteen complete games in two and a half months, usually with two days' rest. During one five-game stretch, I gave up a total of thirteen hits and still lost two of them. We had no hitting.

I was sold again to Baltimore but did not get the promised cut of the sale price. After the 1930 season I needed an appendix operation, so Dr. Booker did it for me free, a sort of in-kind cut.

I hadn't really decided to make a career of baseball until I won twenty-one in 1931 and Baltimore sold me to Washington. The Orioles' business manager, George Weiss, gave me $1,000 of the sale price. Walter Johnson was the manager. The first day I reported, they were taking batting practice when I went out of the dugout and started toward the outfield. He called me back and said, "I want you to take care of yourself just like you've been doing over in Baltimore and pitch like you been doing over there."

That's the last I heard from Johnson. Nice guy. Everybody liked him. I did not think much of him as a manager. Situations would come up, and he wouldn't be ready for them. Say we needed a pinch hitter; he wouldn't think ahead at all. Didn't seem to be in the game.

I was going to start my first game against the White Sox, so I took BP. Johnson threw batting practice and still had plenty on the ball. He hit me on the knee with a pitch, and it swelled up and they had to put ice on it. I guess all that took my mind off what I had to do. I was pretty calm when the game began and pitched a complete game for the win.

I had a fastball that took off and a curve that broke straight down. I would throw that curve on a 3-2 count with three on. If you can't throw your best pitch any time, you're in trouble. We warmed up near the dugout in those days. I would throw nothing but curves so they could get a good look at it, then throw nothing but fastballs for four or five innings. I worked on three days' rest; four was one too many.

I signed for $5,000 in 1932, won twenty-two games, and got a $1,000 bonus at the end of the year from club owner Clark Griffith. The players knew it was hard to get money out of him, but they knew he didn't have it. They all liked him. The Senators were a quiet, sober team, no rowdies. Mr. Griffith would not have any troublemakers on the team.

Moe Berg was a good catcher who helped pitchers by calling what you wanted to throw and giving you a good target where you wanted to throw it. You could spot Berg among the players; he'd be the one with the *New York Times* under his arm after dinner.

I did all right against the Yankees. Ruth hit two home runs off me, but one day I struck him out three times with low curve balls. I beat them one day when Tony Lazzeri doubled into a double play. It was late in the game, and I was ahead by a few runs when Gehrig and Dixie Walker singled. Then Lazzeri hit a long drive to right center. Goose Goslin almost caught it but took it on one bounce. Gehrig had held up at second in case it was caught, and Walker was almost down to second. As Cronin went out to take the relay, Gehrig headed for home with Walker on his heels. The relay came in to catcher Luke Sewell, who tagged Gehrig sliding in, then tagged Walker right behind him.

I made $7,000 in '33, but I hurt my shoulder. Still I won five of six at the end of the year. We had seven .300 hitters and won the pennant, but we went into a slump the last two weeks and were still in it when we went into the World Series against the Giants.

I felt no nervousness before I started Game 4 against Carl Hubbell. We hit a lot of line drives off him but right at the outfielders. Bill Terry hit a home run into the temporary extra seats in the outfield. It was 1–1 in the eleventh inning. Travis Jackson, bad legs and all, beat out a bunt. He was sacrificed to second. Then Blondy Ryan, a weak hitter, was up. I had struck him out twice before; he couldn't hit a sidearm curve ball, but I got one a little too close in, and he fell back and hit it between third and short, and that was the game, 2–1. The losers' share came to $3,019.

At the end of spring training in 1939 I was traded to the Red Sox. Lou Gehrig took himself out of the lineup in Detroit in early May, ending his consecutive game streak and his career. Next time the Yankees came to Boston was May 29. I was behind Gehrig in the runway both teams used to get to the clubhouses. There was a railing on one side. He was over there with two hands pulling himself up the stairs, just dead on his feet. You could've pushed him over with a feather. The next day we played a doubleheader. I had not worked much up to then, and Joe Cronin says, "You're starting the first game." I figured that's funny, but I went out and beat them. Complete game, my only one of the year, and my last win. Then I didn't work again for another month. It turned out that the Red Sox had bought me to send me to their Louisville farm club, but they couldn't get waivers on me. The Yankees kept putting in a claim for me. So the Red Sox figured the Yankees would beat me pretty bad if I pitched against them and they wouldn't want me anymore. But it didn't work out that way. So I had to stick around. The Yankees finally gave up and let me go to Louisville, where we won the Little World Series.

My last year was 1941 at Baltimore; then I went into the army air force, got a commission, went to radio school, and spent two and a half years in a command center near London, in radio contact with fighter group leaders on missions.

The Senators had started training in Orlando in 1933. It was a good place for guys to go fishing, and there was a theater downtown where Sally Rand, the fan dancer, performed for a quarter admission. I owned an apartment building in Washington but decided to settle here, was in the aluminum awning business, then invested in orange groves.

45.

Ted Williams

I was visiting former third baseman Bill Werber in Naples when he mentioned that he was having dinner at a friend's house that evening where Hall of Fame outfielder Ted Williams would be present. Bill said, "Maybe I can arrange for you to talk to Ted before dinner." And that's how I came to be sitting in a basement den with Ted at five o'clock that evening. In his nineteen years with the Red Sox (1939–1960, with two stints of military service), Williams had a .344 lifetime batting average, with a high of .406 in 1941. He never stopped studying the art of hitting. When Bill Werber joined us, the interview became a conversation between two ex-ballplayers—Werber's last four years, including the 1939–1940 Cincinnati pennant winners, coincided with Williams's first four—talking about their favorite subject: hitters and hitting.

Ted Williams filled a room with his presence. He spoke in capital letters, sometimes 60-point headlines, his voice fueled by enthusiasm and underlined by his hand thumping on the arm of the chair. His train of thought was sometimes diverted onto spur tracks before returning to the main line—or not.

When we arrived, Williams was in the middle of telling a story to someone who then left the room with Werber.

WHAT DO YOU WANT to know about me? Let's start out with what you want to know.

[**NM:** Let's start out by your finishing that story.]

In 1939 I went into Detroit stadium for the first time, and I went into the ballpark. It had been redone in the last 3–4 years from Navin Field to Briggs Stadium. I just heard a story about that; they said, "We'll fix the ballpark, and provided you"—Briggs, the owner then—"put up so much money, we'll call it Briggs Stadium." And this is a nice new stadium. And little Tommy Carey—a little duck-butted guy, good infielder, couldn't hit very well—he come out of the third base dugout—and immediately you see right field and this is in May, first year in the big leagues—and he said to me, "I saw Jim Bottomley hit one up against that façade up there." I said, "Oh, horseshit." Now Jim Bottomley was a good hitter; I never saw him play, but I know his statistics are pretty good, had good power, and it's a funny thing: at that time in the American League, in the late '30s and early '40s, there was no good left-handed hitters. There was just none. Charlie Gehringer was still a good hitter but not a power hitter. Gehrig was gone. Here is Charlie Keller coming up, pretty good, strong hitter. Here is Jeff Heath, pretty strong guy. Mickey Vernon. Cecil Travis was a hell of a hitter but not the power hitter. There was no big left-handed power hitters in the American League.

So when he tells me this, I said, "Oh, horseshit." So, gee, the first time I get up, I pull one foul up against the façade. *Foul*. The next time I hit up against the façade—home run. I go around the bases. Now Greenberg, playing first base. This is a true story; it's in my book, just exactly like I'm telling you. Greenberg's still looking at the ball as I rounded first. Charlie Gehringer—it makes a good story but this is true—Gehringer is playing second base, and he has not said hello or goodbye or how do you do to any ballplayers in twenty years. It was the third baseman who said this to me, and that's why I know it was Billy Rogell. I don't know who was playing shortstop. So as I got to third base, nothing's said, but I come around home plate. Now before the pitch that I hit up against the façade, the count was 3-0. And Rudy York had asked me, "You're not hitting, kid, are you?" I said, "Yes, I am." And I hit the ball against the façade. And as I hit home plate, Rudy York said to me, "Kid, you weren't kidding."

So I hit the home run and I come back. And now it's three innings later. I get up again, and I get the count, and now I hit one just a little better, and it's the first ball hit out of Briggs Stadium. Greenberg's still watching the ball. I get to second base, and Gehringer has not said anything for twenty years, so I don't expect to hear anything from him. I don't know who was playing shortstop, but as I got to third base—and I'm sure it was Billy Rogell—he said, "Kid, what the hell are you eatin'?" So now I go around third base and come into home plate and cross home plate. But that's the story about my first appearance in Briggs Stadium. Now—the only reason—why did I bring it up? I don't really know.

I played my first year, and I had a good year. I hit twenty-nine home runs. I led the American League [in RBIs], the first and only time that a rookie ever did that. But I had the circumstances around me. I had Jimmie Foxx, a super guy, hitting ahead of me, Cronin behind me. Here's a young left-handed hitter; nobody knew anything about me. I had all the chances in the world, more than I ever had in any other single season *by a lot*, in the next twenty-three years.

[Red Sox general manager] Eddie Collins, a great player, is the guy who signed me out on the West Coast. He liked me as a young raw kid, innocent as hell, and he's the first one that said he could see big stars in the sky for me as a hitter. Because the first time he saw me—I wasn't even playing—I was in batting practice. He went to Mr. Lane, the owner of the team, and he said, "Who is that kid, that left-handed hitter?" The owner of the club didn't even know who it was. But Collins saw that right away. He knew. Lane said he's three-four years away. Eddie Collins said, "I just want you"—at that time the San Diego Padres were obligated to the Red Sox because they picked up the option for Bobby Doerr, and Collins wanted the option on me—"just promise me the option on this kid." Okay.

I loved Eddie Collins and [Boston minor league director] Herb Pennock; there couldn't have been a nicer man. Herb was big league.

The only three people I ever heard Eddie Collins talk about with more or less reverence were Spoke—[Hall of Fame outfielder] Tris Speaker, a thirty-second degree Mason; Babe Ruth, because he contributed so much to the game; and [Philadelphia Athletics manager 1901–1950] Connie Mack, who he had played and coached for. I gotta say Ty Cobb too because Collins played in that era, and he respected his ability and tenacity and his daring and competitiveness. Anybody who played with Cobb, even the guys that hated Cobb, always said he was the most tenacious competitor this game ever had. I have to think there's been some pretty close but none any greater than Cobb; never will there be a greater competitor in sports than Ty Cobb. So that's pretty good to say when you talk about these young kids, these football players who are pretty gung ho, they'd go through a wall if they could, but when you talk about twenty-five years, that's a different ball game, isn't it?

[**NM:** And 154 games a year.]

You're damn right. That's a different ball game. And, you know, nobody has ever said it like that. You can take some great tough guys, oh they were tenacious on the field; but this Cobb for twenty-five years, the guy that was the best, the guy that everybody either hated or admired so much—and I heard some old players say they hated Cobb. But you can't deny the record; you can't deny what's on paper anyway.

I met Connie Mack in 1940. Al Simmons was one of the coaches. And there was an old pitcher, Lena Blackburne; Christ did he throw good BP! They could waylay the ball from here. But Simmons was his main coach. Simmons stayed on the bench quite a while, then coached third base, and was one of the truly greatest players who ever lived, no question about that. And Mack's son, Earle, was one of the coaches. I remember this so vividly.

I came into the ballpark early one day; you know there probably wasn't that many people there, and Earle said, "Ted, I want you to meet my dad." So we went on up. This little bitty office wasn't as big as this room, about two-thirds the size of this room. He had a little desk there—a 4-by-8 desk—and he's sitting there, a stiff collar, I remember that, big turkey neck. He wasn't a very big man; I would say he was 6-1, weighed 160 pounds. What were his dimensions? I don't even know; I'm gonna say 6-1, maybe 6-2, 160 pounds, frail, skinny guy.

[**NM:** You're talking about a guy who was seventy-seven years old.]

Is that right! Is that right! He let me talk. We had maybe fifteen minutes, twenty minutes to talk. But I remember the one thing he said to me. He might have said, "Kid." Might have said, "Ted." I don't remember. But he did say, "You're going to be one of the greatest hitters pretty soon." I'd played one year, but you know a funny thing. I played eleven or twelve years in Shibe Park, and then they moved to Kansas City. Half of my career I played in Shibe Park, and if I'm not mistaken, my average for those years was .420 or something in that park. And they had some good young pitchers. Why I hit so well I really don't know, but I did hit well. And then I go back to the other most vivid memory of Connie Mack, when—in the '40s and late '30s I absolutely crushed them—doubles, triples, knocking horns down, lights down, everything else. And I hit a ball—did you ever see the old Philadelphia ballpark? They had a high right-field fence, then the stands went up, and they were much higher than they were in left field; then they went around, and there was a pole right at the foul line on the roof. One day I hit one. Jesus did I hit it good! And I hit it right over that pole, and I gotta admit it was that much foul, that much foul. God damn did I hit it! Anyway, I murdered Athletics pitching. I had a .360 average against them at Fenway.

Now my most vivid recollection of Connie Mack—me hitting so well against them and, I want to tell you, him sitting on that bench—little bench, fourteen inches wide in that Philadelphia ballpark—and he had that straw hat on, that stiff collar and tie, and once in a while on a hot day he'd take that off; I wanna tell you something. When he saw me come to the plate and there was some men on, he stretched up about five or six inches, he had the scorecard moving, and he kept going and, Jesus, I thought of that a hundred times in my life how he used to wave that scorecard. He didn't shift on me, but I'm gonna tell you, he walked me, forced the winning run to second base. He did some things that were so crazy at the plate, absolutely—and then Cleveland did the same thing— crazy. I never was walked on purpose with the bases loaded. And, you know, I'm getting to the point where I'm getting a little thin on memory at times, but, boy, I'm telling you, they pulled some things that you wouldn't believe were anywhere conceivable percentage baseball with me at the plate.

Mr. Mack really hurt the club from '47 on because he was just getting too old, not quite up with it, should have been younger thinking, but here he is, he's the owner, the manager. I thought the A's should have won the pennant in '48. They had a young kid, [11-year center fielder] Sam Chapman, a great player. I thought an outstanding player. He had in a lot of ways the ability of DiMaggio, and that's saying something. He could throw, hit with power; not the hitter DiMaggio was because DiMaggio was a super hitter. But this guy looked like he was going to be something. He went in the service, came back, and never picked it up.

But here's the thing. They had a good pitching staff, beat us a doubleheader opening day in Fenway Park. The guy that was the most underrated player in the American League they had that year—Eddie Joost. He had a great year, hit twenty home runs leading off. They shoulda won. They shoulda won! I think they had a hell of a chance to win. They had a good club. It's pretty near sad.

I personally have never heard a bad word about Connie Mack.

In 1946 Tris Speaker was doing some coaching with the Cleveland Indians, and I was hitting like a son of a bitch. And he said, "Ted, you're the greatest hitter I've ever seen." He told me in '47, in '48. But it's been recorded. It's in a book. Somebody got that from Speaker. And Jimmy Dykes too said the same thing. But isn't that a hell of a thing to have Speaker say that? I don't say that. But he did say it. And my greatest regret now is that I don't have a nice picture of Speaker and me.

I didn't see Lefty Grove when he was at his best. But I saw enough of Grove to know he was the best left-handed pitcher I ever saw. What I saw of Grove, there couldn't have been anybody better. And the stories I've heard! Seeing him pitch when he was all done almost and, oh, what a competitor, what control. And he made his reputation with the best fastball a left-hander ever had. Super competitor.

I'm gonna say you have to play the percentages all the time. There's a few guys in life who can play it easy, relax, don't give a shit, won't put out all the way, and still succeed at the highest levels. But most of the guys who succeed in sports and businesses and life's accomplishments get a little dig in the ass going and, God damn it, pushing all the time. They want to be the best; they want to do things; they want to be remembered; they want to be on top of the heap. No question about it. And Grove was one of them sons of bitches. Boy, I'll tell you. He knew he looked good pitching, and every time he threw that ball, he wanted it to look just a little bit better. And the first time I saw him pitching, 1939, '38—'38! Jesus Christ, we're going back fifty years—first time I ever saw him throw, I wrote one of my buddies in school. Here I am a young kid, just played on my high school team two years ago, and now here I am, and I see Grove and I see Foxx and I see Cronin; I see Joe Vosmik, I see Cramer, and I see some other guys in the big leagues, and all I wrote was, "Boy, you should see Lefty Grove." He's the smoothest pitcher I have ever seen. He would pump up, then he would throw, and he would come down. You know, I asked Bill Terry and I asked Gehringer specifically who's the best left-hander you ever saw, and despite the fact that Hubbell was super, they always said, "That guy over in Philadelphia." Both of them referred to him like that.

You know the thing I'll remember most about Grove? I certainly remember his competitive spirit and, oh, boy, talk about business and absolute dedication and absolute win-the-game attitude. The thing I remember about Grove the most—and I forgot what I was going to say just for a second—what were we talking about before then? We were talking about Grove, but just before I started this last statement. Well, everybody, Cronin included, they all said, "Boy, you should have hit against Grove in the morning games they had, eleven o'clock." But there was something else I was on the track about, and I forgot about it.

[**NM:** Did you ever see anybody make an error behind Grove that cost him a game?]

Well, I'm gonna tell you about two incidents about that, and I probably can't tell you anything more. It was my first year. I was hitting between Foxx and Cronin, hitting fourth, and I had all that opportunity to drive in runs. There was three men on one day, first inning. Grove, when I first got there, had 290 wins, and we're trying to get 300 for Grove—289, 290, whatever it was. A ball was hit to right-center. I was playing right field in those days, and Cramer was playing center. Now Cramer had a really great arm, and he was reasonably good and fast in the outfield. Threw like a son of a bitch. Played a little deep, but, boy, I'll tell you, he could throw the ball. They didn't take too many things with Cramer. And this ball was hit between right-center and center field. Cramer come in and we're coming together; he dove for the ball, and it got by him and went to the furthest corner in Fenway Park, and I retrieved the ball and threw it back. Three-run triple.

Now Grove, he was always by himself and did things by himself. He had a locker with a couple of bottles of hooch up there with a lock on it and never touched it but after a game would take a little sip. This particular day this ball gets through, three runs score, and he comes in. Now Cramer is the first man up. I'm the fourth man up. Come in and sit down. Grove is getting his jacket on. Cramer has his bat and is heading to home plate. The great Lefty Grove is there with this young kid, and I heard him say, "He shoulda stuck it in his ass." And I just said, "Oh, horseshit," 'cause I thought he'd made a hell of an effort.

[Bill Werber comes in and sits down.]

Hi, Bill. So finally nothing's said, and Bill asked me the other day how did you and Grove get along. Well, I thought Grove and I got along pretty good. He wasn't overly friendly with me, but he never, never beefed at me. But then I'm going to go one step further with Grove. Grove is after his three hundredth game, and I have one regret. It's that I never concentrated on my fielding as much as I should have. When I first come to the big leagues and you saw me, I had a good arm early. You know? But then I hurt my arm after '46, and I had to deal with that the rest of my career. Now we're after Grove's three hundredth game, and we're playing in Cleveland. He's got 299. Al Smith, a left-hander from the National League, is going for Cleveland. A little curve ball, this and that. Not too bad to look at, I thought. So anyway, we're in the eighth inning. I never brought this story up before. Good story. Might be in my book. I don't know. But anyway, there's two men on, and I hit a double down the right-field line that put us ahead 2-1. Two to one in the eighth inning. Last of the eighth, they get two men on and Ray Mack is hitting. This is in 1940, and Cramer is playing center field. They figured left field was the place for me. I'm in left and Cramer's in center, and that God damn Mack hits a ball, a towering ball, might have been a ton out of the ballpark, but we're in Cleveland; it was 450 feet back there in that corner, so it's a towering high fly. It's a good crowd, Sunday afternoon. The only thing I remember is "Mine . . . mine . . . mine," and Christ, Cramer hit me right there, knocked me flat. Cramer is flat. Home run inside the ballpark, and Grove loses that game!

Now we're in Fenway Park, and Grove is pitching again. It's one of those 8–7 or 7–6 games, but during the game I drove in two runs. In the seventh or eighth inning there were guys on first and second and a left-handed hitter hit a squibber out to me, got by me, and those two runs scored, and it's tied or they go ahead. I'm so mad at myself I could—ooooh. We finally won the game. Doerr got a big hit. Foxx got a big hit.

And this is one of the regrets of my life. Here they're taking the pictures of the great Grove three hundredth win, and they wanted me to pose in that picture 'cause I'd driven in two runs, but I never posed for that picture, and I ain't in that picture, and God damn it, I always felt badly that I wasn't in that picture.

[At this point, the two old-timers got into a conversation about hitting and hitters.]

Bill Werber: Speaker and Cobb were together on the A's in 1927.

Ted Williams: How did they compare with each other in those days?

BW: Well, Cobb didn't particularly like anybody. Speaker was a different person. I was just a kid out of Duke.

TW: What was your recollection of Bob Meusel?

BW: He was an angular fellow, about as tall as you are, a very slim fellow. Right-handed batter. Had a lot of power.

TW: Like Marvin Owen?

BW: No, Marvin choked up on the bat.

TW: Well, so did Meusel. With two strikes, he'd come up a few inches.

BW: He was a good outfielder, a quiet fellow. Never had much to say. One of the best arms. Goslin, as I remember, in his younger days had a hell of an arm, and Meusel had a great arm.

TW: That's what Cronin told me, and I respected Cronin's appraisal of ability. He was all baseball, and he talked about it all the time.

He said that in his book Goslin was awfully, awfully close to being as good a hitter as Gehrig.

BW: But he hit a different kind of ball.

TW: Did he?

BW: Yeah. Goslin was mostly a line drive hitter.

TW: But that's what they always said about Gehrig.

BW: Well, Gehrig was too, but Gehrig hit a ball more often that had a little loft to it, where Ruth was almost entirely a loft ball hitter.

TW: Okay. Now let's you and I get into a little something here. You saw Frank McCormick [first baseman on the '39–'40 Reds]. Just suppose McCormick could hit the ball in the air.

BW: Frank McCormick was an excellent hitter, struck out very few times.

TW: But, you know, nobody ever talks about him. Nobody remembers him. Because he didn't hit the ball in the air enough.

BW: I remember another guy, and you should remember what I'm saying now. Joe Judge. There was a fifteen-year period when Joe Judge hit over .300 for about nine or ten consecutive years.

TW: I'm gonna look him up when I get home. [To **NM:**] Look him up right now.

[**NM:** .297 lifetime.]

TW: .297. That's good. Jesus Christ, they're putting them in the Hall of Fame batting .267 now. How many home runs did he hit?

[**NM:** 71.]

TW: Was he a fast guy?

BW: Yeah. Ran good.

TW: I'll name you some hitters who were God damn good hitters, but because they lacked that one thing of hitting the ball in the air, it kept them from being in the Hall of Fame. Doc Cramer is one. Hell of a hitter. Nobody can ever question that. When Killebrew and Bob Allison—you remember Allison—hit line drives and Killebrew, up in the air. You look in the averages. Allison was a stronger guy and that's saying a hell of a lot, but when you look at the difference, one hit the ball in the air, and the other guy hit the ball on a line.

BW: Here's another thing when you are evaluating players. The guys who could beat you.

TW: You can't tell that from the numbers.

BW: I knew those ballplayers. I knew the guys that you could beat on any given day. I knew the guys you couldn't beat, and I knew those guys up at the bat and I knew they were going to kill us, and I knew the guys on our side who in rough situations were going to deliver. They weren't going to strike out. They weren't going to chase bad balls. Now they might not get the hit, but they'd hit the ball somewhere. McCormick was one of the guys who was a stout fellow. You put him up there in a clutch situation, and he hit that God damn ball for you, and he hit it pretty good.

TW: But he never got any recognition for the Hall of Fame because—

BW: You never hear of him.

TW: The guys, the .258–.260 hitters like Killebrew; he hit more home runs than any player who performed in the American League. Now that's saying something. That's saying something.

BW: I wouldn't have him on my ball club.

TW: But I'll tell you, Billy, he was up there producing home runs. Often. You saw him. I can understand your feeling on him.

BW: Anybody who used a 32-ounce bat, the hell with him.

TW: Oh, boy. And I'll tell you. He had muscles on top of muscles.

BW: Hell, I used a 34-ounce bat.

TW: Well, that's light in those days, wasn't it?

BW: No. Thirty-four ounce, you get good wood in that.

TW: Oh, you bet you can. I used 33 and 34, never went over 34½.

BW: Ruth used a 38.

TW: I know he did. So did Foxx. But you know what—

BW: Foxx could pick him up and throw him over the dugout.

TW: You know what, Bill? Now here's something you don't know, Bill. Lemme tell you something now. Here comes old skinny-ass Williams into Fenway. Now this is true. In my book I wrote twenty years ago, twenty-five years now. I come into Fenway, and I order my bats. I come to the Red Sox, and I use a Cronin bat my first year. No knob, no nothing. Skinny little bat, you know. Good model. But then I started and so I pick up the bat, and when I was in Minneapolis in 1938, I was tired in August. I weighed 172 pounds and 6-foot-4, skinny as a rail, walked 150 times, hit .368. I was on base all the time, led the league in runs scored, bases on balls, everything else, you know, and this is late August, and I'm starting to get tired. In fact, I always got tired in early September. I really did.

So now we go to Columbus, and there's a guy on our club named Stan Spence. Pretty damn good ballplayer too, and pretty good hitter. Played for Washington. So anyway, I go to the batting rack, and we're in Columbus. Columbus! And I pick up his bat. I see the imprint of the ball all over it. Not a small bat, either. Pretty big bat. Banana wood. I saw it, and, boy, it was light, you know. Oh, it felt good. So I said to him, I said, "Stan, do you care if I use your bat tonight?" He said, "Go ahead and use it."

Well, I got up in the first inning. Now this made an impression on me, you know? I think somebody that's successful, more likely than not he sees something that's good or looks good or he gets results from it, and he picks it up quicker than some guys, you know? So I use this bat. I got this bat, and I get up in the first inning. I had this little guy come to me one day and say, "You remember that night?" Little left-handed pitcher. And I was up there with the bases loaded in Columbus. Now the old Columbus ballpark, I'm gonna guess, about 380 to center field. Nice place to hit.

BW: Had a flagpole out there.

TW: That's right. That's right. So I get up there to hit and the Cardinals—I'll tell you who was playing shortstop that night: the great Sammy Baugh—and so I'm up there. I'm hitting. Three men on. Little left-handed pitcher. I get 3-2, and, boy, I'm not going to strike out. I come up on the bat about an inch and I'm over the plate, just guarding that plate, and he throws me a fastball on the outside, and I just went whoom!—like that. Home run. Went out of the park easy. Center field, straight center.

BW: 385 feet.

TW: Well, I thought it was a little closer than that. I thought, "So you don't need a heavy bat to do all this." And that made an impact on me.

So now I come to Boston in '39 and you talk about Foxx. Now Jimmie had just hit fifty home runs for the Red Sox in '38. He was the MVP in the league. And so now here I am coming. I don't hit very well first year. I hit .367 till the All-Star Game, then I ended up .328. I hit .295 from the All-Star Game on. But the thing I'm trying to say is when I got to the Red Sox, because that bat had made such an impression on me, so you know what? We were the first club. . . . I used to get my bats ordered; I was using an O'Doul model now, and I got those bats and I would ask the clubhouse. . . . I ordered them for 33 or 34 ounces, and I don't get them. In fact, we didn't even order the ounces in those days. We'd get the bats and I'd take Johnny Orlando and say, "Take 'em down and weigh 'em at the post office." Eventually we got a scale in there and I started ordering my bats 33.

BW: Is Johnny Orlando still living?

TW: No, he's dead. He's dead. And you know what? He was with the Red Sox the twenty-two years I was there, and the day I quit, they fired him. He'd abused his privileges as a clubhouse boy. Damn it all, he was really a hell of a guy and he loved baseball and he loved a lot of things about it, but he took advantage of the club, and the club was having a hard time about that time. He'd get balls and sell them, he'd get bats and sell them and, you know, he wasn't really doing it right; they warned him about it, damn it all, they warned him about it. Anyway, they had to fire him. So here's Jimmie, fifty home runs. But, you know, that year, I've seen it happen to other ballplayers; he was one of the greatest—*one of the greatest*. I'll tell you one thing—

BW: Drunken bum.

TW: He did drink. He did drink. He wouldn't take care of himself. He was a hell of a guy.

BW: Nice fellow.

TW: So anyway, he was starting to have trouble. Now he's, you know, coming over the hump. He's only thirty-three years old. But he'd abused himself. But he was drinking like hell, and he was having problems at home. He wanted to show the world that he could screw everybody and drink as much as anybody and Babe Ruth, so anyway, you know it's a funny thing. He started to see me coming along a little bit; he picked up my bat and kinda liked it, and you know what? Jimmie Foxx was using a 33-ounce bat. I'm telling you.

BW: Aw, baloney.

TW: I'm *telling you* 33-, 34-ounce bat in 1939 and '40 and '41. Now we traded him. I'm telling you. I know.

BW: He was traded to the Chicago Cubs.

TW: When?

BW: In either '41 or '42.

TW: I said '42.

BW: He was catching there in '42.

TW: When they traded Jimmie Foxx, I could not believe it.

BW: Let me tell you something. Foxx was catching a ball game for the Cubs in '42, and one of our pitchers threw in there; it was a holiday game, he was up at the plate, and he didn't see the ball because it came out of the shirts.

TW: Hard to see there.

BW: Yeah, hard to see, and it turned the brim of his cap. And when I came up to bat—always liked Jimmie—I said, "Jim, why in the hell don't you get out of there?" I said, "You're gonna get killed." And he laughed and giggled and said, "A guy gotta eat, don't he?" And that was his response: "A guy gotta eat, don't he?"

TW: You know the most money he ever made was $35,000 with the Red Sox. As far as I'm concerned, I'll always love him, and he was a hell of a nice guy, his own worst enemy.

BW: I told Norman the story how Jimmie almost wound up with the Yankees.

TW: I didn't know that.

BW: Oh, yes. Frank "Home Run" Baker told me when we were hunting down on the Choptank. He owned Foxx's contract in the Eastern Shore League, and he took him up to sell him to Miller Huggins; he kited Foxx and told Huggins that Foxx could perform with the best he had, and Miller Huggins said, "I don't think we can use him, Frank." So Frank went down and he gave Mr. Mack the same spiel that he had given Huggins, and Mr. Mack said, "If he's half as good as you say he is, Frank, he's worth $2,500." And that's how Foxx got with the A's and did not get with the Yankees.

TW: You know where he hit the ball in Yankee Stadium.

BW: I saw him hit one in Cleveland one day that was over the tops of those bleachers. This was in old League Park. There was a great big enormous oak.

TW: I didn't know anybody ever hit one over there.

BW: Listen, it was a great big white oak tree, and it was beyond the Lux toilet soap sign on top of the bleachers. Foxx hit it over the bleachers, over the Lux sign, and over the top of that—

TW: Were you in Cincinnati the day he hit one off Vander Meer?

BW: No.

TW: Well, he hit one off Vander Meer in Cincinnati they're still talking about. I wasn't with them. I was sick and had to go to Boston.

BW: We all ran out of the dugout in Cleveland. I can remember Dusty Cooke was right beside me, and when the ball disappeared over that oak tree, he turned to me—I was on his right—and he said, "It's a God damn lie." That's all he said.

TW: Well, I've seen him hit some balls that I. . . . No way that the ball could take any more than he put to it. We went to Cleveland right after that, and Foxx hit one way way back; you know there was a corner way back. Off Harder he hit that. I was on second base, and he hit another one on that trip. I can't remember right now. Chicago, I think. He hit one way the hell up in left-center.

BW: Chicago had two decks.

TW: Oh, Jesus, he hit them a ton. There's only one guy right-handed that I think could hit a ball as hard as Jimmie Foxx: Mickey Mantle. Only guy, and they're both built the same, and they both sounded like charges in their bat when they hit it. It sounded like firecrackers—*whack*!

BW: Did you know that Foxx could run?

TW: As good as anybody.

BW: He beat me in a hundred-yard dash in Boston. I cheated. When the gun went off, I was about as far as from here to that lamp. There wasn't anybody could catch me back in those days. But he did. He caught me before I got to the—

TW: Mantle could run like hell, and Foxx could run like hell. They were both built well. Six foot. Two hundred pounds. And they had strength. And quickness. And when they got that bat going, I'm sure the bat speed of those two guys was probably as fast as. . . . I seen Foxx hit some balls. . . .

[Voice from above: "It's time for dinner."]

TW: Let's go eat.

46.

Gene Woodling
MEDINA, OHIO, FALL 1989

Outfielder Gene Woodling was a key member of the New York Yankees' five consecutive World Championships (1949–1953). The career .284 left-handed batter played for six teams over eighteen years (1943–1962), with two years in the navy. We sat and talked at the dining room table in the farmhouse outside Medina where he had lived for almost forty-five years.

I CAME OUT OF a poor neighborhood in East Akron, Ohio. Rough neighborhood, every color and nationality. My people were from Germany. They broke away from all the religious wrangling and came to Pennsylvania—Pennsylvania Dutch. I had good parents, taught me right from wrong, pay your bills. My old man bought nothing unless he paid for it. He told me, "If you ever get in serious trouble, I'm not coming to help you."

I had fun when I was a boy, wouldn't trade my boyhood for all the money in the world. If you misbehaved in school, you had to beg your teacher and principal not to tell your parents. They were strict, and I don't see anything wrong with that. Those teachers were doing you the biggest favor of your life. We were a family of outstanding swimmers. My brother was a national champion at Ohio State. After 20 years in the major leagues, I was put in my high school Hall of Fame—for swimming.

I was a good student in high school but had no money to go to college. If I couldn't play ball, it would be the tire factory. We were Cleveland Indians fans—still are. Cleveland scout Bill Bradley signed me. They sent me to Mansfield, Class D, about sixty miles south of here. Eighty dollars a month. People in the rubber shop were making twelve dollars a week, and I was making twenty dollars a week playing ball.

Baseball can be cruel. I was seventeen, never been away from home. Scared to go into a restaurant. Rough old-time player named Willy Stover was the manager, scared me to death. I'll never forget him. I showed up, and he said, "What position do you play?" I said, "In high school I played in the outfield." He said, "You're playing third base." I'd never played third base. That lasted for about a week. I did everything wrong. But I led the league in hitting.

The next year I wound up at Flint, Michigan, played the outfield, third base, even pitched a few innings, and led the league in batting again.

In 1942 I broke my ankle in May in Wilkes-Barre in the Eastern League. Went back in '43 and played for Tony Lazzeri, the old Yankees second baseman. We were just kids, 19–20 years old. I couldn't have played for a better guy than Lazzeri. Great handling young people. You were family; that's the best way I can put it. He and his wife were very good to us. You just couldn't play for better people. Tony was an epileptic. He had a winding stairway in his home in San Francisco. One day he had a spell and fell on that stairway, and that's the way he died. His wife wrote me a letter and told me what happened.

[September 30, 1948, Woodling was sold to the Yankees. Casey Stengel became the Yankees' manager in 1949.]

Casey Stengel was a hell of a psychologist. Don't you kid yourself. That guy made me successful. [Outfielder] Hank Bauer and I used to tell him we wanted to play. And when we didn't play, it made us mad. We told him to go to hell and everything else. What's wrong with that? I coulda killed the old man a lot of times. He loved it. He was thinking, "That pair of squareheads. When I turn them loose, they're gonna go out and beat somebody." When you take inventory of your career and come to him, you say, "This guy made me a good ballplayer." How can you hate him? There was no hate. I wanted to play and got mad when I didn't get to play.

After we won a World Series, I went into his office. I was going to say I was sorry I got mad at him during the season. But he said, "Get the hell out of here. You ain't coming in here telling me you're sorry for making me look good all year." That's Casey. Simple as I can say it.

He knew who to stir up and who to leave alone. I didn't know this at the time. I found out later. He wound up being my best PR man when I left New York. I told him, "Why didn't you say those things when I was in New York? I'da made more money."

Stengel was the toughest manager you could play for. When you went to that ballpark, it was no nonsense. The first time a pitcher walked around the mound, dilly-dallying like they do today for the TV camera, Casey would tell the pitching coach, "Go get him. He's afraid to throw the ball."

I never thought Casey was funny. Not until he went to the Mets.

They said anybody could have won with that team. That's not true. Some other guys didn't win with players like us. Handling twenty-five temperamental guys, that's hard. After we won the first one [in 1949], he said, "That was the easy one. Now everybody in the league is gonna be out to beat you." We won a second one, a third—five in a row.

They talk about those Yankee teams with all those hitters and pitchers. But we were the biggest bunch of red asses; we got on each other. If somebody made a mistake in the field, we got on him. When we went out there, we gave it everything we had to give. You'd see Vic Raschi off the field and think he's just a perfect gentleman. In a game he'd cut your throat. They used to tell Yogi Berra to go out and talk to Raschi on the mound. But Yogi said, "No way." Raschi would tell him, "Get outta here, Dago."

Bobby Brown was an agitator. I'd be sitting down by the water cooler when I wasn't playing and Brown would sit next to me and say, "The old man is going to be on your ass." I'd say, "What the hell you talking about? You better go back to those medical books." And he was right; Casey would get on me.

Frank Crosetti was the best coach you could have on any club. With him a spade is a spade, and there's no deviation. No partygoer. He said, "I'm hired to do a job," and did it better than anybody else. I let anybody know where I stood. Stengel said I was the only one who didn't talk behind his back. And Cro was that way.

Guys who were not red asses? Yogi, Jerry Coleman, Joe Collins. That didn't mean they wouldn't say anything or I wouldn't get on them. Don't kid yourself. Only Joe DiMaggio didn't have to say anything. He just had to look at you. Didn't say ten words all season.

But when we left the clubhouse, we were the nicest guys. And twenty-five, thirty years later, there were no closer bunch of old-timers than us Yankees. Course winning made it a lot easier.

When Casey was with the expansion Mets and he took me from Washington in the draft, they had a press conference in New York. He told the writers, "You guys said I didn't like this fella and he didn't like me, and that's a bunch of bull." He turned to me. "Did you dislike me?"

I said, "Well, at times I'd like to kill you, but as far as saying I didn't like you, that's a bold statement."

He said, "Hey, who's the only guy I brought back here to the Mets? We ain't going anywhere. I'll tell you guys something else. He wanted to play all the time on that other side [the Yankees]. He can play all he wants over here."

I handled the press real well: write what you want. If I do it on the field, you gotta print it. If I got three hits that day and a writer knocks me, prove the guy wrong. I kept a lot of those articles knocking me. They're amusing to me now.

I was traded to Baltimore in 1955. Paul Richards was the Orioles manager. June 15 he traded me to Cleveland. They said I left Baltimore because I didn't want to play with a losing team. They knew I left there because I didn't hit. They said I didn't care if I got a hit. Every guy who goes up to bat wants a hit. I had the opposite reputation from what they wrote. And that bothered me. You talk about a mean guy. I could be mean. Threw a typewriter in the whirlpool one day.

I got booed out of the city my first time there 'cause I was getting one base hit a week. When Paul Richards brought me back to Baltimore three years later and I did well, proved them wrong, they gave me a day. I was thirty-six. Richards knew I came to play hard, booing or not. I prolonged my career because of that attitude. I had my best years thirty-five, forty years of age. The 1959 season was a magic year for me, won a lot of games in the eighth and ninth innings. I don't know why. I was blessed with good health, good eyesight. I didn't cheat myself. If I didn't play well that day, I didn't have to make any excuses when that was the best my body would let me do.

I didn't give a damn for managers, owners, or anybody else.

I'd go to the ballpark—tell them to leave me alone, play hard, and when I left that ballpark, I'd say stick the baseball up your butt and they'd shake their heads, and you know the best way to describe that? Richards would say, "Yeah, and who's going to play better than him tomorrow? When he goes home, he forgets it with his family. But when he comes here tomorrow, get out of his way."

My kids weren't raised in a baseball atmosphere. I never took the game home with me. I could go 0 for 4; they wouldn't know. I could get fifty hits; they wouldn't know. In 1953 my daughter was in school. The kids were talking about the World Series between the Yankees and Brooklyn. She didn't know. A kid said he was rooting for Brooklyn. So she said she was for Brooklyn. I had to explain it to her. But I'm proud of that.

In mid-September 1960 the Orioles were going into New York for our last series against them, tied for first place. I came home on that Thursday, sitting right at this table. Nothing was said. I said, "Can anybody at this table tell me what's going on in New York this weekend?" My wife, my children didn't know I had a chance to be in the World Series. Isn't that nice?

I played with Roger Maris in Cleveland before he went to New York. He became a lot better hitter and outfielder than I thought he would be. By nature he was a quiet guy, didn't want to smile. He was a good person. The pressure he got from the New York writers! If you thought Roger was bad, I'd have been a hell of a lot worse. You can only do what your nature is. If you were going to write a book about the way your attitude should be in baseball, at the ballpark, away from it, and living your life, I'd single out Roger as one of the best. Brooks Robinson too. I'd like to have each of them for a son.

Bob Feller was our main AL player rep. I was the rep for pension matters for seven years. We were given a lot of hell for not picking up old-time players who made baseball. When we started, we didn't have the money. As soon as we were able to go back money-wise, I was the first guy going back and picking up the old-timers who made the game.

I played in the older era and lasted long enough to play in the younger era. The guys playing today don't remember that we started all this and the hardships we had. The owners wanted to get me out of baseball, but I kept hitting. I told them, "You guys keep getting me mad and not liking me, and I'll stay around and hit .300." I got condemned for being honest. You try to be honest, and you'll be in trouble.

I had no wish to be a coach, but when Hank Bauer became the Orioles manager, I could help him by seeing to the clubhouse, the players. If somebody was fooling around in practice, I'd go at him. That was what Bauer hired me for—to see that a situation was handled without it getting to him.

I was there when Frank Robinson came over from the Reds. In '66 he had the most amazing year I ever saw: forty-nine home runs, two more in the World Series. He played all out, looked mad all the time, didn't laugh much. Did it all on the field. Wasn't the fastest, but would steal a base when you needed it. Not the strongest arm, but threw out a guy when you needed it. Frank was a real leader. It's tough to put into words. He made center fielder Paul Blair a much better ballplayer. If Blair made a booboo in the outfield, Frank ate him up. I thought Frank would be a good manager.

I didn't enjoy coaching. I said to myself, "What am I doing away from my family, my beautiful farm?" When they fired me, I was the happiest guy in that clubhouse. I had plenty of calls from former teammates and managers to be a coach. I thanked them all and told them for some reason I love my farm better.

My wife and I had grown up together, two poor kids. We were going to come back to Ohio after baseball, and we'd always wanted a farm. So when I got traded back to Cleveland in 1955, we started looking. I couldn't live in the city. You can't describe the life we've had here. It's work, but I love it. At first the neighbors laughed at me. I said, "I'll raise the best hay around here," and I did. We don't farm or have any animals any more, but I do all the maintenance. I tell people I scrape five weeks, then paint six. But I enjoy it.

I was asked to run for Congress from this district. I expressed interest but didn't do it 'cause my wife would divorce me.

It's changed now, but when we first came here, we were among farmers whose families had been here for 150 years. You don't come in here as ballplayers and do anything but mind your own business. We've had a nice life. Very fortunate. Count our blessings.

I'm tickled to death every day that I was a ballplayer. I wasn't the greatest ballplayer, wasn't the nicest guy, didn't have the greatest attitude. But I had a winning attitude. I stayed honest, got in a lot of trouble, and I'm sitting here right now, very proud of what I accomplished.

47.

Don Zimmer

LEGENDS FIELD, TAMPA, MARCH 2000

Infielder Don Zimmer was a baseball lifer; twelve years a player (1954–1965), half of them with the Dodgers; twelve years a manager for the Padres, Red Sox, Rangers, and Cubs; and twenty-five years a coach, the last eleven for the Yankees (1996–2006). We sat in the dugout of the Yankees' spring training field one morning, and I asked him how it all began.

I SIGNED WITH THE Dodgers right after graduation from high school in Cincinnati in June 1949. I got on a train and went to Cambridge, Maryland, in the Eastern Shore League. Class D. They had told me to go to the hotel in town, an old white building. The first thing I always did, from that day on, whenever I went into a town, I went to the local newspaper office and had the paper sent to my father.

I called the ballpark. The general manager said, "Where are you?"

"I'm at the hotel."

"Be out in front and I'll pick you up in twenty minutes."

It's about four o'clock in the afternoon, and it was hot. He came in a pickup truck. I got in, and we go to the ballpark. He introduced me to the players. In Class D baseball you were allowed so many veterans and so many limited-service players. The rest were rookies, like me. The manager said to me, "You ready to play tonight?"

"Yes, sir."

They had a veteran third baseman, Hank Parker, and a veteran pitcher, Zeke Zeiss. He was twenty-eight, the best pitcher on the team. About my fourth game, I was playing shortstop. Zeiss is pitching. Here came a ground ball, took a bad hop, and hit me in the neck. You figure it's called a hit. The next ball I went to field took a bad bounce and hit me on the right shoulder.

There was a wooden outhouse over beyond first base. The third ball hit to me, I finally caught one. I threw it over the first baseman's head and hit the outhouse. I figured that was my first real error. Two innings later another ball's hit over my head between me and the left fielder. I go back figuring the left fielder's going to run me off the ball. I don't hear him. I reach out. The ball hit my glove and fell on the ground.

Later I make another error and we lose. I had botched up the game. As we're walking off the field, I happen to be walking behind Parker and Zeke Zeiss. The pitcher said to Parker, "What are we doing with this guy? He can't play a lick."

Parker said, "Let me tell you something. You're twenty-eight years old. This kid played in high school a week ago. Give him a chance."

I never forgot that. I always respected Hank Parker for kinda sticking up for me.

A few days later I got a call from my dad. He said, "Well, it didn't take you long to set an Eastern Shore League record."

I said, "What's that, dad?"

"You made six errors in one game."

"Well, I remember making three legitimately."

I had a room in a boarding house. We rode in yellow school buses, straight backs, for road trips. It was quite an experience. Eighteen years old, scared to death, going away for the first time, guy picks you up in a truck to take you to the ballpark.

INDEX